CARING FOR THE FUTURE

The Independent Commission on Population and Quality of Life

Caring for the Future

the Future

Making the Next Decades Provide a
Life Worth Living

*Report of the Independent Commission on
Population and Quality of Life*

Oxford   New York

OXFORD UNIVERSITY PRESS

1996

Oxford University Press, Walton Street, Oxford OX2 6DP

Oxford New York
Athens Auckland Bangkok Bombay
Calcutta Cape Town Dar es Salaam Delhi
Florence Hong Kong Istanbul Karachi
Kuala Lumpur Madras Madrid Melbourne
Mexico City Nairobi Paris Singapore
Taipei Tokyo Toronto

and associated companies in
Berlin Ibadan

Oxford is a trade mark of Oxford University Press

British Library Cataloguing in Publication Data
Data available

Library of Congress Cataloging in Publication Data
Data available
ISBN 0–19–286186–7

10 9 8 7 6 5 4 3 2 1

Typeset by Hope Services (Abingdon) Ltd.
Printed in Great Britain by
Mackays PLC
Chatham, Kent

PREFACE

When I accepted the invitation to chair the Independent Commission on Population and Quality of Life (ICPQL), I had in mind what Norway's prime-minister Gro Brundtland had written in the foreword of *Our Common Future* (1987): 'The questions of population—of population pressure and human rights—and the links between these related issues and poverty, environment, and development proved to be one of the more difficult concerns with which we had to struggle.'

Indeed, the same was going to be true for ICPQL. Where was our work to begin? At which level were we to establish the links developed in the Brundtland Report? To start with macro-problems would be almost useless since the political and media languages had made these connections too broad and too abstract. To describe the concrete situation of population growth itself, when there were many outstanding analyses and guide-lines from sound institutional sources, would be nothing but a mere recapitulation of reality.

The common way of understanding linkages by adding two complementary terms—population *and* development, population *and* poverty—was scientifically limited and unsatisfying. The way out was for us to attempt to establish more concrete and partial correlations among all the elements that converge into what is called population dynamics, to look from new angles at their interface, and to determine in each case the 'point of entry' into the matter.

This approach did not prove easy. I was going to rediscover how the mentality of specialization remains widespread, and how it functions as a dike against new thinking, new ways of acting. Interdisciplinary knowledge, an inter-sectoral grasp of problems, integrated policies for action: these asked for a quantum leap forward. The Commission was clear in this regard: we would not extricate ourselves from the population problem by remaining within its boundaries. Its task of 'situating population matters within the socio-economic context' asked for analyses of, and proposals for, the main elements of a diversified framework.

For some of those around us, the preparation and realization of the Cairo Conference on Population and Development (1994) seemed, at first sight, to drain the Commission of its *raison d'être*. Commencing its work only two years before Cairo, at a time when the regional meetings and global preparatory committees for Cairo were already under way, the Commission could not aim at having an impact on the Conference itself.

This did not worry me, however. On the contrary, I felt great relief in seeing that some of the major components of the 'population' issue were going to be integrated in the conferences of the United Nations: namely, the issues based on demographic analyses and on the assessment of services and methods, falling within the general context of *population programmes*, were covered comprehensively. The women's movements had seen clearly the importance of these series of events. They became, therefore, strongly involved in the Cairo Conference. This proved to be decisive: it led to a shift away from the voluntaristic approaches of governments and other institutions to the rights of women as the subject of decisions concerning them directly. It was obvious that, with the participation of women, *population* should be seen in a broader context. The Cairo event itself thus represented a turning-point in the way the 'population' question was to be approached in the future. The Commission felt, in that shift, a confirmation of the correctness of the road it had chosen since its beginning.

⁊

After the Cairo Conference two facts seemed inescapable. First, all the data pointed out that population growth was an added burden on poverty, and that the projections for the coming decades showed that the overwhelming suffering of the poor was to be inflicted upon many more millions of human beings. How could we relate population and quality of life, then, if not in a new and consistent linkage? Secondly, the Rio de Janeiro Conference (1992) had already made abundantly clear that the 'population problem' of the world is equally one of over-consumption and the accumulation of wastes in the industrial countries. This was affirmed again and again throughout the Cairo Conference. We were thus not dealing with a mere 'environmental problem', one to be listened to condescendingly by politicians. Because of the obvious sequence:

$$ecology \rightarrow environment \rightarrow Nature,$$

much of the discourse on the environment sounded idealistic to many people, and not touching the heart of the issue.

Several paradoxes involved in the problem were, however, fairly apparent:

- on one side was the enlargement of women's rights, particularly their central role in fertility, and on the other side, the persistent, weak political will of governments and agencies in this respect;
- the enormous inequity between North and South, despite the overwhelming acceptance of, and compliance with, a single model of development;
- the unanimous acceptance of sustainability as a basic principle in dealing with Nature—and yet too slow a process for creating technologies capable of reducing stress on the environment.

These, among many others, were aspects which, once the new way of dealing with population matters was open and accepted, had to be tackled as intrinsically connected with population dynamics.

The Commission was made acutely sensitive to the need for a new type of industrial 'equation', one that would change the patterns of production and consumption. How to deal with it, I did not know. But I did know that the terms of the equation would not go unchallenged either in themselves or in what concerned their links. The scandal of *absolute poverty* and the *irrationality of consumption patterns* intrinsically linked to population growth could be overcome only by a new type of economic growth.

~

The Mission Statement for ICPQL was one of great ambition: a *fresh vision* of international population matters had to be elaborated, taking as its main references human rights and socio-economic conditions. To think of a fresh vision was *exhilarating*—but how could one pretend, from the outset, to provide new concepts, new strategies, new tools?

Then I remembered a visit that I had made in 1986 to the Salk Institute in California. After a fascinating talk about men and women, biology and the human sciences, Jonas Salk offered me a copy of the book *World Population and Human Values*, published by him and his son, Jonathan, in the early 1980s. This gave me a clue. The sigmoidal curve, used traditionally to describe the transition period in the evolution of population size, was taken by the authors as a metaphor: a symbol of changes in the aspirations to, and in the perceptions of, quality of life. While the first part of the curve—with its tendency towards the infinite—spoke of unlimited growth and unlimited perspectives, the segment of the curve following the transition zone 'spoke' of a ceiling, a contained or closed 'space'. Aggressive competitiveness thus could cede its place to co-operation, fierce independence would give in to interdependence, expansion to equilibrium.

In the geographic regions where the stabilization level of population has already been reached (i.e. most of the northern countries), there is little evidence that the awareness of a civilization with limits—one in which we have entered—permeates decisions and choices being made. The North's dominance over earthly resources and knowledge creates the illusion that we are still in the 'unlimited' part of the curve. Being constantly wrapped in this illusion, it is easy for the North to continue reasoning as if the planet's capacities remain without limits. The South, by adopting the same model, embraces similar illusions. Hence, both in population growth and in consumption patterns, there is the same need for a change in values.

It was then clear that the urgency to move towards stabilization of the population was linked with another one that Salk indicated as *balance*. 'Balance will become evident in relationships among human beings and in the relationships between human beings and Nature'. It was this suggestion that led me to the idea that to tackle the question of *population* in every society is no longer to be done in terms of demographic transition alone, or in terms of the direct means to accelerate this transition. Rather (I came to believe), the issue was for society to come to grips with all the elements contributing to *dynamic population balance* in harmony with the environment and allowing life its fullness for future generations.

Such a balance was then expressed, at the global level, by one of the Commission's members, who put the stress in a way that became a fundamental framework of the vision and policies that the Commission sought: quality of life for all can be found only by taking into account *the carrying capacity of the Earth* and *the caring capacity of humankind*. Population, in this context, is not simply one factor; it is the key factor. In *population* the human person is central, and people cannot be interchangeable with *things* (energy, inflation, and so forth). The linkages to be analysed, in other words, should never short-circuit the human being.

Although the scrutiny of specific population policies and programmes was definitely on our agenda, the Commission did not envisage covering exclusively the conventional areas of analysis. The Commission members had decided from the outset to articulate all the interrelated issues within a single framework.

This they found could be done within the second qualification of the Commission's name, *quality of life*. By unanimous decision, this expression became the guiding and ultimate goal (and even conceptual tool) permitting us to formulate our findings in what we hoped would be an innovative way.

Throughout the three years of the Commission's life, the notion of *quality of life* worked its way forward through all the stages of our work. *Quality of life* was seen to be the goal once that the threshold of *quantity* (beyond the level of mere survival) was crossed. Quality of life became, in this way, the guiding principle in regard to sustainable consumption—increases in which often lead, paradoxically, to a lessened quality of life. Little by little, quality of life emerged as a combination of rights and duties, clear indications for both decision-makers and the dynamic components of civil society.

~*~

Against this background, the main strategic decisions of the Commission proved, already during its first session, to be extremely important. Instead of dealing only with a secondary search, or relying on the well-known experts in the many fields to be covered, we decided to give a preponderant role to testimonies taken in several Public Hearings conducted within the world's main regions. Thus the 'people's voices' became our main testing-ground of the views emerging but not yet consolidated in cohesive form. Little did we realize at the beginning that these very voices would become the driving force in our effort.

It was the people's voices, indeed, that, although giving the Commission a most illuminating picture of the cultural diversity that we had to address, represented a convergent outlook. They provided the elements for a realistic approach that was not ours to ignore. They brought evidence that *population matters* have to be integrated in a new perspective, one leading to new approaches to governance and leadership, to policies and strategies, and to concrete actions and specific measures that need to be taken.

Everywhere the individuals and groups to whom we listened took for granted that the ICPQL was tantamount in itself to Quality of Life, connoting improvement in their own concrete situations. The first of these hearings, held in Zimbabwe in December 1993 (with people present from English- and Portuguese-speaking countries of Africa) set the tone. A large poster there announced: 'We deserve a better Quality of Life.' This confirmed the virtual motto for the Commission's work.

The Public Hearings, which gave the Commission the opportunity to listen within the context of their region to people from fifty countries, raised an enthusiastic response. Humanitarian organizations involved with the most diverse issues, and encompassed within the general designation of NGOs, included members of the scientific community, representatives of donor agencies in the field of 'population programmes', directors of public services, and (last but hardly least) the destitute people who came to present testimonials of their situation. The Public Hearings had another characteristic: in six of the seven cases, they were organized by the member(s) of the Commission belonging to the region, and in close collaboration with the NGOs.

Two practical lessons came from the hearings. The first was the *level of integration* at which policies and services made sense for both individuals and communities. Even in the most destitute areas, people do not wait for isolated, discrete actions to occur. They want to see *together* what they experience *as a whole*, whether stepping-stone or impedance to a better quality of life.

The second was a *warning signal*. In all regions the Commission sensed a revolt against institutions that had come equipped with their own recipes for reducing the rates of population growth, and yet often failed to see the overall, interdependent conditions in which people lived.

—ᴓ

What was needed was not only a fresh vision but also an authentic empowerment of people in the process of improving quality of life. In its composition, the Commission was equipped to deal with both vision and empowerment: there was the balance of the Commission, with North and South equally represented. And for the first time in any international undertaking, there was parity of representation by men and women. This parity was not in numbers alone, as the women and men of the Commission had the same level of reputation in their own countries. Their experience, in the political, social, and scientific realms, paralleled their reputations.

Besides their own special fields, the members of the Commission provided a wide spectrum of experience: professors, several former or current members of parliaments, several former or current ministers of development, health, social affairs, or foreign affairs. Moreover, most members of the Commission were activists.

I need to express here, however, the bitter regret of the entire Commission for the fact that Olusegun Obasanjo was not allowed to join the sessions from March 1995, when he was arrested, jailed, and later secretly tried and condemned for his alleged implication in a plot. The Commission has reason to know that General Obasanjo was in no way involved as charged.

To all members of the Commission I extend my gratitude for their generosity in sharing ideas, experience and work, for their stimulating creativity and steadfast commitment, and for the unwavering support they gave me in difficult moments.

It is true that we went through such moments—the search for new ground to explore, the resistance encountered, the methodology required for building evidence, the working-out of concepts as we moved along, the uncertainty that all this created. All of these difficulties proved to be stumbling-blocks along the way. But these very obstacles cemented further the cohesion amongst the

Commission's members as we moved towards a new vision of international population matters. A body of thought came to be created collectively and, as one member expressed it, the 'ownership' of the Commission by its members was assured.

⊸

In this book the Commission provides the main lines of its vision, with the hope that these lines may be developed both by those who are working in the field and by other specialists. By bringing 'population matters' into a much wider context than has been the case with more piecemeal approaches, we also hope that current polarizations may be reduced. We trust that all who are involved will come to regard population as a fact not only at the crossroads of public policy but (most of all) as the continuous expression of the dynamism of society in terms of human phenomena, life and death, stability and mobility, and in the context of the sheer survival of humans and the Earth itself.

We would like also that this attempt at a fresh vision should stimulate action at all levels: of people, especially the poor, empowered to improve their quality of life; of those involved in education, to look for alternative concepts and methods; of enterprises, seeking forms of compatibility between social suppleness and economic flexibility; of the scientific community, to elaborate further the systemic approach as to what concerns population and the elements of quality of life; of the activists in all the areas evoked here to build pilot-projects creatively, based on suggestions that they have found useful; and of politicians, to take seriously and act upon what they may at first sight find idealistic.

The Commission is convinced, very deeply, that either population matters must be taken in hand in their entirety, or else that no breakthrough will be possible. All who know that population growth must be slowed also realize that this cannot happen if there is not a radical shift in the way that population matters are integrated with fundamental governance.

MARIA DE LOURDES PINTASILGO

CONTENTS

� Caring for
the Future

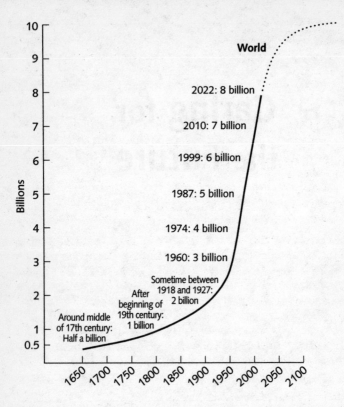

Frontispiece. *The march of the billions.* The S-curve shows the growth in human population, estimated for the period 1650–1980. Between 1825 and 1925 a second billion was added to the first. The third billion came in the next thirty-five years, the fourth during the fifteen years following. The United Nations expects a population of 5.8 billion in 1996, perhaps 8 billion by 2025 on certain assumptions of fertility and mortality. After Jonas and Jonathan Salk, *World Population and Human Values, A New Reality* (New York, Harper & Row, 1981).

INTRODUCTION
A WORLD IN TRANSITION

> ✒ *Population and quality of life have to be seen in the context of development, that is, improving the conditions of life at the individual and collective levels. It is important to go beyond the traditional oppositions between North and South, development and under-development, between communities and individuals, among sectors within countries and even communities.*
>
> Ricardo Melendez Ortiz, Colombia
> Latin American Public Hearing

> ✒ *Assessing our demographic situation, the important problems are: environmental deterioration in many regions, nearing catastrophic proportions; poverty bordering on indigence for most of the population; intense social differentiation, hastening the disintegration of society; loss of a system of values, with disorientation of much of the population; growing criminality, with no guarantees of safety; disappearance of the country's labour potential. Reforms are carried out with no understanding of the close correlation between economic and social transformations.*
>
> Natalia Rimachevskaya, Russia
> Eastern Europe Public Hearing

Never was the expression *unprecedented change* more pertinent to a historical period than to the decades following the Second World War, a period in which the new and unknown became the norm—characterized by a multitude of unforeseeable events. Our century has also seen a spectacular growth in population.

In 1830 the number of human beings reached the 1 billion mark, but the next billion came along within a hundred years. Post-war growth has been on an altogether different scale. In the 1960s the annual growth rate was over 2 per cent, compared with 0.5 per cent in the first half of our century and 1.5 per cent during the first half-decade of the 1990s.

Thus the acceleration rate in the world's population growth has begun to taper off. The world has reached, in terms of the population-growth curve, an inflection point. This point lies in the middle of a demographic transition period stretching, more or less, over two generations.

Jonas Salk interprets the human predicament in the form of a curve, its two sides depicting the evolution of any species in finite volume. Before reaching the curve's inflection point, the appearance of limitless expansion seems to prevail: it is based on independence, competition, power, either/or reasoning, fierce individualism, and realities only half perceived. After passing the inflection point the curve begins to reflect interdependence, collaboration, consensus, balance, the both/and way of thinking, and a perception of the whole.

This typifies the shape and character of a great transition period of civilization. Nothing of this nature has been experienced before. And never before has humanity experienced such a radical change in its composition, on such a scale and in so short a time. It is even probable that our species will never again experience such radical change.

In terms of composition, today's 5.7 billion humans are very 'different'. Only 16 per cent live in the industrialized countries. About 45 per cent of the population in developing countries is below the age of 15. And the number of older people is rising everywhere from its current level of 10 per cent.

Even with a declining growth rate, the world's population will continue to grow for several decades because of the 'population momentum' inherent in today's absolute population figures. Tomorrow's parents are already born, so that billions more people will be added. Therefore the world will emerge from the demographic transition with a much larger population. Even if growth has stabilized by 2040 (i.e. with the fertility rate at the replacement level of 2.1), there will be between now and 2050 an addition of more than 4 billion people.

We live in a time when social forms, tested methods, and values disappear before new forms and methodologies have had the time to take shape. Accepted traditions and values are challenged, while the changes themselves remain undefined or not yet systematically articulated. But as acceleration shifts to deceleration in our growth rate, as economic growth rates stagnate, the image of power and the fear of losing it are at their greatest. For some, the old values are unable to hold, while others cling desperately to them. The new values, however, are slow in establishing themselves; at times when they seem finally irrefutable, other new solutions suddenly appear.

The world is caught, at the same time, in a multifarious process of accelerated transformations in almost all realms of life, although the different transitions are not necessarily linked through a causal relationship. They seem even to move in many, often contradictory, directions. The old world 'order' has gone, with a new one yet to evolve. We are witnessing, in essence, transition from a limitless horizon to a limited, if not finite, space in search of balance. There is little doubt that there is an intense conflict between the two sets of values marking this transition. The conflict often results in an impasse—one having an adverse effect on societal stability, on equity in the relations between nations and peoples, and on individual security.

Tensions are further exacerbated by the consequences of the acceleration in scientific progress. This progress has also given rise to the emergence of a global culture, one tending to reduce diversity in value systems.

The United Nations (UN), in its Charter adopted in 1945, defined its objectives thus:

- to save succeeding generations from the scourge of war;
- to reaffirm faith in fundamental human rights, in the dignity and worth of the human person, in the equal rights of men and women and of nations big or small;
- to promote social progress and better standards of life, in greater freedom.

This represented nothing short of a package of values and principles to facilitate a transition towards a more peaceful and prosperous world than before. It defined, for the first time, a quest for collective security in the military as well as the social and economic spheres.

In the fifty years following the last World War, global product has more than quadrupled in real terms, meaning that industrial product grew fortyfold, energy consumption twenty-twofold, cereal production more than three times, and external trade seven times. The global product in current dollars was US$2.6 trillion in 1950 and £22.3 trillion in 1990, whereas world trade was $60 billion in 1950 and $3,400 billion in 1990. Cereal production in 1950 was 631 million tonnes, 1,971 million tonnes in 1990.

This growth imposed serious strains on our natural resources, in proportions unthought of only a few decades ago. These changes triggered, furthermore, new stresses and conflicts: unfettered exploitation of natural resources, the accumulation of waste material, pollution, poverty, and famine—to name but a few.

The high expectations for peace did not materialize. The arms race and the politics of the Cold War kept alive differences and conflicts, even exacerbating them. The capacity to destroy the world many times over was built up by the rival power blocs, diverting resources from human welfare. The importance claimed by defence security tended to neglect other elements of human security relating to food, health, employment and income, and the environment.

~

All these factors are by no means unrelated phenomena; they are integrally part of the tensions represented by the processes of global transition. They question existing production and consumption patterns—unsustainable and too long unchallenged. They point to the need, also, of giving to social policy a much higher priority than heretofore in overall decision-making and policy formulation. This demands a transition of its own, in terms of the nature of public policy at the national and international levels.

All these transitions interlock with two overarching transitions. One pertains to the political processes, seeking a transition from top-down regimes to securing a democratic basis for nation-states by empowering the people. The second transition, one affecting all other developments, is fuelled by the revolution in global communication. Cultural transition, thus buttressed by improved communication, plays a crucial role in interconnecting people, facts, and ideas; it easily 'globalizes', furthermore, all dimensions of the transition process.

Achievements in health care, and success in producing food as well as other goods and services, have had their direct impacts on population growth. The ongoing transition processes already described may facilitate, or else pose obstacles to, efforts intended to improve the quality of life; yet they influence, even if indirectly, population dynamics.

Demographic transition lies at the heart of all transitions—if it is not, indeed, the very basis for turmoil, especially in terms of life and death, the way we work and love, how we move about and interact. There prevails no isolated logic, one upon which an accelerated pace could be imposed by sheer will.

All these processes are affected, in turn, by demographic transition and the conflicts that this causes. Demographic behaviour in Eastern and Central Europe after the demise of communism, for example, illustrates the immediate effects of political, economic, and social transformation on demographic conditions, especially fertility and mortality rates.

If properly managed, all the transition processes can help reduce the time required by demographic transition and its related turbulence and uncertainty. Smooth management of the entire process of transition is a huge challenge, but still greater is the challenge of getting it under way.

～

The ideological rifts of the past have lessened with respect to democracy, human rights, and patterns of economic management; but the danger of new ideological confrontations and tensions still looms large.

For all these reasons, the Independent Commission on Population and Quality of Life (ICPQL) chose to link inseparably the issues of population and quality of life. A holistic view of demographic transition transcends any simplistic notion that a solution rests solely on stabilization of the global population. The Commission's integrating view emphasizes, instead, *all* the processes that affect the quality of life. (To shed further light on all the dimensions involved, ICPQL commissioned a number of studies, the list of which is found in the Appendix.)

'The world of tomorrow can be tamed either through outside force or through shared values', according to one political scientist and environmentalist. Indeed, it is because the total process of transition cannot devolve from catastrophic events, or even the impact of extraneous forces, that it requires a new value-system—a set of principles to manage the transition process smoothly and speedily. The Commission's vision is reinforced by the fact that the international community has agreed, as regards population issues, on *choices* and *rights* at the personal level. Implicitly, this stresses the role of normative values in guiding choices and strengthening rights.

Now that we stand both on the threshold of the new millennium and at the crossroads of all the transition processes, we still face two unresolved challenges of overriding urgency, challenges to be taken up simultaneously.

The first is an old conflict, begun with the Industrial Revolution and strongly reiterated fifty years ago with the birth of the UN, but not yet won: freedom from want. This is the most fundamental aspect of human security; it is tied up intricately with work, income, health, and environmental security. Eradication of poverty is thus a challenge to what we call humanity's *caring capacity*, to our ability to empathize with others, and to a commitment to do what is needed to provide fellow beings with at least the minimal quality of life consistent with dignity and our concern for the Earth's continued viability.

The second challenge goes even deeper—braking the degradation of the environment. This is a fundamental danger. It threatens the quality of our life, and, worse, puts the survival of humankind in jeopardy. It is a challenge to our ability to stay within the carrying capacity of the planet's habitats.

> ❧ *Quality of life is directly related to the quality of the natural world, so we must move towards standards of living that recognize the natural constraints.*
>
> Phyllis Creighton, Canada

Part I

Context and Challenges

1 The Population Challenge

> ❧ *A one-sided view of the problem looks at population in terms of numbers of bodies, ignoring the fact that these bodies consume food and use energy. This split view predominates even in international fora, where rich countries point at the fast rate of population growth of poor countries as the main problem in sustainable development—while the poor countries stress the high per-capita consumption by rich countries.*
>
> Maximo T. Kalaw, Jr., Philippines
> South-East Asia Public Hearing

> ❧ *Fair estimates suggest that if we go the way we are going, two billion people—one-third of humanity will be the absolute poor. One half of this—one billion—will live in the cities. It is not only a question of the cost of living, but the cruelty of the cost of survival.*
>
> Anwar Fazal, Malaysia
> South-East Asia Public Hearing

Numbers and Growth Rates—Facets of Population Dynamics

Few issues have aroused more controversy and political, social, and moral divisiveness than the question of population, although few bold actions have been taken so far. World leaders express deep demographic concerns, but the meagre results of these concerns show that population must be affected by more complex factors. We do not solve population problems by *tackling population alone*. It has become, in a real sense, a strategic factor in national and international politics. Because the manner in which demographic transition takes place will have enormous future significance, it may be useful at the outset to retrace population development and look at likely further trends.

Population began to grow in the wake of the Agricultural Revolution, although its ascent was punctuated episodically by famine, epidemics, war, and the occasional collapse of civilizations. By 1750 the world's population numbered 700 million.[1]

During the eighteenth and nineteenth centuries the Industrial Revolution in some European countries and in North America shifted the pace of growth into higher gear, although this was tempered by high mortality rates—which in fact rose. It took one century, 1830–1930, for the total population to move from 1 billion to 2 billion.

Mortality in the developing countries began to fall rapidly after the Second World War, as populations continued to increase. This is attributable to progress in industrialization combined with advances in medicine and health care. The overall trend was uneven, however, for four reasons:

- variations in the type and spread of industrialization;
- disparities in the availability of services such as health care and education;
- varying demographic features, such as size of the group of reproductive age; and
- the impact of traditions.

After a slow descent, mortality fell to a rate of 2.1 per cent in 1990.

In the industrialized countries population growth tapered off rapidly. While it had grown at an annual rate of 1.2 per cent from 1950 until 1980, it dropped to 0.6 per cent by 1990.

The period of fastest population growth coincided with swift advances in technology, health, education, and material well-being. The average real income in developing countries, measured in constant purchasing-power parity dollars, rose almost threefold from $950 per person in 1960 to $2,730 in 1991. These rises were substantial in all regions except Africa and South Asia.[2] ('Purchasing-parity' equivalence seeks to relate how much in earnings it takes to buy the same product or service in different economic settings; it is probably the most equitable of currency relationships.) In terms of health, life-expectancy at birth in developing countries rose from 46 years in 1960 to 63 years in 1992, although the latter figure contrasts with the 76-year average in the industrial nations.[3] There were striking improvements in education too, the drops in illiteracy coinciding with advances in enrolment in primary and secondary schools.[4]

Despite the popular impression of an accelerating explosion, therefore, the growth *rate* in the world's population as a whole has passed its peak. This was reached roughly thirty years ago (1965–70), when it ran at over 2 per cent/year. The rate slowed to 1.54 per cent/year during the period 1990–5. Figure 1.1, prepared by the UN, expresses these changes in graphic form.

In absolute numbers, total population rose from 3.7 billion in 1970 to 5.7 billion in 1995—two additional billions in a mere

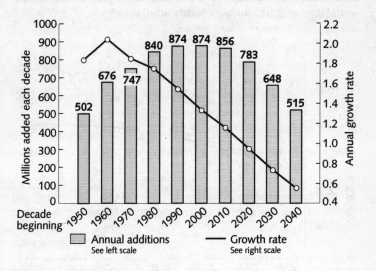

Fig. 1.1. Passing the population hump: addition, growth by decades. The growth *rate* reached its peak about 1965; the increment in *numbers* may reach its highest towards 2010.

Source: United Nations, Population Division.

twenty-five years. Thus an even smaller growth rate will translate into larger absolute figures, and this 'population momentum' will continue for several decades because tomorrow's parents are alive today. Until the year 2000 the absolute increase is projected at an all-time historical peak of 88 millions on average. This is the equivalent of *ten new Swedens* every year or an *entire Latin America* every five years.[5]

The range of what could realistically happen, demographically, is broad enough to allow alternative projections of scenario. The UN Population Division prepares projections based on a variety of assumptions concerning, for instance, female fertility in the future. Based on present trends, the *most plausible scenario* may be the UN Population Division's medium projection, estimating that total population will reach 9.8 billion by the year 2050 (see Fig. 1.2). Its central assumption is that female fertility, averaging about 3.1 children per woman in 1995, will fall to the replacement level of 2.1 children by 2040. To stabilize world population at a plateau of 11 billion would then require another century, until 2150.[6]

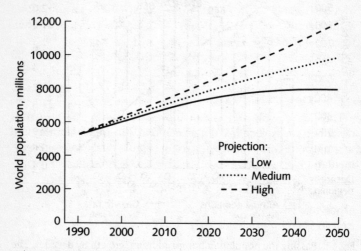

Fig. 1.2. Alternative futures in demographic increase: high, medium, and low projections.
Source: UN, Population Division.

Thus between 1995 and 2050 another 4.1 billion people would be added, the *equivalent of the world's population in 1975*. We would have to find ways to feed, clothe, shelter, and provide livelihood and other resources for the likely addition of 4 billion more people while endeavouring to preserve local and global environments. This should present immense challenges to policy formulation, finance, human-resources development, the building of institutions, and the development of new technologies.[7]

Using the UN's high projection, female fertility would level at 2.5 children from about 2040 onward. Since this is above the replacement level of 2.1 births, the population would continue to grow indefinitely, with world population attaining levels of 11.9 billion in 2050, 18–19 billion by 2100.

According to the UN's low projection, the replacement fertility of 2.1 children per woman would be reached as early as 2015 and then begin to fall—as it has done in most European countries. By 2050 the typical woman would have 1.57 children, the current European average. Should fertility remain at this level—not an unrealistic assumption—then human numbers would peak at nearly 8 billion by 2045 and diminish after that time.

In the early years of these projections differences in growth will be small. Even ten years hence, the gap between low and high projections would be 295 million. But, as the decades pass, the gap would widen until the total reached massive proportions by 2050.

The future, however, is not graven in stone. The scenarios described are projections, not *predictions*. The implied fertility and mortality rates may change as a result of individual choice, governmental policies, unforeseeable disasters, or scientific breakthroughs.

Mortality, too, could follow different paths. It could be lower than expected, yielding higher totals of population—should life-expectancy improve even faster than projected.[8] Mortality rates may decline, on the other hand, more slowly than expected. Old diseases such as malaria and tuberculosis are already in resurgence, and growing resistance to antibiotics and pesticides may bring new problems. AIDS could slow the population's growth in some African countries as well as radically change demographic composition if adults die in their prime.[9] Climatic change, too, could affect mortality if crop yields are depressed or if severe droughts occur.

The future world population's age-composition signals new problems. The under-15 age-group now accounts for a sizeable part of the population; it is expected to grow further.

Between 1950 and 2025 the number of old people (i.e. those 60 years and over) may increase sixfold, from 200 million to 1,200 million: a rise from 8 to 14 per cent of the global population. The number of people aged over 80 years is expected to rise from 13 to 137 million. Never before has there been such a prolongation of human life.

All but 1 per cent of future population growth will be concentrated in today's developing countries, and no less than two-thirds of this will occur in only two regions: Africa and South Asia. These areas are the world's poorest; they have the lowest quality of life and the most regrettable situation for women. Women are also in a disadvantaged position in Western Asia and North Africa, regions expected to experience the fastest demographic rates of growth.[10]

The stereotyped view that population growth occurs only in developing countries, however, is false. Four industrialized nations—the United States, Canada, Australia, and New Zealand—are also projected to continue growing. Most of this growth will derive from immigration and high fertility among recent immigrants. Future demographic growth in these and other industrialized countries will depend, also, on their immigration policies.

Populations in Europe may diminish within the decade 1995–2005, creating a different set of problems. Among the industrialized countries, trends in ageing may put severe pressures on social sustainability, and the benefit levels of social-security systems could well be affected. In developing countries the challenge of ageing should be even more daunting because their capacities are already insufficient to deal with their needs.

Population as Numbers, Population as People

A difference in numbers should make a huge difference in the quality of life to be experienced by future generations. It is equally true, however, that improvements to the quality of life, especially that of women, would be a function of total numbers. It is this two-way link, quality of life/population growth, that makes imperative the taking of action on both these fronts.

A balance is needed, therefore, on how population is viewed, in terms of both numbers and human beings. *Population* means *people*. As one witness in our South Asian consultation remarked: 'Women have children; they do not have population.'

Population means *numbers*, too. While numbers matter, they do not matter in themselves. Numbers are important because of the effects they have on many elements of the quality of life. It is all too often that people are forgotten in favour of abstract, macroeconomic targets: low inflation rates, balanced national budgets. If population is considered in numbers alone, isolated from the other aspects of life, this is *wrong* in both human and scientific terms. The quality of life of *population as people*, therefore, should be the central focus of all policy-making.

Responsible governments need, of course, policies based on population-as-numbers, the very fundamentals of demography. They must take a stand, for example, on whether their rates of growth, migration and territorial distribution are acceptable. But to bring about change in such parameters, governments are obliged to develop corresponding strategies. Policy regarding population-as-numbers, in other words, cannot overlook its primary goal—improving the quality of life of population-as-people.

> ✎ *In Ho Chi Minh City nearly 100 per cent of the dwellings are shabby, almost 100 per cent of the families are without toilets, 80 per cent of the poor people are migrants from rural areas, 70 per cent of the poor people have only a primary education, 29 per cent of the poor over 5 years of age are illiterate, 65 per cent of the population works temporarily for less than 6 months of the year,*

and the average floor space in the country is 3 square metres per capita.

Nguyen Thi Canh, Vietnam
South-East Asia Public Hearing

References

1. Colin McEvedy and Richard Jones, *Atlas of World Population History* (Harmondsworth, Penguin Books, 1978).
2. UN Development Programme, *Human Development Report 1994* (Oxford, Oxford University Press, 1994).
3. Ibid.
4. On literacy, UN Development Programme, *Human Development Report 1994*; on school enrolments, UNESCO, *Statistical Yearbook* for various years (Paris).
5. UN Population Division, *World Population Trends as Assessed in 1994* (New York, UN, 1994).
6. Respectively, UN Population Division, *World Population Trends as Assessed in 1994*; UN Population Division, *Long Range Population Projections* (New York, UN, 1992).
7. UN Population Division, *Long Range Population Projections*.
8. Wolfgang Lutz (ed.), *The Future of World Population* (London, Earthscan, 1994).
9. John Bongaarts, 'Projection of the Mortality Impact of AIDS', in ibid.
10. UN Development Programme, *Human Development Report 1995* (Oxford, Oxford University Press, 1995).

2 The Social Challenge

Facing Poverty

> ❧ *I have a suggestion. Environmental impact reports are required internationally for projects at all levels. Why not make it compulsory to prepare reports on impacts to correct inequalities?*
>
> Maria Teresa Augusti, Brazil
Latin-America Public Hearing

> ❧ *I am a parent in a very poor family of seven children in Ormoc City, Leyte. My husband's low wage as a sugar-plantation worker is not enough to feed us, so that two of our children go to elementary school while the five eldest work to help support everyone. Our eldest son left home in 1988 and has worked ever since as a clandestine employee in a piggery at Bulacan.*
>
> Enrica Albes, Philippines
South-East Asia Public Hearing

> ❧ *Our children leave school because it is expensive, fathers cannot find work, prices keep rising. There is nothing to collect from the forest to help our unemployed husbands. While the land we till becomes smaller—reduced grazing lands have made our animals disappear—our families become larger. What will happen to our children, and what can we do for them?*
>
> Sibonelelo Group, Zimbabwe
Southern Africa Public Hearing

Faces of Poverty, Multiple Deprivations

Half-a-century after the UN pledged to abolish hunger, millions of people (with their numbers growing daily) still live a life of destitution. There remains a great amount of avoidable suffering in the world, an unfinished agenda of massive proportions.

Poverty in many developing countries has shown that it cannot be reduced and absorbed through the efforts of integrated development. The structural poverty in industrialized countries adds to the realization that the current economic model is unable to cope with the demographic changes happening in different regions of the world.

It is now nearly three decades since the rights to health, education, work, and freedom from fear and hunger were declared fundamental in the International Covenant on Economic, Social, and Cultural Rights. Although the aim of ending poverty world-wide has been affirmed and restated insistently through international agreements and actions, the rights do not affect more than a billion people. The designation of 1996 as the International Year for the Eradication of Poverty provides a new opportunity for the international community to rally its energies, to work towards the realization of an objective now long overdue.

There were some 944 million people in absolute poverty, according to UN estimates, in 1970. By 1985 this total had risen to 1.156 billion. By 1994 the UN Development Programme (using a different methodology) placed the total at 1.3 billion.[1] These millions are not mere numbers. They stand for individuals, each with his or her own hopes and fears, each with an equal right to self-respect and freedom from suffering and anxiety. The numbers mean that all the misery in the world has not shrunk despite three decades of development effort. Quite the opposite: this misery has grown in certain respects.

Living a hand-to-mouth existence, the poorest of the poor have a higher rate of mortality, and their infant mortality rates are much higher than those of the rich. The affluent in many countries have more children, and first-generation immigrant families who experience new security and improved health have a higher growth rate. And yet the period of our fastest growth, since 1950, has also witnessed the most rapid advances in technology, health, education, and material well-being. We have already seen how average real incomes, measured in international dollars at purchasing-power parity, rose three times between 1950 and 1991. The rises have been substantial in all regions except Africa and South Asia.[2]

Poverty, a blatant attack on dignity, has many faces. It implies low income but goes far beyond: poverty also means malnutrition, persistent ill health, lack of education, bad housing. It means chronic unemployment or underemployment; lack of access to social, legal, and many informational services; and inability to assert legal or political rights. Indeed, the poor are often denied access to legal or political redress.

Poverty appears in other ways: lack of control over one's life and future, the humiliation of powerlessness, and the corrosive effects of despair, cynicism, and loss of faith in the future. Poverty can mean not simply one brief episode of deprivation, but repeated or continuing privation. More often than not it is the same people who suffer from several (often all) privations.

So poverty is synonymous with poor quality of life, a quality failing to meet the minimal acceptable standards. And poverty exists in developing and industrialized countries alike. In the developing regions poverty is not a temporary phenomenon. Rather, it has

Poverty in the Industrialized Societies

Any night of 1993 in New York, 23,000 men and women slept on the street or in public shelters—a small part of the 3 per cent of the city's population which had no roof over their heads during the preceding five years.

(*The New York Times*, 16 Nov. 1993)

In the United Kingdom 400,000 were officially classified as homeless in 1989.

(*Human Development Report*, 1992)

Levels of unemployment in the 1980s were more than 20 per cent in Britain, over 40 per cent in Spain, and 46 per cent in Norway. (*UN World Survey*, 1989)

become a persistent structural feature in the development process—trapping poor people inside poor countries.

⟶

And poverty is on the rise in the industrialized countries. Vulnerable minorities—the ageing and retired, the young, those unemployed who are also beyond their prime, recent immigrants— all of these are experiencing levels of insecurity, deprivation, or exclusion that may last decades. There are more and more people without sufficient income to enjoy a minimal quality of life, as reflected by the rising number of 'street people' almost everywhere.

The dimensions of privation are staggering and frightening. They shake our complacency to the point of outrage or paralysis. In 1990 an estimated 406 million children of primary- and secondary-school age in developing countries could not exercise their right to education, and UNESCO expects this figure to rise to 450 million by 2000.[3]

While the rate of adult illiteracy in developing nations fell from 55 per cent in 1970 to 33 per cent in 1990, the absolute numbers climbed to 905 million (essentially as a result of population growth). Two-thirds of these were women.[4] And illiteracy is by no means confined to developing areas. Illiteracy in industrialized countries has been estimated, using different criteria, at 15–20 per cent of the total population. (Note that illiteracy in industrialized countries corresponds to the phenomenon that, in spite of a few years of schooling, the ability to decode a message is almost non-existent.) These figures embrace youths older than 15 years together with those younger than 15 who are not enrolled in formal education. World-wide, there may be an estimated 1.5 billion illiterate or functionally illiterate people.

The number of jobs world-wide has grown, but this has been insufficient to provide livelihoods for all. Combined with unemployment or underemployment, poorly rewarded, degrading, or exploitative work still characterizes the lives of many. In 1995 an estimated 120 million people were unemployed, with perhaps another 600–700 millions seeking additional work to eke out a minimal standard of living or to improve the prospects for their children.[5] According to the International Labour Organization, the number of children who are estimated to be at work world-wide is 100 million. There is no reliable count of the other categories of deprived, marginalized, and often invisible workers. Global studies—by industry, profession, and occupation—are badly needed.

⤙

Around 1 billion people are out of reach of the basic health services. Some 1.3 billion must drink unclean water, while 1.9 are without *rudimentary* sanitation.[6]

Between 1988 and 1990 some 786 million people were estimated to be chronically undernourished. While this represented a drop from the 941 million estimated in 1969–71, all the improvement took place in Asia only. The numbers held steady, or grew, in the other regions. In Latin America, for instance, the figures rose from 54 to 59 millions. In Africa the count climbed steeply from 101 to 168 millions.[7]

In daily life, each of these aspects of poverty overlap. Unemployment and poor income, illiteracy, hunger, ill health, inadequate shelter and social services do not strike randomly. They usually visit the same persons, the same families, the same shanty-towns and other slums, the same marginal or rural areas. Illiteracy is bred by lack of schooling, and then leads to difficulty in finding work and having a decent income. Low revenue itself means overcrowded habitat, poor diet, lack of access to clean water and sanitation; all of these mean fragile health.

Multiple privation often combines with discrimination on the basis of race, gender, 'class', or handicap. Taken altogether, these prejudices constitute *social exclusion*, or multidimensional and cumulative disadvantage.

Yet exclusion is not a state; it is a process by which humans are disinherited—dispossessed of the basic rights that help constitute dignity. These rights belong to every member of society,[8] yet the different aspects of a poor quality of life overlap because poverty in its different forms locks people into a situation from which escape is difficult, for them and for their children.

Not only is the level of the quality of life inherited by the next generation, but poor nutrition of mother and child assures a bad start in life. Poor parents have difficulty in keeping children in school, and illiterate parents cannot help children with their studies. Chronic malnutrition, furthermore, leads to physical and mental underdevelopment at school, ill health, or a handicapped existence later: in essence, a lack of control over one's own life. Poor children, as the ultimate victims of such circumstances, are doomed to perpetuate the inequalities of pauperdom and multiple privation. These conditions pose grave risks to social harmony. Increased violence and rising crime (which hit the poor hardest) add to a lowered quality of life for everyone.

The Causes of Poverty

The reasons why so many people remain deprived of basic needs are complex. The primary causes are of a political, economic, structural, and social nature, abetted by a lack of political resolve and wrong attitudes regarding public policy and the deployment of resources.

- At the individual level, people are handicapped by lack of access to resources, skills, or opportunities to make a decent living.

- On the societal plane, the major causes are inequalities in the distribution of resources, services, and power. These inequalities may be institutionalized in terms of land, capital, infrastructure, markets, credit, education, information, and advisory services. The same is true in the provision of social services: education, health, clean water, and sanitation. Inequality of services leaves rural areas the worst off, so that it comes as no surprise that an estimated 77 per cent of the developing world's poor live in rural zones.[9] Yet the urban poor are mired in even worse conditions.

All these problems affect women more than men, reinforcing the existing gender problem. Despite legal or institutional protection, this inequality persists and is spreading. The world's poverty has, indeed, an increasingly feminine face.

Poverty becomes further entrenched by worsening inequalities in the distribution of income and wealth, within and among differ-

Table 2.1 *Comparison of living conditions between slum and non-slum areas in greater Manila ('Metro Manila')*

	Slums	Non-slums
Student drop-outs before secondary school (%)	35	20
Birth-rate/1,000 population	177	33
Infant mortality/1,000 live births	210	76
Tubercular patients/100,000 population	7,000	800
Third-degree malnutrition (%)	9.6	3

Source: South-East Asia Public Hearing.

ent countries. The gap between the richest 20 per cent and the poorest 20 per cent, therefore, is widening. In 1991 the industrialized countries, with 22 per cent of the world's population, enjoyed 61 per cent of the *real* gross domestic product (GDP), leaving only 39 per cent for the developing countries with their 78 per cent of the population.[10]

Some countries have managed to combine economic growth and give attention to easing the disparities in levels of equality by investing in human resources. The levels of inequality within countries vary enormously. In developed nations the gap between the richest and poorest fifths of households range from 4.3 to 1 (Japan) to 9.6 to 1 (United Kingdom). Among the poorer countries, the disparities are within the same range in much of Asia, where they average 6 to 1, and in western Asia, where the average is 7 to 1.[11] But differentials are higher in most of Africa, where they average 13 to 1. They are most pronounced in the Latin American average, 17.5 to 1.

Widespread are the inequalities between urban and rural districts. There remain glaring gaps in the provision of health, educational, and family-planning services among rural and urban incomes. To illustrate, in Latin America the gap between the two has averaged 2.8 to 1, in Asia 4.2 to 1, and in Africa almost 8 to 1.

Eradicating Poverty

Narrowing the gap in income distribution becomes central to any policy aiming to eradicate poverty. Access to wealth and services needs to be made more equal than before. The present situation, inherently unequal distribution, is not the unavoidable result of economic processes; it is the outcome of the history of choices made in public policy—and the situation can be changed only through altered public policy.

A distribution of income and access to services that is essentially unfair breeds a sense of injustice and unrest, a feeling quite different from that of envy, but one that harbours the seeds of discontent. An equitable distribution of income and resources is essential, therefore, for co-operation, solidarity, and social cohesion.

It is noteworthy that the non-fulfilment of economic and social rights does not arouse the same indignation and advocacy as does the violation of civil and political rights. Either the international community will prove itself capable of launching effective action to eradicate poverty, or else its repeated concern for the population explosion will prove to be mere rhetoric.

The situation is changing, nevertheless. A sense of outrage against injustice has been a source of inspiration in ethical and ideological development, and for major movements of reform or even radical change. Pressure from the groups involved has come increasingly through the growing number of UN conferences dealing with environment and development, population and development, social development, human rights, and the role of women (the last held in Beijing, 1995). This pressure has accelerated interactions between governments and civil society—all the non-governmental organizations representing live, independent forces in society, focused on societal issues. Our view is that such movements will be ever more needed and decisive if 'Rights to Quality of Life' are to become real, if a sense of active social responsibility is acknowledged as an indicator of social and political development.

Radical change is inevitable. In recent years the formulation of national strategies to reduce poverty has attracted the support of both governments and international mechanisms. The Copenhagen Summit, in particular, succeeded in giving political weight and push to these approaches. They must now be followed up in earnest, and translated into reality.

The Commission is keenly aware that the battle against poverty is a demanding one—the battle of our time. Population growth can deepen poverty; it leads, combined with laws on inheritance, to a fragmentation of land-holdings and living below subsistence levels. Although it is usually seen as the cause of poverty, demographic growth is, in fact, but one of the reasons for the persistence of poverty.

The resources clearly exist to end poverty and exclusion, within countries and internationally, and they need to be used to relieve the growing number of poor nations. Poverty, untenable as it is, is unlikely to be eradicated without adding substantial additional resources—a problem raised specifically by the Commission in this report.

> ✎ *Too many of those children born to children are hungry. Every night in the richest country in the world we have five to eight million children to go to bed hungry. Every morning we have the same number to go to school hungry. We have too many of our children that are healthless or have no health care. We have many children that are born and left in hospitals. Many children who are at homes who are unplanned and unwanted, that are hugless. Nobody cares about them. It is easier in our country sometimes to get drugs than it is to get hugs. . . . We've to make sure that every child born anywhere in the world has an opportunity to grow up healthy, educated, motivated and full of hope for the future.*
>
> Jocelyn Elders, former Surgeon General of
> the United States
> North America Public Hearing

> ✎ *Forty-seven years of independence and many promises. The majority in India still have no idea whether they will have a job tomorrow, whether their child will survive, whether women will have safety of health and life.*
>
> Imrana Quadeer, India
> South Asia Public Hearing

Improving quality of life for poor people must consider a spectrum of problems simultaneously. We want to see no more people on the streets without a place to live. We do not want to hear that people don't have food. We don't want to see that women have no health care or are dying from unsafe abortions or sexually transmitted diseases or unsafe anything because we have the capability to do otherwise, go to the moon—build weapons that can wipe out the human race. We have not been able to resolve this issue.

Cece Modupe Fadope, United States
North America Public Hearing

The poor, too, have dreams; they have solved an immense mass of problems; they have survived, as have indigenous peoples. They can offer solutions.

Rigoberta Menchu, Guatemala
Latin America Public Hearing

Mahatma Gandhi said, 'When you are deciding a matter, have the picture before you of the poorest man you have met and ask if the decision will help him. If the answer is in the affirmative, take the decision without hesitation.' This remains eternally and universally sound advice.

Nirmala Buch, India
South Asia Public Hearing

The fight against poverty today is at the core of the relationship between population and quality of life. The more we gravitate around sectoral issues like education, health or violence, the more we return to poverty as the fundamental point of attack . . . Latin America is not a poor continent, it is one marked by injustice.

Rosiska Darcy de Oliveira, Brazil
Latin America Public Hearing

One of the main vices of the reformers who determined socio-economic policy in our country since 1992 is their extreme negligence regarding social policy. They

[thought] social problems could be resolved after . . .
revival of the economy. Our politicians have an excep-
tionally quantitative approach to the problems of social
protection.

Anatoly Vishnevsky, Russia
Eastern Europe Public Hearing

➤ *I am fourteen years old, eldest of five children of a shoe-*
maker. I became one of eight child laborers in the
Young's Town sardine factory [where] we worked from
seven in the morning until four the next, sometimes
fainting at work, many days sleeping only two hours.
We ate noodles (our owner had a noodle factory, too),
sometimes cooked with maggots and cockroaches, or
else family leftovers. We inserted fish into cans, as many
as 3,000 a day. We slashed our fingers on the tins and
fish bones, our blood sometimes dripping into the cans.
After work, we were locked in our bunkhouse, could not
leave on Sundays or holidays, and were not paid our
wages for months because the employer deducted the
bus fares he said we owed him for our travel from the
provinces. The National Bureau of Investigation raided
the factory and freed us.

Josie Caberos, Manila, Philippines
South-East Asia Public Hearing

➤ *The real quality of life of ordinary people results from*
maldistribution; it is only partially related to population.
Overemphasizing population growth sometimes works
against the interests of the people when non-performing
politicians and the ruling elite try to use it as an alibi.

Devendra Raj Panday, Nepal
South Asia Public Hearing

➤ *Poverty has to be ascribed to the perverse distribution of*
income and the absence of land reform, penalizing
chiefly that part of Brazil's population that is of African
origin—especially the women.

Edna Roland-Geledes, Brazil
Latin America Public Hearing

> ❧ *Payatas in Quezon City is a dump site to which many urban poor have migrated. Its 635,000 population lives by scavenging, the cause of deaths or hospitalization. These people cannot get out of their vicious poverty.*
>
> Anita M. Celdran, Philippines
> South-East Asia Public Hearing

References

1. UN, *1989 Report on the World Social Situation* (New York, UN, 1989).
2. UNESCO, *World Education Report 1993* (Oxford, Oxford University Press, 1993).
3. Ibid.
4. Ibid.; 1970 figure from UNESCO, *Compendium of Statistics on Literacy* (Paris, 1993).
5. World Bank, *World Development Report 1995* (Oxford, Oxford University Press, 1995); UN Development Programme, *Human Development Report 1992* (Oxford, Oxford University Press, 1992).
6. UN Development Programme, *Human Development Report 1994* (Oxford, Oxford University Press, 1994).
7. Food and Agriculture Organization and World Health Organization, *Nutrition and Development—A Global Assessment* (Rome and Geneva, 1992).
8. G. Room *et al.*, *Observatory on National Policies to Combat Social Exclusion* (Report to the Commission of the European Communities, Lille, 1992).
9. UN Development Programme, *Human Development Report 1994*.
10. Global real GDP is calculated by multiplying average regional real GDP per person by regional population.
11. Regional averages calculated by the Commission on the basis of data found in World Bank, *World Development Report 1994* (Oxford, Oxford University Press, 1994).

3 The Ecological Challenge

❧ *The poor in growing numbers add to the destruction of the environment. These are the* kaingineros *doing subsistence agriculture after the loggers have clear cut the forests. They are the marginal fisherfolk resorting to dynamite fishing in overfished waters, or the urban squatters displaced from the countryside. Most are victims of inequitable access to natural resources in their communities. This is the root cause of their poverty which our church functionaries and those in political power are embarrassingly silent about.*

> Maximo Kalaw, Philippines
> South-East Asia Public Hearing

❧ *It is not the poor who are responsible for deterioration of the environment. When people have fewer resources, they husband them more carefully, because that is all that they have to fall back upon. Small farmers are a lot more efficient. They care for their land a lot better. It is the greed of the affluent which is using more of the resources than the poor do. Gandhi said: 'In this land there is enough for everyone's need but there is not enough for some people's greed.'*

> Vijay Vyas, India
> South Asia Public Hearing

Pressures on the Environment

Poverty is at the root of deforestation, land degradation, and the destruction of coastal habitats. Hundreds of millions of poor people are forced, all over the world, to over-use their habitats in order to survive. This problem is exacerbated by growing populations. The destruction of the natural-resource base is doomed to continue as long as the conditions of poverty remain unaddressed.

❧

Since the beginning, nature was taken as given, limitless. For too long regeneration of the natural environment was also taken for granted.

The scientific and industrial revolutions brought about a radical change in the relationship between Nature and human beings. Man found ways to uncover Nature's secrets and thus conquer Nature.

Riding as it does on the extensive exploitation of natural resources, modern industrial civilization made Nature subservient to economic purposes and forgot Nature's need—that of self-renewal. Within the economic paradigm of unending growth impelled by the Industrial Revolution, Nature, instead of being the main resource as in agrarian societies, became one of several assets. It lost its claim to favoured treatment that had long been institutionalized, even ritualized, in agrarian cultures.

As science discovered the hidden and complex life processes of Nature, in the economic calculus of the Industrial Revolution Nature became an increasingly inanimate factor—one to be exploited. Ignored was the importance of the natural environment as space integral to human existence, one needing nurture and care, a bequest to be made to future generations.

In the agrarian cultures respect for Nature's bounty as the primary means of human survival (and even fortune) engendered harmony between human needs and the natural environment. The main guardians of this symbiosis were the peasantry and its women. The transition of agriculture to mass-production industry, with its intensive chemical inputs, led to the 'death of the peasantry in the second half of the [twentieth] century',[1] and lent further impetus to the destruction of a harmonious relationship with the environment.

❧

The consequences of ecological depredation affect the entire world, even people still in its agrarian phase, and the responsibility of the industrialized world, at its peak in industrialized societies, is undeniable. Today the world as a whole faces the awesome task of establishing a new and sustainable equilibrium. This means that the environment is no longer to be treated as a warehouse of resources and as a disposal sink, but rather as the site of life and habitat. We want it to be as clean, healthy, and attractive as we can make it, and then bequeath it to those who will follow. The environment's quality is a crucial dimension, whether directly or indirectly, of the quality of life.

Until the 1950s pollution was a circumscribed problem, dealt with by production and sanitation engineers, localized to the extent that its consequences tended to have a local impact. Since then, the profligate use and waste of natural resources at every social level have changed drastically.

The cumulative effect of the unbridled use of resources has created a problem unparalleled before in its scope and severity, a global challenge being faced by all. Rupture of the old equilibrium has been great enough to affect what we understand about the relationship between Nature and human beings.

In the 1970s the problem was dealt with regionally at first, and then globally. Concern for spreading deserts, deforestation, soil erosion, acid rain, and pollution of urban air appeared on the international agenda. By the 1980s it was clear that human activity was the cause of disruption on a planetary scale. Added to the earlier list were the ozone hole, global warming, reduced biodiversity, and the sequels to over-fishing and ocean pollution.

The question of responsibility for degradation of the environment has created new ideological divides, between North and South on the international plane; between the affluent and the poor (or those who speak for them), at the national level. Poverty is at the root of deforestation, land degradation, and the destruction of coastal habitats. Hundreds of millions of poor people are forced, all over the world, to overuse their habitats in order to survive. This problem is exacerbated by growing populations. The destruction of the natural-resource base is doomed to continue as long as the conditions of poverty remain unaddressed. Hence what is urgently needed is a plan of action to offer to these many hundreds of millions of households—primarily in the South—alternatives to slash-and-burn and similar subsistence activities.

Compromising the Integrity of Nature

Some features of the environment, such as biodiversity and access to natural resources, are immediate constituents of the quality of life. Others have a less direct impact on quality through their effects on health and nutrition, livelihood, the labour burden, community ties. These features apply not only to the industrialized countries. They threaten the quality of life everywhere, the livelihoods of the poor, even the survival of our species. It is not sufficient, therefore, that a few countries establish clear and cautious norms for environmental conservation. The effort must be global.

Population growth is implicated in all such problems. Demographic growth is not an isolated phenomenon, since it combines with two other dominant factors:

- the pattern of consumption and prevailing production schemes; and
- the types of technology employed and the resulting wastes.

It appears that these problems have to be tackled together, as they are intrinsically interlocked. The integrity of Nature's basic elements, too, has come progressively to be compromised as can be seen in the cases of air and water quality, biodiversity, and forests and deforestation.

Air and Water Quality

Air and water, fundamental components of Nature, are subjected to pollution from a variety of sources: on a large scale by factories and electrical power stations or other production units, by vehicles and other transport modes, and by households.

Following dramatic surges in levels of pollution—characterized by the detrimental effects of sulphur dioxide (SO_2), low-level ozone, chlorofluorocarbons, and other pollutants in the air; and poisonous discharges of heavy metals into water—the industrialized countries embarked on clean-up programmes.

In the process the quality of air and water has clearly improved. Emissions of smoke and SO_2 diminished in most cities since 1980 (in some cases dramatically). SO_2 levels dropped by more than 50 per cent during the 1980s in Finland, France, Germany, the Netherlands, Sweden, and Switzerland. And in most countries the concentrations of heavy metal have also fallen steeply.[2] Emissions of nitrogen oxides and low-level ozone (both produced by motor vehicles), however, continue to grow; they exacerbate cases of asthma in many cities. In most countries there has been a rise in concentration in water of nitrates, produced by fertilizers washing off farm-lands.[3]

The problems are repeating themselves in the newly industrializing countries of Asia and Latin America. During the 1980s there were striking rises in air pollution as SO_2 emissions rose by 50 per cent or more in China, India, Indonesia, Pakistan, and Thailand. Some concentrations in Xian, Shanghai, Beijing, Jakarta, Lahore, and Tehran, for instance, were by then four to eight times higher than in Tokyo.[4]

In the mid-1980s an estimated 1.3 billion people—mostly in the developing countries—were exposed to outdoor smoke ceiling-levels higher than those set by the World Health Organization (WHO). Had the levels been lowered to those advised by WHO, between 300,000 and 700,000 premature deaths could have been averted each year.[5]

The poorest households face an additional hazard in the form of air pollution indoors. Besides producing smoke, wood, straw, and dung fires give off nitrogen oxides, SO_2, carbon monoxide, and carcinogens. These can lead to acute respiratory infection and chronic bronchitis—conditions that kill some 4 million infants and children annually. Between 400 and 700 million people, most of them women and children, may be exposed to indoor-smoke levels as much as ninety times higher than WHO's peak guide-lines.[6]

Atmosphere

Perhaps the greatest challenges to our survival are posed by human-induced changes in the atmosphere: oxygen depletion, global warming caused by increased emission of the so-called greenhouse gases (like carbon dioxide and methane), and by deforestation.

Even if climate change caused by global warming proves to be gradual, the consequences will be serious. Based on probable trends until 2100, the Intergovernmental Panel on Climate Change (IPCC) predicts a rise in average temperature of about 2.9°C (nearly 5° Fahrenheit) and a rise in sea level of between 30 and 100 centimetres. Low-lying island states in the Pacific Ocean could be submerged, and in China's populous coastal zones as many as 76 million people might be affected. In Bangladesh, one-tenth of the population could be displaced.[7]

Planet-wide, precipitation should become more erratic; new patterns of water deposition, soil moisture, and rainfall may emerge. There would be unprecedented changes in crop production: with a doubling of carbon-dioxide levels, rice yields could fall by 2 to 5 per cent and maize production might fall by 15 to 24 per cent.[8] Plants would suffer increased heat stress, and pests and diseases will spread. Any adaptation to the new climatic realities should be dramatic.

All these changes could affect, too, the circulation of the oceans, with the risk of significant shifts in global climate that could, in turn, trigger mass migrations and conflicts.

Global warming should hit developing countries especially hard. Cereal production could be cut by 9 to 12 per cent below what it would be otherwise, and cereal prices could rise anywhere from 10 to 100 per cent.[9] The numbers of people menaced by hunger in developing countries (an estimated 640 million by 2060 if there is no climate change) could rise to 823 million. The irony here is that the millions risking hunger will not have contributed to atmospheric change since they are too poor to use the sources of the toxic emissions. Yet it is they who will bear the brunt of change.

Climate change, too, could multiply many times over the already devastating effects on biodiversity. With the shifting of rainfall and temperature zones, many species would be displaced. Some biological species, such as trees, would be unable to 'move' fast enough. Others might find the route barred by swathes of human settlements.[10]

Forests

Forests are in crisis in tropical, boreal, and temperate zones. Throughout the 1980s the 1,756 million hectares of the world's tropical forests were shrinking at a rate of 11 million hectares/year (1980) to 16 million hectares/year (1990). This is an area equal to five Belgiums, and the rate is accelerating.

The highest rates of loss during this period were in Asia (11.4 per cent during the decade), West Africa (9.6 per cent lost), and Central America (14 per cent lost). In countries such as Bangladesh, Malaysia, Pakistan, the Philippines, Thailand, and several countries in Central America and the Caribbean, the Food and Agriculture Organization of the UN reports that more than 18 per cent of tropical forest disappeared during the same decade.[11]

Forest degradation and deforestation have particularly serious effects on global warming. The burning of forests accounts for some 20 per cent of global carbon emissions: 4.6 gigatonnes of carbon dioxide are emitted into the atmosphere annually. Deforestation is at the heart of the loss of habitats and biodiversity. Where loggers and farmers cut down virgin forest, soil erosion increases, fish die in streams and rivers, and there are fewer animals and plants for local use. These processes reduce, in turn, crop-yields and variety in diet.

Also causing concern is the plight of 200 million cultivators in tropical countries who have migrated to inland watersheds in search of arable land. While traditional slash-and-burn agriculture cut down the trees, farmers left the land fallow so that it could rejuvenate. But growing populations now force a reduced gap between cropping times. Productivity diminishes, especially in hilly forests where the soil is usually of poor quality. Even where the traditional system has given way to terraced cultivation, productivity remains low.

Deforestation in hill areas, furthermore, triggers erosion of the soil and expansion of wasteland; it reduces rainfall and lowers the water table below ground, often producing acute scarcities of water in the area. Women and girls, inevitably responsible for fetching water in rural areas, then travel longer distances. In dry areas this can require two to three hours daily.[12] Deforestation means, besides, the disappearance of forest fruits, fuel-wood, and fodder, so that the nutrition in households dependent on wooded land is affected. Building-poles, herbs for cooking or of medicinal value, and other forest produce all provide a livelihood for the poor who market them—'as is', or after processing.

Deforestation thus means, for the poor, a spiralling descent into poverty. It is this cumulative dependence on forests as their life-support system during the non-agricultural seasons that absolves the poor of blame for most deforestation. The poor, on the other hand, are reported to prove much better conservationists than State forest authorities.

As journey times for the collection of wood and water increase, children (especially girls) are recruited to help their mothers. This reduces the adequacy of their calorie intake and may keep the youngsters away from school.[13]

Forests are in crisis in the boreal and temperate zones too, regions playing a pivotal role in the sequestration of carbon. Extensive ecological damage is caused by pollution and wasteful forest-harvesting practices. The rapidly increasing industrial demand for timber heightens the pressure on loggers. Large areas have already been irreparably damaged by clear-felling and inadequate investment in reforestation.

Insufficient scientific knowledge on how forest ecosystems function, and complex issues concerning the relationship between forests and climate change, make for constraints on conservation and regeneration. Without a holistic approach that integrates biological, physical, economic, and social variables not much progress is to be anticipated.[14] A second constraint is the lack of institutional mechanisms at the local level to combine public accountability with popular participation. Innovation in joint forest management by the government and the people in some Asian countries is drawing much attention internationally. A particular example comes from peasant women's groups in one Indian region (West Bengal) who demanded, and received, a 50 per cent representation in village Forest Protection Committees.

Biodiversity

The biggest threat to biodiversity—the number and variety of genes, species, and ecosystems—is the loss of natural habitats. These are being lost at record rates as farm-land expands in developing countries and as land for urban expansion (housing, roads, work-places) is lost to Nature everywhere. Thailand, for example, is estimated to have lost 87 per cent of its original mangroves, 96 per cent of its wetlands. Australia has lost 95 per cent of its marshland and other wetlands, whereas the figure for the United States is 53 per cent.[15]

Population density is a highly significant factor in the loss of natural habitat. Among fifty selected countries in Asia and Africa, the 20 per cent of the countries worst affected by loss of habitat have average population densities of 189 people per square kilometre; by 1990 they had lost an average of 85 per cent of their original wildlife habitat. The least affected 20 per cent, by contrast, lost only 41 per cent of this habitat, and population density averaged only 31 persons/sq. km.[16]

The progressive disappearance of tropical rain-forests poses a particularly urgent problem because they contain more than half the world's plant and animal species (insects included) and related genetic resources. It is estimated that annual loss in tropical forest resources may lead to the extinction of another 13 per cent of the remaining species by 2015.

The preservation of biodiversity is crucial to the future supply of food and nutrition. Although not more than some 200 of the planet's 250,000 plant species have been domesticated, their wilder relatives possess an important gene pool for plant breeders of the future. Some of the most important centres of crop diversity in western Asia, Ethiopia, the Indus basin, and the Andean highlands are threatened by a severe degradation of the land.[17]

Biodiversity also assures a rich source of pharmaceutical and other medicinal products of the future; it has important functions, too, in the regulation of biosystems. Many plants depend on specific animal pollinators or seed-dispersers, so that the loss of animals thus means the loss of plants. Some 120 modern medications are derived from plants, and four out of five persons in developing countries rely on traditional (mainly herbal) medicines as a first line of treatment. Yet much of this biological wealth is vanishing, along with knowledge about its use, because of both loss of wild habitats and the decay of indigenous cultures.[18]

People prize biodiversity for its direct value, therefore, but for its aesthetic qualities as well. As urban areas become more and more congested, citizens value increasingly all unspoiled wilderness. Many communities, and all religions, cherish most living things on the spiritual plane.

In Search of a New Equilibrium

The ecological challenge represents a new stage of human awareness as we embark on defining a new paradigm of the equilibrium between Nature and human beings. We are in the midst of a period properly called an *ecological transition*: from the notion of an always-renewable Nature (and naïve confidence in its permanence) to a revolt against over-exploitation of its resources, its purity, and its beauty.

The passage from Nature 'out there' to an environment that is part and parcel of human existence calls for a drastic change in our values and attitudes. The latter are best translated into terms such as sensitivity, respect, reverence, harmony, and careful nurturing, alongside more technical expressions such as protection, conservation, and rehabilitation—the last words invoking fewer emotions. Essential to the new understanding required is a recognition that the human being shares a common destiny with Nature, that our lives depend upon and are even interwoven with Nature's basic ingredients of air, water, land, and trees. The search for harmony and mutual sustenance is meant to guarantee that *people* remain at the centre of all societal processes, including the preservation, renewal, and enrichment of Nature.

More philosophically, our species has witnessed the passage of Nature from a merely linear evolution to a stage in which we have subordinated Nature to our own mastery, and onwards to a cycle in which we affirm a need for Nature's renewal. Policy and practice of conservation and efficiency are the new imperatives for the survival of Nature's capacity to support human life.

During this period of ecological transition, production schemes and consumption patterns (analysed in the next chapter) require transformation in such ways as to replenish Nature's losses. This will require, among other changes, strict regulation of industrial activity—even a ban on certain processes and products whose environmental fall-out can no longer be managed on the basis of existing knowledge.

Still another task is to harmonize the patterns of human settlements with those of Nature. Mega-cities and their evolving urban fabric impose excessive demands on Nature, the threatening and even devastating consequences of which can be seen in centres such as Mexico City, Shanghai, Bombay, or Cairo.

As with all other processes of transition, the ecological one will be a period of confusion, false solutions, disarray. We cannot bypass, either, the fact that the complexity of the factors involved may tend to make population the *flexible factor*, much in the way that Nature in the past was made the disposable factor. Before we tamper further with population, however, we need to look at other causes of difficulty.

There is now a citizens' movement against golf courses, proliferating as the playgrounds of the newly rich in many Third World countries. The citizens' groups believe that these playgrounds are at the expense of the environment and of the poor.

Anwar Fazal, Malaysia
South-East Asia Public Hearing

Our children no longer know wild animals, they are now extinct. We now use our bare hands to plough because of lack of animals to pull the plough; that is difficult. People just kill wild animals randomly. Respect for wild animals, which God created to beautify the world, is gone. Our children are unemployed, because of ESAP (economic structural adjustment programmes).

Sibonelelo Group, Zimbabwe
Southern Africa Public Hearing

References

1. Eric Hobsbawm, *The Age of Extremes: The Short Twentieth Century* (London, Michael Joseph, 1994).
2. UN Environment Programme, *Environmental Data Report 1993–94* (Oxford, Blackwell, 1993).
3. Ibid.
4. Ibid.
5. World Bank, *World Development Report 1992* (Oxford, Oxford University Press, 1992).
6. Ibid.
7. IPCC, *Climate Change: The IPCC Scientific Assessment*, updated by J.T. Houghton (ed.) (Cambridge, Cambridge University Press, 1990); *Climate Change 1992* (Cambridge, Cambridge University Press, 1992); the *Guardian*, 6 Apr. 1995; F. U. Mahtab, *Effects of Climate Change and Sea-Level Rise in Bangladesh* (London, Commonwealth Secretariat, 1989); Norman Myers, *Environmental Refugees* (Washington, Climate Institute, 1995).
8. Martin Parry and Cynthia Rosenzweig, 'Food Supply and the Risk of Hunger', *The Lancet*, 342 (Nov. 1993), 1,345; Cynthia Rosenzweig *et al.*, *Climate Change and Food Supply* (Oxford, University of Oxford Environmental Change Unit, 1993). Numbers cited are derived by averaging the results across the three main climate models.
9. Parry and Rosenzweig, 'Food Supply'; Rosenzweig *et al.*, *Climate Change*. Numbers cited are derived as explained in n. 8.
10. Robert Peters and Thomas Lovejoy (eds.), *Global Warming and Biological Diversity* (New Haven, Yale University Press, 1992).
11. FAO, *Forest Resources Assessment 1900* (Rome, 1993).
12. UN, *The World's Women* (New York, 1991).
13. Actionaid, *Listening to Smaller Voices* (London, 1995).
14. For a detailed discussion, see *World Commission on Forests and Sustainable Development: Proposed Work Programme* (Woods Hole, Aug. 1995).
15. These and related data are available on diskettes of the World Watch Institute.
16. Paul Harrison, *The Third Revolution* (London and New York, Penguin Books, 1993). Data sources: Jeffrey McNeely *et al.*, *Conserving the World's Biodiversity* (Gland, International Union for the Conservation of Nature and Natural Resources (IUCN), 1990), 268–9, with population-density figures from World Resources Institute, *World Resources 1990–91* (Oxford, Oxford University Press, 1990).

17. World Conservation Monitoring Centre, *Global Biodiversity* (London, Chapman and Hall, 1992), 331–40.

18. Ibid.; IUCN, *Global Biodiversity Strategy* (1992).

4 The Economic Challenge

A New Production and Consumption Model for the Globalized Economy

🙖 *Unless we come to terms with how global market forces shape our future, government and citizens will find themselves relatively helpless . . . The challenges posed by a non-sustainable population that distributes resources inequitably [means] finding ways to . . . regulate these global forces.*

Richard Falk, United States
Southern Africa Public Hearing

🙖 *The job market is now flooded and qualified young people can no longer get good jobs. We end up being underemployed, badly employed, misemployed, or worse still, unemployed. Young people have suffered the most. The economic crisis, ESAP, the AIDS menace, drought, desertification, deforestation as well as environmental pollution are threatening people's health, especially the poor, women, and young people.*

Brigitte Hlatshwayo, Zimbabwe
Southern Africa Public Hearing

🙖 *Our country has decades of experience in development programming: policies and planning to improve the national economy. The people, however, have not had the opportunity to say how they wanted to earn a living. Top–down consultation of the people is not enough . . . Let the pace of the economy be the people's choice.*

Nirmala Buch, India
South Asia Public Hearing

Pursuing Economic Growth—A Succession of Development Models

Population growth, extreme poverty, and ecological degradation are each and together rooted in the economic systems with which the world has been operating for the last fifty years. Economic and social development has been the principal quest of all nations, individually and collectively, during the past five decades. Development became equated with economic growth, progressively the exclusive pre-occupation of policy-makers everywhere. This resulted in a proliferation of development models, strategies meant to boost economic growth.

In the aftermath of the Second World War, and with memories of the Great Depression still fresh in people's minds, most Western countries relied on market principles to:

- bring mass unemployment to an end;
- ensure the free flow of capital and goods;
- create equality of opportunity for all;
- establish a system of health care, education, and social security;

and thus create the welfare State.

As political independence came to the developing regions, there was an equal determination to industrialize and achieve rapid economic growth for the attainment of social goals. The same goals were sought in communist countries through central planning.

During these decades the developing countries succumbed to raging fashions, each of which offered differing points of entry to the many facets of development—often encouraged, if not pushed outright, by the industrialized nations and the international development-funding agencies. The range of policies pursued in this respect is breath-taking:

- providing basic needs; generating flows of savings and aid;
- development of infrastructure, with a focus on construction;
- industrialization via import substitution;
- 'corporatizing' various public functions;
- reinforcement of development administration;

- trade instead of aid;
- revolutionizing agriculture;
- integrating rural development;
- growth through redistribution;
- human-resource development;
- structural adjustment programmes;
- attracting direct foreign investment;
- sustainable development;
- guidance based on the needs of this 'sustainable, human' development; and
- rediscovering the private sector.

Between 1945 and 1973 the world's economy experienced a long upswing, providing a favourable setting all over the world. The situation changed in the 1970s as the shock of rising petroleum prices triggered a long cycle of faltering growth, payment imbalances, and trade disturbances throughout the global economy. Government deficits rose, as did inflation and public debt.

In the Third World models of parastatal domination of economic activities, including import substitution behind high tariff walls, were clearly failing. In Eastern Europe and the former Soviet Union, State-ownership, repression, and centralized planning failed to deliver the goods and services promised. State intervention in the social and economic processes came under serious scrutiny in all countries.

Concurrently the development agenda of the 1970s centred on the affirmation of national sovereignty in the economic field, endogenous development, and a diversity of economic systems enshrined in the Charter of Economic Rights and Duties (adopted by the UN General Assembly in 1974). Later, the end of the Cold War and the globalization of economic activity contributed to the disappearance of the development alternatives that had begun to be defined in different regions and countries.[1] Today, rapid and full integration within the global economy is a principal target of all development efforts.

Against this background the principles of democracy, the primacy of market forces, and the pluralism of initiatives came to dominate the political scene of the 1980s and 1990s. These forces culminated in the end of the Cold War and the collapse of central planning in the Soviet Union and among its allies. Within less than two decades all countries have radically shifted in their national economic policies.

Balanced budgets and an endless sequence of cutbacks in health, education, and social-security entitlements became the order of the day. The State was interpreted widely as assuming a minimalist role, one of ensuring public safety and national security, facilitating at the same time an unimpeded functioning of the markets through deregulation. State enterprises and services were cut, and often privatized.

The debt crisis compounded the difficulties. The debt of the developing countries soared from $658 billion in 1980, to $1,375 billion in 1988, to $1,945 billion in 1994. Massive obligations were incurred during the petroleum crisis of the 1970s and at the collapse of commodity prices in the early 1980s, when the recycling of petrodollars made loans easy to obtain. Besides, world-wide interest rates rose to record highs. Debt-servicing, as a consequence, became onerous; fresh loans were used to service prior debt rather than for productive investment.

There were wasteful investments as well as corrupt practices, to be sure, but the decline in commodity prices was numbing. In 1993 they were 32 per cent lower than in 1980 and, in relation to the price of manufactured goods, they were 55 per cent lower than in 1960. Result: there was a sharp deterioration in the terms of trade affecting developing countries.[2]

The debt crisis formed the setting for the introduction of structural-adjustment programmes that debtor countries had to undertake, with the advice and supervision of the Bretton Woods institutions. These programmes often required deep cuts in public spending: public employment itself, and reduced access to public health care, education, family planning, food, and housing. Many of the undertakings were too harsh, sweeping, and sudden; they invariably failed to take into account social factors and local conditions. The policies pursued could be characterized as 'adjustment at any cost'.

The structural-adjustment process thus intruded into the caring social services. Social services crucial to the quality of life and economic growth (e.g. health and education) were not protected against such cuts, and they thus made easy economic targets. Regulation and subsidies—sometimes indispensable to ensure equity—were scuttled, sometimes indiscriminately. The abrupt slashing of subsidies on food and energy, for example, raised the cost of living for the urban poor and the rural landless. Reductions in public spending also increased unemployment.

The immediate impact of all this on the quality of life was often cruel, especially in Africa where the Commission's two hearings heard a torrent of bitter complaints against structural adjustment. In many countries primary-school enrolment rates dropped, and life-expectancy fell.[3]

Most of the former communist countries of Eastern Europe and the former Soviet Union suffered, too, from an application of free-market principles often too abrupt and overly zealous. This entailed sweeping budgetary cuts and privatization, compounded by the collapse of trade among these countries. In Russia and seven Eastern European nations real wages fell between 17 and 54 per cent from 1989 to 1993. The proportion of people in poverty rose from between 4 and 24 per cent in 1989–90 to between 25 and 61 per cent in 1993. Most countries experienced a rise in mortality rates (especially among adult males), whereas life-expectancy diminished. Marriage and fertility rates, too, experienced steep declines, a phenomenon more commonly seen in wartime. Crime rates rose from 1989, by between 68 and 295 per cent within three years' time.[4]

The Impact of Globalization

Globalization, as a process, has a long history: the creation and expansion of the United Nations and many other multilateral organizations, steady growth in world commerce, development of internationalized knowledge systems in symbiosis with social evolution—implying changed patterns of communication, technology, production and consumption, and the promotion of internationalism as a cultural value. Few sections of the globe's population escaped the effects of two world wars and the

Depression between them, despite wide differences in the various degrees of participation or even interest.

The technological revolution lies at the heart of an accelerating globalization process; it has introduced fundamental changes in the international system. International market forces increasingly shape economies and national cultures. Capital, information, and images flow round the globe at the speed of light. Trade, finance, science and technology, mass media, consumer patterns, and social and environmental problems are all globalizing swiftly.

Globalization, therefore, presents a political challenge. The various modes of globalization are tantamount to a universalization of power, now being concentrated into the hands of new multinational actors. These transcend the sovereign nation-state and supplant the spirit of internationalism developed in earlier decades. The new structures and protagonists of world power are relatively anonymous; they lack accountability and often operate without controls—given the absence world-wide of effective, accountable regimes of regulation and supervision.

Deregulation has been the pivot of economic globalization and has radically reduced the power of individual governments. This is best exemplified by the unsettling effects of international currency speculation on national economic policies. Governments, less able than before to choose policies in the national interest, must be able to react effectively to new international economic perceptions. In an effort to strengthen controls over public spending, many governments are compelled to reverse gains made by the Welfare State by tightening their own social policy and its benefits.

Simultaneously there has been a globalization of labour, in the sense of global competition among work-forces. Labour does not 'flow' freely at the international level, however, given the restrictions on labour migration. Instead, capital flows freely to where competent labour is cheapest and least subject to regulation. This has weakened both labour laws and the bargaining power of trades unions to fight for better conditions and pay.

Globalization appears to de-link the fate of corporations from the fate of their employees. Hitherto increased profits meant job security and higher wages. No more. Today it is quite common that a firm announces profits in parallel with major lay-offs.

Similarly large firms are becoming de-linked from their countries of origin.

⤴

The changes transforming the world's economy occur so fast, and they are so far-reaching, that they generate widespread confusion and fear among employees while presenting new opportunities, and raising expectations and benefits for employers.

- On the one hand, the huge and fast-growing markets of the emerging economies are quickly becoming the major loco-motive of a period of unprecedented economic growth. They create jobs and prosperity, raising incomes and material stan-dards while providing their consumers with cheaper goods and services.

- There are costs, on the other hand. Transferring certain kinds of jobs abroad raises fears and opposition to free trade, stimu-lating an isolationist nostalgia. Countries exporting primary commodities and people (who lack market access or the skills and other resources to profit from the market) are increasingly marginalized. People and social groups everywhere, possess-ing little education and few skills, are being devalued by the increasingly competitive economy.

- The mega-competition that is part of globalization leads to winner-take-all situations.

In tandem with the globalization of information, a universaliza-tion of culture is under way as Western consumer patterns and American mass media invade the world. Cultures everywhere erode. Other problems take on global proportions: terrorism, or-ganized crime, and the drug trade acknowledge no frontiers. Dis-eases old and new spread across the planet faster than before, and environmental risks cross national boundaries and affect all of Earth.

Globalization can neither be stopped nor can any country avoid its consequences. The challenge now is how best to manage the autonomous processes involved, mitigate the threats that they rep-resent, and transform their benefits to best advantage.

Winners and Losers in the Information Revolution

Globalization is bringing about a control of knowledge by new actors and their power, replacing the traditional ways of internationalizing knowledge systems. Knowledge systems, with all their implications for quality of life, are now a commodity. The intellectual-property regime is firmly controlled by actors from industrialized countries, offering little opportunity to developing nations. Without review and revision of these new mechanisms, continued globalization will leave the developing world at ever-growing disadvantage.

Global knowledge systems, technologies, and capital combine to dominate the information revolution. Control of Hertzian frequencies and of hardware and software will determine the creation of livelihoods well into the twenty-first century. Control today will translate into further domination tomorrow. Global reach and aggressive marketing should allow the new media to influence, furthermore, public perceptions, attitudes, and values as well as material demand everywhere.

Some contend that developing countries would have a comparative advantage in regard to new technologies. Having not invested heavily in industrial-society structures, these countries should be able to leap-frog into the knowledge society. But to do this would require a minimum of capacity in science and technology—a capacity lacking in most developing countries.

Deficiencies in Current Strategies

The pursuit of economic growth as the *raison d'être* of our economic system has resulted in dramatic increases in global output, trade, and investment. Owing to deficiencies and failures in the development models applied, however, there have appeared widening disparities, growing inequalities and inequity among nations.

Growth based on GNP (as the Commission stresses elsewhere in this book) is an imperfect concept. Because GNP offers an aggregated summary of all the goods and services that a nation produces, it has been mistaken for a comprehensive guide to a nation's well-being—often taken as the leading expression of the quality of life and the prime standard to compare with that of other nations. As a road-map, however, GNP is inaccurate. It does not tell, for example, if the well-being is sustainable, and international comparisons do not in themselves reflect relative states of the quality of life.

The utilitarian and transactional character of the market system (inherent in various models), moreover, has proven incapable of capturing satisfactorily the manifold dimensions of *quality of life*— including preservation of the environment. It has created, thereby, a glaring global mismatch. One-fifth of humanity consumes four-fifths of all the Earth's resources. While the industrialized and rich countries have not paid for the ecological damage resulting from their activities, many of the consequences and their costs (e.g. global warming) will fall upon developing, poor countries.

A world economy that thrives on relentless exploitation of natural resources, depending perilously on fossil fuels, causing limitless waste, and remaining oblivious to the precepts of equality and equity among different societies, is neither sustainable nor tolerable. It is headed for disaster. The situation demands fundamental economic reorientation and restructuring—a transition that will require domestication of market mechanisms in terms of environmental and social objectives. Every human being of the present and the future, regardless of where he or she lives, must have equal and inalienable opportunities to profit from the Earth's natural resources.

The situation is aggravated by the prospect, by the year 2025, of the largest addition to human population in history, meaning also the greatest additional demands to be made by human consumption. The world's economy must be guided, henceforth, by production that emphasizes quality more than quantity: it must adapt its patterns of consumption to satisfy the requirements of global sustainability. Such a transition should prove even more profound than the agricultural and industrial revolutions of the past.

Two conflicting goals need to be reconciled, that is, sustainably improving the quality of life while ensuring a high level of economic activity capable of expanding the economic base and the livelihoods that it generates. An underlying precept, quite obviously, will be *sustainable consumption*.

- Sustainable consumption is the use of goods and services that respond to basic needs and bring a better quality of life while minimizing (i) the use of natural resources and toxic materials, and (ii) the emission of wastes and pollutants during their normal life-cycles, in order not to jeopardize the needs of future generations.

Towards Sustainable Consumption Patterns

Present consumption patterns are characterized by direct and indirect use of fossil fuels, unfettered use of natural resources in manufacture and food production, rising levels of waste and pollution, short life-cycles of products, and resource-insensitive behaviour.

Increased consumption accounted for 75 per cent of the increase in air pollutants in Western countries between 1970 and 1988 and 74 per cent of the carbon-dioxide emissions between 1965 and 1989. The philosophy of *ever more*, synonymous with social aspirations, drives over-consumption in utter disregard of the potentially irreversible environmental consequences.

Consumption depends on the choices made by the individual in the contexts of both the community and global society. Consumption patterns normally depend on what is available: the resources available to the individual or a group. They also rely on saving for the future, and deferring immediate wants in order to enjoy a better life later, within the context of present and future generations. Current consumption patterns tend to disregard these checks on behaviour, making one's identity status dependent on consumption styles.

Decrying consumption is not to pass moral judgement on others' life-styles. Consumption highlights, rather, deficiencies in society's behaviour and in the state of the political, economic, social, and engineering sciences. Unless we find new ways to prevent consumption from becoming a more growing threat to the quality of life, slowing the growth of population will not do the job for us. The whole world cannot sustain the Western level of consumption. If 7 billion humans were to consume as much energy and other resources as do today's industrialized countries, five planets Earth would be needed to satisfy everyone's needs (according to a Norwegian analysis made in 1994).

◆

The impact is shown most markedly in the United States, a frontier culture rich in resources, where production schemes and consumption patterns tend to be more wasteful than in other industrialized countries. In 1991 the United States consumed almost three times as much energy as Japan in order to produce $1 of GNP.[5] With only 4.6 per cent of the world's population, the United States produced 22 per cent of the global carbon-dioxide emissions in 1991—more than those of China, India, South America, and Africa together.[6]

Using energy consumption as a surrogate for environmental sustainability, a baby born in the United States represents twice the environmental impact on Earth's life-support systems as one born in Sweden, three times one in Italy, thirteen times one in Brazil, thirty-five times one in India, and 140 times one in Bangladesh.

During the period 1986–90 the average person in a developed country used nine times as much fossil fuel and twenty times as much aluminium as his or her counterpart in developing countries. In terms of waste, he/she produced four times as much household refuse, eleven times more carbon dioxide, twenty-six times more chlorofluorocarbons, and seventy-five times more hazardous wastes.[7] Average Americans use forty-three times as much petrol as average Indians, forty-five times as much copper, thirty-four times as much aluminium.[8]

If we are to achieve sustainable patterns of consumption, individuals must be prepared to pay the full environmental costs of what they consume. This means that housing, meat, and travelling by car will be more expensive. The charges for energy, and sewage and other waste clearance will have to be raised. It is almost inconceivable that, without major technological advances, the Earth could support a doubling of the number of private vehicles by 2015 (as currently projected)—quite apart from an anticipated eightfold increased by 2100.

Just as the division of the globe into rich and poor nations no longer reflects a world of growing diversity, so the idea that overconsumption is confined to the North is an oversimplification. The South has its own expanding 'North'—an affluent élite leading life-styles that resemble in material terms more and more the Western ones.

To state in other terms what is mentioned elsewhere in this volume, the richest fifth of Chileans, Mexicans, Venezuelans, and Malaysians enjoy incomes higher than the average German or Japanese.[9] The change in the situation is noteworthy as incomes in the South rise. China, the world's third largest economy measured in dollars of purchasing-power parity, is also the third largest emitter of carbon dioxide from industrial sources. India, the world's seventh largest economy in real terms, is the world's sixth largest emitter of the same greenhouse gas.[10]

The size of the emerging consumer class in developing countries—those with enough disposable income to spend on large consumer-durables—is already enormous. Some idea of the size of this emerging class can be derived from data on television-ownership, an essential good of our civilization that is now deemed a necessity. (Television-ownership, that is, no longer reflects individual life-style.) In 1985 there were already 570 million people in television-owning households throughout the developing countries. By 1991 this figure had almost doubled, to 1,120 million: the total population of the industrialized nations. During the six years in question, the number of TV sets grew by 12 per cent annually—an extra 134 million owners, a growth rate almost six times greater than that of the population.

Although television serves in many countries to inculcate a wasteful Northern-style model of consumption, the medium also offers unused opportunities for information and education on sustainable patterns of consumption. Eventually, the promotion of alternative life-styles may become reality. And although the process of consumption cannot be halted, it can be influenced, shaped, as a global phenomenon with global impact.

❧ *I would like to see more emphasis on community development: people trusted, given funds to explore*

> *their talent. In Bangladesh, for instance, everyone talks*
> *about a bank that lent money to women. The bank*
> *earned a good return on its loan, and the women devel-*
> *oped an income-generating activity. The women felt*
> *empowered.*
>
> Cece Modupe Fadope, United States
> North America Public Hearing

·❧

The effects of over-consumption should continue to pose a threat long after the slowing of population growth if the current paradigm of development↔economic growth remains unchanged. The adoption of sustainable patterns of consumption in the North, on the other hand, may serve as an ideal for more sustainable development in the South. We need an 'efficiency revolution' in how we use energy and materials, one that will require regulations and the introduction of economic incentives and disincentives.

As the growth of population slows and family-size diminishes, there is a shift in focus from reproduction to satisfaction of other human desires—more emphasis on consumption. Even where demographic growth is negligible (as in the rich countries), changes in population continue to exert an upward pressure on the rate of consumption per person. Age at marriage, divorce rates, and life-expectancy all rise. More and more people live in one- or two-person households, each of which requires its own energy and water supplies, furnishings, and other possessions. (Population slow-down may not at first produce changes in the totals of population × consumption.)

Moving towards a life of sustainable consumption should be a lengthy process, partly because there is already in place a vast infrastructure of housing, shops, offices, factories, and roads. Governments can speed the transition by ensuring that new or replacement facilities take advantage of energy and other resource efficiency. This can be done through regulation that affects lighting, ventilation, heating or cooling, and so on; by promoting balance in the composition of communities; by government's own influence as purchaser and builder; and through campaigns of research and public education.

Because sustainable consumption affects not only the North, the South can avoid the North's past errors. Sustainable consumption is an ideal for even poor countries via (for instance) fuel-efficient wood-stoves, agroforestry, and inexpensive soil-conservation methods. The North can lead the way by insisting on urgent reduction of emissions before the year 2000.

Moving Ahead with Sustainable Production Schemes

The functioning of economies must be reoriented by questioning and adapting current production processes, as seen through their impact on the environment. This calls for analysis of how, and how efficiently, they use resources and create wastes, how they damage nature, and how they integrate aesthetic factors.

The task to be accomplished is to find ways of satisfying the same end-use but with less damage to the environment.[11] Retrofitting and stop-gap measures will not be sufficient. Instead, growth in GDP must be de-coupled from growth in energy consumption; products with long life-span and reuseability must be developed; manufacturing discards and other waste should be recycled; private transport also needs curbing; and farming should be based on sustainability.

Improving efficiency should lower the throughput of minerals, fossil fuels, and other resources. It is to be noted that prices often do not reflect real scarcity, and thus induce misallocation of raw materials or semi-finished products. Many governments, for example, subsidize the use of fossil fuels, pesticides, chemical fertilizers, and other products for the farm. Natural resources under governmental control (water, forests, range-lands, mineral deposits), furthermore, are frequently available at such low royalty levels that they subsidize—in effect—over-use and environmental damage. Conversely, official incentives should induce more sustainable practices.

Technological development, in this respect, should prove critical: new production processes need to reduce significantly the quantities of natural resources used, thus lowering the emissions and other wastes produced and thereby meeting the criteria of current risk assessments. A pro-active industrial policy, balancing incentive with interdiction, should promote the design and application of environmentally safe techniques. It is in the interest of industry itself to collaborate.

Coping with Waste

The principal challenge here is to reduce the mounting volumes of solid, liquid, and gaseous wastes produced by households and industry. This means reducing the bulk of the materials required, from extraction to finished product, for the goods and services sought by clients—the slogan for which might be: 'Reduce, Re-use, Recycle.'

The mining sector provides a figure that speaks for itself: mining yielded nearly 46 per cent of the solid wastes produced in 1990 in Western Europe and North America. While it is unlikely that we shall run out of minerals, we may well poison ourselves with the detritus coming from mining, refining, transporting, and consuming them if use continues at the present rate. A total of 2,951 *billion* tonnes of mineral waste dwarfed the 344 million tonnes of household waste produced at the same time.

Future population growth will, of course, make the problem of mineral waste more critical: bigger spoil-heaps, more scarred land, larger quantities of water polluted not only by mining waste and production but also by the very use of mining's products. The last affects atmosphere, water, biodiversity, and the quality of life itself.[12]

Hazardous and other toxic wastes pose a special problem in regard to exports, so that it must be ensured that such materials are not exported to—'dumped' in—developing countries.

Reducing Emissions and Other Pollutants

We are unlikely to run out of fossil fuels, but the threat of climate change is forcing us to reduce their use drastically while massive reserves are still underground. Changes in technology policy and the use of these fuels should make a big difference if we follow three main avenues, thereby reducing carbon-dioxide emissions too:

- increase energy efficiency;
- alter the 'mix' of these hydrocarbons, descending to lower carbon content (i.e. less coal, more natural gas);

- introduce and aggressively promote the renewable energies.

Shifting from fossil fuels to renewable energy sources will entail major restructuring of the economy, pushed by policy change at national and international levels. If the adjustment proves successful it will result not only in lowered greenhouse-gas emissions but also offer a long-term solution to the problem of energy needs in developing countries. To this end, the industrializing nations will require substantial financial support and advantageous terms of technology transfer.

The Imperative of a New Economic Rationale

We confront a disconcerting paradox. The poor increase their consumption in order to escape poverty, while the non-poor aspire to even greater material prosperity. All governments advocate higher consumption as a means of stimulating the economy and reducing unemployment. Yet higher consumption, under present conditions, is bound to result in an unsustainable level of energy use—energy coming from fossil sources and poisoning the air and water.

The chain: economic growth–employment–political success in the form of democracy–increased resource consumption–waste and environmental damage, must be broken if we are to achieve sustainable improvement in the quality of life. Economy based on quantity must make way for economy founded on quality—producing quality goods and more and better services, ensured by labour of high quality too.

The Commission considers, therefore, that it is urgent and even imperative to change production schemes and consumption patterns, a shift amounting to no less than a new economic revolution. Because this will affect the future and perhaps the very survival of the world, the effort can be nothing less than one of joint responsibility and joint undertaking by industrialized and developing countries alike.

The major shortcoming of today's economic system is shortsightedness: how decisions, primarily investments, are made. We constantly discount the future. An enormous challenge is to develop a macro-economic framework for the long-term consequences of economic activity.

> *Mankind can accept only those processes—whether they are economic, social, political, or cultural—that incorporate the entire population. No longer can we admit that these mechanisms devised by humans (because it was not God who created the economy) be called modern, rational, logical, scientific . . .*
>
> Herbert de Souza (Betinho), Brazil

> *You, ESAP,*
> *You are a two-headed snake,*
> *You lie to me that all will be well,*
> *Aren't you ashamed of yourself?*
>
> *You, ESAP,*
> *You have a two-coloured back.*
> *Food and clothing are now expensive because of you,*
> *Get off!*
>
> *You, ESAP,*
> *You beat about the bush,*
> *Yesterday you got me retrenched from work,*
> *I say pack and go!*
>
> *You, ESAP,*
> *You clean up like Vim, the scouring powder*
> *I can't borrow money to start an income generating project,*
> *What do you want me to do?*
>
> *You, ESAP,*
> *I am now carrying a heavy load*
> *Hospital and school fees are now too high,*
> *Oh, it's a hard life.*

Song from Tsholotsho Group (illiterate), Zimbabwe
Southern Africa Public Hearing

> *The World Bank and IMF talk about 'structural adjustment' in monetary terms. My own feeling is what we*

*really need is adjustment to sustainable life styles, that
the Bank would not recommend. Because their structural adjustment is in money terms, not value terms.
But if developing countries have to undergo such an
adjustment in terms of financial problems, living
within the budget and so on, industrialized countries
will also have to go through a structural adjustment
process.*

M. S. Swaminatham, India
South Asia Public Hearing

References

1. Rajani Kotari, 'The Yawning Vacuum: A World without Alternatives', *Alternatives*, 18: 2 (1993).
2. World Bank, *Global Economic Prospects and the Developing Countries* (Washington, 1994); *World Debt Tables 1994* (Washington, 1994).
3. *World Debt Tables 1994*; UNESCO, *World Education Report 1993* (Paris, 1993).
4. International Child Development Centre, *Crisis in Mortality, Health and Nutrition* (Geneva, 1994); UNICEF, *Transitional Regional Monitoring Report No. 2* (Florence, 1994).
5. World Resources Institute, *World Resources 1994–5* (Oxford, Oxford University Press, 1994).
6. Ibid.
7. Ibid.; Paul Harrison, *The Third Revolution* (London and New York, Penguin Books, 1993).
8. *World Resources 1994–5*.
9. Calculation based on real GDP in 1992 at purchasing-power parity and income distribution; see World Bank, *World Development Report 1994* (Oxford, Oxford University Press, 1994).
10. The real size of an economy equals real GDP/person at purchasing-power parity times total population; World Bank, *World Development Report 1995* (Oxford, Oxford University Press, 1995); *World Resources 1994–5*.
11. Norwegian Ministry of Environment, *Report of the Oslo Symposium on Sustainable Consumption* (Oslo, Jan. 1994); Oslo Ministerial Roundtable, *Conference on Sustainable Production and Consumption* (1995).
12. John Young, *Mining the Earth* (Worldwatch Paper No. 109; Washington, Worldwatch Institute, 1992).

Needed: A New Way of the World

Population, not only in terms of numbers but more importantly as *people*, needs to be viewed within the interpenetrating contexts of debilitating poverty, environmental degradation, and economic globalization. Sustainable improvement in the quality of life must become our central goal—respecting the limits of the Earth's carrying capacity and responding to needs through rediscovery and reassertion of the *caring* capacity of humankind. This vision can become reality only if it is translated into policy by socially caring States and all the international community. A minimum of policy requirements demand a paradigm shift in population policies, a redefinition of our concept of work, conceptualizing and implementing alternative directions for health and education, providing for reproductive choices and the empowerment of women. Nothing less than a new social contract, in other words: one that will mobilize social forces and other resources.

Part II

Towards a Fresh Vision

5 Focusing on the Goal

Sustainable Improvement of the Quality of Life

> ❧ *This is Bamako today: our houses are too small, and there are too many people in the houses. People deposit their garbage outside containers, and the smell of dead sheep and dogs thrown in ditches irritates people. Children go to the toilet on other people's properties, and there are not enough street lights.*
>
> Modibo Diakite (aged 10), Mali
> West Africa Public Hearing

Time for a New Focus: Sustainable Improvement in the Quality of Life

We have seen that the pursuit of economic growth has become a dominant concern the world over. Development is equated with, or even held to be synonymous with, economic growth only: it is thus evacuated of all social implications. This focus has by now overshadowed all other considerations, such as equity, environmental sustainability, employment, and social cohesion.

The very word 'development' has not been very helpful. It implies movement towards a goal. The contrast found between 'developing' and 'developed' countries suggests that the goal is a certain plateau of affluent consumerism—one already reached by industrialized countries and yet to be attained by the others. There is no such plateau. Human reality is multidimensional, and is not to be squeezed into the single dimension of economic growth. Clearly the time has come for an alternative, more holistic, approach to attaining our policy goals.

The Commission proposes, therefore, that the concept of sustainable improvement in the quality of life become the central focus for policy-making in all countries. This would be an ongoing, dynamic task, leaving no room for *status quo* politics or excuses for inaction.

A limitless increase in the number of people, or of material goods per person, is impossible. But quantity and quality diverge somewhere along the horizon of what is possible. And while quantity and increase in quantity can no longer be the overriding precepts guiding the processes associated with human activity, quality can always be deepened and reinforced. 'We need a transition from quantity to quality', Gro Brundtland maintains. This is why it is possible to imagine sustained improvement in the quality of life (which, in fact, could be practically limitless). Indeed, sustainable *improvement* in the quality of life could become the touchstone of both industrialized and developing countries.

In seeking sustainable improvement in the quality of life, highest priority should be accorded to meeting the basic, minimal survival needs of the population; and this should not be negotiable. At poverty level and below, quantity is of the essence for both incomes and services. Indeed a certain, minimal quantity is essential before there can be meaningful quality of life. Above survival level, however, quantity is significant to people in so far as it contributes to quality of life—helping to reduce discrepancies and close gaps. (Pursued to excess, quantity may not be sustainable at all and may lead to deterioration in the quality of life.)

Sustainability need not limit the horizons of developing countries to mere satisfaction of the most basic needs, or limitations on the processes inherent in industrialization and consumption. Nor should sustainability assume a stable, final state for the industrialized countries, or perhaps the continuation along a path towards 'always more'. Sustainability is not a ceiling to be imposed on the many nor an open space reserved to a limited few. It allows, on the contrary, for progression towards ever-improving quality in all of life—for nations as well as individuals.

There are many elements to the quality of life. They are based on the secure enjoyment of health and education, adequate food and housing, a stable and healthful environment, equity, gender equality, participation in everyday life, and dignity and security. Each of these elements is important in its own right, but lack of fulfilment of even one of them can undermine the subjective sense of 'quality of life'.

Quality of life cannot, furthermore, be 'summed up' or 'averaged out', so that the defining and measurement of quality of life is far from easy. Much of what people call their quality of life is culturally defined. Even within a single society, views concerning what makes for quality of life differ widely among its subcultures and its individuals.

So the notion of quality of life may always retain an element of subjectivity as well as of cultural diversity. Within a single culture or one of its components, reduction of one's material wants (or even greed) may be sought as a rite of passage. In another subunit of the same society or in another society altogether, such abnegation would be seen as not only foolish but as a kind of self-torture. A dichotomy between the selfish and altruistic orientations exists, it is true, in most cultures. So the near-universality of such ethical tension, even among today's fast-changing belief systems and values, provides the foundation for the Commission's choice of sustainable improvement in quality of life as a central policy goal.

Towards a Secure and Sustainable Quality of Life

In recent years the disquiet sensed with the concept of 'development' has led to two major efforts that (a) are of the utmost importance and (b) translate adequately the changes in the contemporary world. The report of the Brundtland Commission, *Our Common Future* (Oxford, 1987), responded to the discovery of a limited world, adding a decisive tone and urgency to the concept of sustainable development. Since then it has become obvious (we quote the report) that 'the content of economic growth would have to change', and that 'even consumption of material goods should be ranked according to a scale of sustainability'.

Likewise, the disappearance of the military threat that hung over many nations for almost fifty years has led to acceptance of the primacy of *human security*, one that the security of the State had managed to keep in the background.

Enhancing Human Security

Traditionally governments were concerned primarily with safeguarding the sovereignty and security of the State, and the ending in the early 1990s of a bipolar world has by no means resolved all conflicts based on this precept. Instead, the new combination of a monopolar world together with fragmented societies here and there has given rise to numerous smaller conflicts between opposing interests—struggles accompanied by widespread civic violence. These conflicts are fed by a resurging militarization of life. The peace dividend anticipated during the post-Cold War period, furthermore, has proved elusive. Reconversion of the military-industrial complex in the developed countries, especially those of the former Eastern bloc, and progressive demilitarization in the Third World are proving to be complex and difficult.

The emergence of a new and expanded concept of human security (i.e. downgrading the military side but emphasizing explicit social, economic, and environmental aspects) is an important breakthrough. The Commission shares the view that it is indispensable to adopt a new vision of security, our present one being still State-centred and one whose main instrument is the military. So when we discuss security we still think of the security of the State, in both its external and internal contexts. The Commission found that the effects of this view of security in Latin America, for instance, were most devastating.

So now we must move towards a more human dimension of the notion of security, placing people at its very centre. Security is, after all, making life secure for *people*, and not only from outside threats. People can, just as well, help make their own lives secure: everyone undertakes all kinds of things to assure this more personal security, but conditions favourable to security must pre-exist. One does not simply 'deliver' security to someone else; this is to say that the social conditions must be present that will assure its acquisition. Therefore maintaining a statist attitude towards security is unlikely to transform that security into a genuinely humane one. A very 'secure' State can, indeed, contain a host of insecure people.

Populations find themselves caught today in a sort of structural insecurity—one stemming from poverty, exclusion from the community's services. There is often an absence of the opportunity to work, combined with a disregard by the State's machinery and its 'powerful' class for social rights. The overwhelming majority of people, the Commission found, are less worried about the risk of war than about whether:

- there will be food on the table;
- they can gather enough wood to cook or keep warm;
- they will be attacked on the street or at home;
- they will find shelter from eviction or earthquake;
- they will be protected against flood, drought, unemployment;
- they can manage to send their children to school; or
- they can avoid illness or count on minimal health care.

Insecurity is thus felt most at the personal level, with many people confident that local officials can help when there is distress. In fact, however, guarantees of security can no longer be assured by the immediate community because the real threats tend to spill over administrative boundaries and even national frontiers. Problems of the environment, migration, drugs, and terrorism require primarily awareness and cohesion so that solutions can be found.[1]

⤙

The Commission endorses a comprehensive definition of security that is rapidly gaining acceptance at the international level: one that transcends the traditional concept by explicitly stipulating the safety and security of people from injury, accident, disaster, disease, and violence, as well as from the loss of livelihood or damaging environmental change.[2]

The security of the human being is thus what counts perhaps most in the quality of life. People have a right to it—not simply the right to be free from avoidable harm, but to be free of the fear of harm. Personal security is linked intimately, therefore, with economic security. A threat to one's livelihood is also a threat to everything that income and property provide: nutrition, health, housing, and the like. And among the poorest of people, threats to livelihood are threats to life itself.

Environmental security grows in importance because environmental change can affect health, livelihood, and sometimes survival. Soil erosion can threaten a farmer's resource base. Water- and air-pollution threaten health and may, indeed, cause conflict. The ozone hole, increasing the risks of skin cancer or cataracts of the eye, threatens individual health. Global warming may threaten us with floods and hurricanes, and rise in sea-level could leave millions homeless and (literally) landless.

Besides killing people, war uproots lives; cripples farming, industry, and commerce; disrupts education; creates famines, and drives waves of refugees from its locale. War between States, we have already seen, has become less common than conflicts within States: the number of contemporaneous civil wars rose from less than ten in 1960 to thirty-four by 1993. Annual deaths from warfare between 1980 and 1992 were averaging some 450,000 annually.[3] In 1993, indeed, all conflicts registered were civil wars—in the former Yugoslavia and Soviet Union, nine out of forty-three nations in sub-Saharan Africa, and several Asian countries.[4]

It is a mistake to believe that high military spending protects against the risks of war. High budgets can precipitate wars because of a nation's fear of the growing power of another. Within countries, high arms budgets may encourage governments to intransigence, ignoring the needs and demands of their own marginalized regions or social groups.

Military spending damages human security. The comparative priorities that governments give to State security as opposed to security of people finds expression in planning, the commitment of human resources, political campaigning, and the like. From its peak in 1987, it is true that military spending fell dramatically from $995 billion to an estimated $767 billion in 1994. All but $27 billion of this peace dividend of $228 billion accrued to the benefit of industrialized countries.[5]

Among developed countries the security of human beings now has higher priority than defence needs, the average industrialized country spending twice as much on health as on the military. But, among the ninety-four developing countries for which data are available, no less than fifty-two spent more on the military than on health in 1990. Overall, the average developing country spent 2.5 times more on arms expenditures than on health.[6] The Commission joins in the international campaign to lower military budgets world-wide, especially in developing countries.

Industrialized nations now need to contribute more actively, more credibly, to the demilitarization of international life. It is not enough to admonish developing countries to reduce their military expenditures and to introduce new forms of 'conditionality' to foreign aid. Military assistance to developing countries must diminish further—and be phased out. While arms sales by the ten top exporters fell by more than half between 1988 and 1992, the supply should be halted, at least in those regions most mired in actual or potential conflict. No profits accruing to the State can convincingly argue for peace. The production and sales of arms through clandestine channels should be banned.

The Commission is convinced that broad acceptance of a new definition of demilitarization must be complemented by its introduction into mechanisms to merge military and socioeconomic concerns. The Commission proposes, therefore, that the concept of collective security should be expanded in such a way that the body most competent in the maintenance of international peace and security—the Security Council of the UN—shall deal also with threats to the socioeconomic security of humankind.

Universal understanding of this expanded scope of the Security Council's responsibilities can be laid down by a resolution voted by the General Assembly of the UN, obviating prolonged discussion about otherwise necessary amendments to be made to the UN Charter of 1945.

Redefinition of security should affect security priorities at the national level that encompass personal, social, economic, environmental, and military security. This will necessitate shifts from military spending to areas having great impact on human security such as health (particularly reproductive health), environment, and crime prevention. As a minimal first step, governments not already doing so should aim to spend at least as much on health and education as on military affairs.

Fostering Sustainability

Quality of life may be the forgotten part of modern life. In order to take the next step forward in civilization, what we should aim at is quality of life as *the future of humanity*. So, for the century to come, humanity's main task should not diverge from an intense, operational search to define and make quality of life real.

Sustainability is a concept that accumulated knowledge has made timely, one flowing directly from our awareness of Nature and our acknowledgement that its resources are limited. It is the basis of the survival of the environment, of society and its individuals, and of their economies.

The Commission holds that sustainability is both a precondition for and an integral part of quality of life. If livelihoods and prosperity cannot be sustained, they cannot be secure. Security therefore implies sustainability. The quality of life at any level, and any improvement in this quality, must be sustainable, otherwise the quality will decline and—for future generations—be worse than at present. This is an important dimension of our *caring capacity*, discussed further along.

Sustainability has many dimensions, and the Rio de Janeiro Accord known as Agenda 21 covers many of these aspects. (The Agenda 21 final document was signed by virtually all States participating in the UN Conference on Environment and Development, held in Brazil in June 1992.)

In economic terms, sustainability means keeping our stock of natural capital intact. Any income derived from drawing on capital, we all know, is not sustainable in the long run. In environmental terms, sustainability means that we must avoid depleting Nature's stock of natural resources and imperilling its waste-absorbing sinks. Biodiversity, for example, needs to be preserved as much as possible, in as many natural habitats as possible. Solid, liquid, and gaseous wastes, to take another example, should not be produced in excess of the capacity of waste sinks to absorb them.

❦

There is also a social facet to sustainability. We need to preserve the diversity of human beings by allowing them to develop their personalities, mainly through health and education. It might even be said that the capital invested in people's health and education (some call this *human capital*) becomes an important economic factor—especially in a time of global competition. This sort of capital should be sustained by maintaining or raising the level of investment in education, health, and other social services.

Sustainability is also the capacity of our human race to support mutually every one of us, overcoming any sense of loneliness that otherwise would be testimony of the shrinkage and loss of the potential of people.

Communities and entire societies also build (to speak more abstractly) a social capital constituted by cohesion, cultural identity, and discipline; these are essential for our peaceful collective survival. Such capital can, in itself, be depleted by inequality, unemployment, insecurity. Situations of this kind are socially unsustainable over the long term, because they may lead to (among other consequences) the abuse of chemical substances and crime. Not only do these sequels reduce everyone's quality of life; they lead inevitably to social collapse.

Sustainability, therefore, is not only an effort to be incorporated in governmental policy. It is a basic ingredient of the individual's duties towards society.

What is the Quality of Life?

In my country our greatest enemy is our mentality. To change it, we need to be informed and understand—not deceived by ideologists and politicians. This is the key factor in quality of life.

We cannot assume that indifference to human suffering is part of the solution to the problem of putting people at the centre of things.

Just as we cannot talk of life that does not survive, we cannot talk about quality of life without survival of life itself.

If there is no quality of life and no human development in the South, it will be impossible to restrain migrations.

An official of Colombia

Individual and Collective Dimensions of Quality of Rights

Needs, Rights, and Responsibilities

What we have come to call quality of life, however difficult to define, finds its origin in the individual basic rights slowly developed during the last three centuries and since proclaimed by the United Nations. Because human beings are interconnected through a structured society, there are fundamental rights that correspond to humans' material, social and psychological needs. Even in society's simplest forms, these rights are always individual or collective (or both). When societies become States, national rights spring forth from the needs of the corresponding social institution. And as within each society, there are 'individual' and 'collective' rights for communities of nations.

Today's conditions make it urgent that we proceed to reflect deeply on the interweaving of these individual and collective rights. As much as we declare the uniqueness and autonomy of each conscience—and the right of everyone to follow the dictates of his or her conscience—we also affirm that collective rights need clear definition in this era of globalization.

Many individual rights have been codified in international legal instruments, whereas almost all collective rights are enunciated only through resolutions and action programmes adopted by the UN and other international organizations; the latter type has no legally binding force. The different categories of rights are not always in harmony with each other: dichotomies and contradictions exist.

Rights represent formal acknowledgement by the collectivity—whether State, family, employer, or international community—of basic needs. They also seek to define (a) content and (b) the limits of the two-way relationship joining individuals and communities at different levels. Civil and political rights are considered among *basic* rights because they enable citizens to participate in decision-making in different roles, at many levels.

Fulfilling needs depends on all the parties involved carrying out their obligations in a responsive, responsible manner. Without an implicit acceptance of responsibilities on all sides, the rights may remain little more than moral directions for social relations. Such directions never acquire the political and juridical weights necessary to influence effectively the behaviour of human beings.

In stressing *rights*, one should not lose sight of the concomitant *responsibilities*. Individual responsibility is not only the basis for *caring*; it embodies the very concept of the *human* being. A society of extreme individualism will have little possibility of assuring fulfilment of human rights.

Needs and their Expression as Rights

Quality of life responds, as we have seen, to material, social, and psychological needs. There is little contradiction between the needs of the living generation and those of the future. In order to translate our various needs into an 'operational' mode, however, it is necessary to express them in terms of rights that are aimed at satisfying individuals' requirements.

The rights to life and personal security are, as we have said, fundamental. To ensure freedom from fear, States have been ceded the duties of maintaining law and order and of assuring a nation's external security.

The right to freedom from hunger is a *basic necessity* for one-fourth of our species, explicitly recognized in the World Declaration on Nutrition (1992): 'We recognize that access to nutritionally adequate and safe food is a right of each individual.' This implies the need to ensure adequate nutrition, in particular for mothers during pregnancy and lactation—not only for survival, but for an active and healthy life.

People consistently rate good health as the element paramount in assuring quality of life. The International Covenant on Economic, Social and Cultural Rights (ICESCR) of 1948 recognizes 'the right of everyone to the enjoyment of the highest attainable standard of physical and mental health'. According to the constitution of the World Health Organization, the standard is not merely absence of disease or infirmity, but 'a state of complete physical, mental and social well-being'. More recently, health rights have been interpreted to mean the right to social and environmental conditions conducive to health. The right to health thus implies a right of access to basic preventive and curative health-care information, education, and services. Since adoption of the Health for All programme of action, access to primary care has become an explicitly recognized right.

Education, as a fundamental right, enables people to satisfy several material, social, and psychological concerns regarding quality of life. Literacy, for example, is essential for the assertion of political and legal rights, and education overall serves more and more as the path to work and better pay. The ICESCR recognizes the right to compulsory and free primary schooling and to equal access for all to secondary and higher education; this is supplemented by the right to basic education for anyone who missed the primary level. The Jomtien Declaration on Education for All introduced an additional element, furthermore, one calling for the right to lifelong education and training.

In order to survive, people must work. An overwhelming majority of the population produces its own food, providing housing and first-level health care for itself. Above the subsistence level, however, people need access to additional income for access to resources such as land or capital in order to generate additional income. The ICESCR recognizes 'the right of everyone to an adequate standard of living for himself and his family, including adequate food, clothing and housing, and to continuous improvement of living conditions'.

The right to work thus translates into earning an income. This is the very first of the rights evoked in the ICESCR, 'the right of everyone to the opportunity to gain his living by work which he freely chooses or accepts'. This right obliges States to pursue policies to achieve 'full and productive employment', employment being considered not simply as a 'job' provided by an employer. It includes self-employment in farming, small enterprises, and (more and more) the services. And work is not simply a means to an end; it also serves as the social environment for much of an adult's waking hours. Hence the *conditions of work* become an important aspect of the quality of life. ICESCR also recognizes rights related to quality of employment: fair wages, safe and healthy working conditions, equal opportunities for promotion, rest, holidays, and other leisure.

Governmental obligations concerning the right to work are clarified in the International Labour Organization's Convention No. 122 on employment policy, adopted in 1964 and since ratified by eighty-three countries. This states that members 'shall declare and pursue, as a major goal, an active policy designed to promote full, productive and freely chosen employment'.

The right to adequate housing translates into shelter against the elements, safety from attack and theft, and access to services assuring good health—including water and sanitation. Since most housing is self-provided, the essence of the right to housing is the right to security of tenure, that is, protection against arbitrary eviction; it also implies a right of at least basic *affordability*.

The right to marry and found a family is enshrined in the Universal Declaration of Human Rights (1948). The right to determine the size of one's family freely and responsibly is recognized in the Convention on the Elimination of Discrimination against Women (CEDAW); it includes the right of access to family-planning information, education, counselling, and services. The same convention recognizes other reproductive-health rights, for example, rights to pre-natal, confinement, and post-natal services. These rights were elaborated in the action programmes adopted at the Cairo and Beijing Conferences.

Concern for the physical environment is of recent vintage. The right of life implies that support systems for human life (water, soil, forests, biodiversity, oceans, and atmosphere) should be preserved. The condition of water, soil, and trees also affects nutrition and the labour of women who collect water and fuel. Biodiversity is important for its own sake, of course, but also as a source of aesthetic pleasure. All these points are recognized in the World Charter for Nature, adopted by a resolution of the UN's General Assembly in 1982.

An expanded statement covering environmental rights could include (among others) rights to clean water, food free of pollutants or poisons, clean air, information regarding toxic elements affecting water, food, and air, as well as more general information on environmental hazards, together with the right of access to national and international remedies for environmental damage.

Political rights provide the framework within which social needs can be met—the reason why political rights are an intrinsic part of the quality of life, as well as being a means to assure other rights and support the dignity of the human. They are recognized in the UN's International Convention on Civil and Political Rights (ICCPR) and include the rights to life, liberty, and security, along with the freedoms of opinion, speech, assembly, association, and movement. There are also the rights to vote and to be elected through elections. The edifice of orderly life is built on the rule of law, making the latter the first goal in all established societies.

The right to equality, too, is embodied within the ICCPR, one fundamental in the defence of other basic rights. The right to equality is realizable, however, only if there exists a right to easy and affordable access by everyone to legal information, advice, and representation.

But of greatest importance to 'ordinary people' is probably the right to participate in decisions affecting everyday life at home and at work. Thus far, however, this right has not been defined sufficiently clearly to guarantee its exercise. The ICCPR does recognize, none the less, 'the right to take part in the conduct of public affairs either directly or through chosen representatives'. CEDAW, furthermore, implies a strengthened right for both men and women 'to participate in the formulation of government policy' and 'to participate in the elaboration and implementation of development planning at all levels'.

❧

A fundamental issue in the enjoyment or enforcement of rights is the quality of gender, guaranteed by international law but violated in most countries. Women continue to be discriminated against in the exercise of political power, seeking redress through the legal system, finding work with adequate remuneration, establishing property rights, exercising reproductive rights, pursuing education—and in virtually every other endeavour.

The Convention on the Rights of the Child recognizes the child's need for love and understanding. From infancy and throughout a long period of life, humans require *love and care* within the family and the community to ensure growth and development. Those deprived of care may grow up psychologically damaged, people more likely than others to do damage in society.

Special attention is to be paid to the quality of relationships inside the family itself. Power relationships that can often lead to emotional, verbal, and physical violence (and most often directed against women and children) deserve particular attention. The family usually cannot thrive without the support of a wider community. Communities possessing positive attitudes provide material and emotional support, often helping with the burdens of work. People need the assurance of the community's commitment and support, a reassurance that permits them to enjoy networks of friendship around both home and work-place.

Responding to psychological needs contributes to enriching the quality of life, especially those needs relating to leisure, rest, or play. These are recognized for children in the Convention on the Rights of the Child (CRC) and for workers in the ICESCR and various conventions of ILO.

Most of these psychological needs are rights in the moral sense, although many are not amenable to being treated as juridical rights. They cannot be directly served by any well-defined institution: juridically, no one has a societal obligation to be held accountable. Governments, nevertheless, should strive to create a conducive and enabling atmosphere, one making it increasingly likely that such psychological demands will be recognized and met. Such psychological demands can be met by the action of courts.

International Recognition of Rights to Quality of Life

Without losing its humane and highly diversified meanings, the term ' quality of life' must be given an operational meaning, beyond the confines of subjectivity and cultural relativism, if it is to be used by governments to set policy and by the people to demand and control action.

We have seen that needs translate into rights. All rights are indivisible and interdependent, and they establish the parameters for meaningful human existence. Civil and political rights cannot be exercised fully unless social and economic rights are fulfilled. There must be a balance between civil and political rights on the one hand, and economic and social rights on the other. As we have elaborated earlier, many rights are already codified in four great UN treaties: the International Covenant on Economic, Social and Cultural Rights, and the International Covenant on Civil and Political Rights (both of 1966); the Convention on the Elimination of All Forms of Discrimination against Women (1979); and the Convention on the Rights of the Child (1989). Table 5.1 highlights the principal rights laid down in these treaties, complemented by elements taken from the UN Charter.

In legal terms, only nations that have ratified the treaties shown in Table 5.1 are bound to apply them via national law. Even those States that have ratified a treaty, however, may enter a reservation with respect to certain clauses. The reach of the four treaties is broad. By April 1995 a total of 112 nations had ratified all four instruments, and another fifteen had ratified three. Ten countries have ratified none.

In terms of governments, 129 States were parties to ICCPR, there were 131 signatories to ICECSR, 140 to the Convention on the Elimination of All Forms of Discrimination against Women, and 175 to CRC. The Commission believes that a major international effort should be mounted to make these four treaties universal by increasing the number of nations signing and ratifying them, and by persuading countries that have expressed reservations to withdraw the latter. At the least, each State should indicate its reasons for non-signature or reservation and outline the conditions that might help overcome the obstacles.

Still, signatures and ratifications alone will not suffice. Rather, the focus (both national and international) should be on the degree of enforcement of implementation of the various treaties' stipulations.

To raise the pressure on countries to honour their commitments, the committees established under treaty provisions (which heretofore have reviewed reports prepared by individual States) should be requested and enabled by the signatory States to prepare regular, analytical summaries on the fulfilment of the different rights as well as on obstacles encountered.

Table 5.1 *Rights to quality of life recognized in legal instruments of the United Nations*

Right	Instrument
Dignity	Charter, preamble
Right to life	ICCPR, 6.1
Security of the person	ICCPR, 9.1
Freedom from fear	ICESCR, preamble
Adequate food, freedom from hunger	ICESCR, 11.1–2
Maternal nutrition	CEDAW, 12.2
Right to work	ICESCR, 6.1
Quality of work	ICECSR, 7
Full and productive employment	ICECSR, 6.2
Health	ICECSR, 12.1
Access to primary health care	CRC, 24.2.b
Pre-natal, post-natal maternal health care	CEDAW, 12.1, CRC, 24.D
Access to family-planning information, services	CEDAW, 14.b, 16.e
Preventive health education	CRC, 24.e
Education	ICECSR, 13.1
Compulsory, free primary education	ICECSR, 13.2.a, CRC, 28.a
Secondary education: available, accessible to all	ICECSR, 13.2.b
Adequate housing	ICECSR, 11.1
Maternity leave	ICECSR, 10
Social security	ICECSR, 9
Gender equality	Charter, preamble; CEDAW
Family protection	ICCPR, 23.1
Political rights	ICCPR, *passim*
Participation	CEDAW, 7, 14.2.a

Abbreviations: CEDAW = Convention on the Elimination of Discrimination against Women; Charter = Charter of the UN; CRC = Convention on the Rights of the Child; ICECSR = International Covenant on Economic, Social and Cultural Rights; ICCPR = International Covenant on Civil and Political Rights.

Sources: UN, UNESCO

From the outset the ICCPR has had its own policing body, the Human Rights Committee. This unit hears reports from States, as well as complaints by States against other States. An optional protocol (introduced at the same time as the Covenant) allows the Committee to receive complaints from individuals or groups that are victims of violations. While States' reports about themselves may be complacent, the complaints reveal more reality. Complaints also accumulate a body of precedents that strengthen interpretation of the Covenant.

In contrast, the ICESCR had no monitoring body until 1987. In that year was set up the Committee on Economic, Social and Cultural Rights. Member States must report every five years on their efforts. The Committee makes brief, general comments on the principles of economic and social rights; it cannot hear individual, group, or inter-State complaints. The two other treaties, on Elimination of All Forms of Discrimination against Women and on the Rights of the Child, have their respective committees. They too receive country reports, but they are unable to hear complaints raised by individuals, groups, or other States.

The Commission urges speedy completion of an optional protocol for the ICESCR, one permitting complaints by affected individuals and groups.[7] Similar optional protocols should be prepared for the other conventions. Such protocols should be extended to include the right of States to bring complaints against other States. This would create the same *right to complain* as currently exists in the International Covenant on Civil and Political Rights.

As regards enforcement, practically no machinery exists. New, direct and indirect approaches have to be devised. First to be dealt with are obstacles built into the conventions. While infractions of civil and political rights would have to be processed immediately by all States having ratified the Covenant, the ICESCR contains an escape clause already used to excuse delays in implementing rights. Article 2.1 of this Covenant affirms that States should take steps 'to the maximum of their available resources, with a view to achieving progressively the full realization of the rights recognized' in the Covenant. This has been taken to imply that poor countries cannot be expected to apply the rights immediately but would do so gradually—as and when the means permitted. This would allow almost indefinite postponement of application of the rights. The Convention on the Rights of the Child contains similar caveats about economic and social rights, but not about civil and political rights.[8]

The Committee on Economic, Social and Cultural Rights has

firmly rejected such lax interpretation, holding that every State party to the Covenant has a 'core obligation to ensure the satisfaction of, at the very least, minimal essential levels of each of the rights'. Thus, for example, a State in which a significant number of individuals are deprived of essential foodstuffs, primary health care, shelter, and minimal education, must be judged prima facie as failing to discharge its obligations under the Covenant.[9] (In Anglo-American common law, prima facie refers to judgement made on its evident merits, without previous investigation.)

Poverty can be no excuse for inaction. A State that is party to a covenant, maintains the Committee, 'must demonstrate that every effort has been made to use all resources that are at its disposition in an effort to satisfy, as a matter of priority', its minimal obligations.[10] While deciding whether a State has failed to respect a right, the Committee may consider whether

- the government concerned has made effective, equitable use of its resources;
- access to its services is equitable;
- it has given proper priority, when compared with other programmes, in applying the rights.[11]

It is utopian, however, to suggest that international procedures alone will change dramatically the reality and practice within countries. Torture, imprisonment without trial, indefinite postponement of elections: these abuses persist despite the ICCPR and its enforcement system. The Covenant *has helped to improve* civil and political rights, an effect produced by a variety of moral, economic, and diplomatic pressures coming from NGOs, media, and other governments. These have been motivated by the natural desires of nations for a good international image, to promote tourism and investment from abroad, fear of exposure in the international media, and fear of consumer boycotts of exports. Pressure from other governments through diplomatic channels includes, of course, possible sanctions by the Security Council.

The UN's rights system can provide allies abroad for local citizens, community organizations, trade unions, women's groups, and other non-governmental bodies. Knowledge of the existence of international rights adds strength to any of these, the strength of knowing that they are not alone in their struggle for freedom and justice.

Just as a complex of pressures has worked for civil and political rights, so can they work in behalf of economic and social rights—once such pressures are used widely, well publicized by the UN, member governments, media, and NGOs. Much as some donors have begun providing aid to strengthen democratic institutions, so could donor aid be given in favour of economic and social rights. International pressure is a proven persuasive force.

To that end, development agencies and NGOs concerned with such issues as food, housing, health, family planning, or education, should make much greater use of the internationally recognized rights. They should add the rights argument to those based on justice and equity, need and interdependence, and they should submit evidence to the committees established under authority of the treaties. The more that rights are talked about, the more will knowledge of them spread, and inevitably the more impact they will have.

Other rights of individual or collective nature, especially those pertinent to economic and social spheres, are dealt with by a variety of resolutions, declarations, and action programmes adopted by the UN, its specialized agencies, and global conferences. It should be borne in mind that, contrary to the treaty as legal instrument, these categories have no legally binding force.

Towards a Single, Comprehensive Concept of Quality of Life

Asserting quality of life can become a force to end poverty because it is the poor, the vulnerable, and the powerless who are most often denied their rights. Rights are a compelling framework in which people can raise claims when the State infringes upon their rights, or fails to promote and protect them. Rights have a built-in bias towards those excluded. If they are widely known and discussed, rights *can* empower the powerless and hold accountable those otherwise unaccountable.[12] Rights can also be the basis for alliances capable of strengthening civil society, inspiring activists to collaborate closely in the pursuit of their own advocacy—abandoning, thereby, the separate and even isolated ways of the past.

The Commission suggests integrating all relevant rights—irrespective of whether they have been codified in international legal instruments or adopted by governing bodies of international organizations—into a single, all-encompassing instrument. A holistic approach means capturing the most important economic, social, and political dimensions of the quality of life in a systematic, measurable, and implementable way. This should replace the fragmentation and piecemeal procedures of the past, introducing a quality compatible with reality. Such a step should, in turn, serve as a meaningful tool for policy-making, evaluation, and enforcement.

This new concept is in line with recent efforts to give practical meaning to the rhetoric of the past. Action plans adopted by global conferences include explicit requirements to draft national action plans, submitting periodic reports on the status of implementation to an acceptable responsible body. Such action plans can also be made available to the committees established under the four treaties already mentioned.

All these requirements can have galvanizing effects—perhaps costly, it is true; but they will succeed in enlisting the co-operation of all elements of governance and civil society.

Strategies for Achieving Sustained Improvement in the Quality of Life

To reach sustainable improvement in the quality of life (based on our comprehensive approach), countries need a practical and feasible strategy. This should be based, first, on setting minimal quality-of-life standards that would apply to all nations, measurable and verifiable. Secondly, a timetable should be agreed upon for bringing these minima to everyone. Thirdly, once the minima are attained, progressively higher standards may be set. Emphasis should then shift from quantity to quality, as would a corresponding responsibility to assist others seeking minimal standards of *quality*.

This will require firm commitment, nationally and globally, to *pro-active social policies*. Minimal quality-of-life standards must be non-negotiable: they should become goals of the highest priority, for everyone, and as soon as possible. For each element of the quality of life, an international effort should be mounted to establish indicators and minimal standards per indicator. Below minimal levels, the right to quality of life should be considered unfulfilled.

Minimal standards should be defined precisely and in as measurable a way as possible. A minimum of education, for example, might be a specific number of years of free schooling. In the domain of health the standard might be *affordable* access to clean water and public sanitation, together with certain nutritional norms, basic health care, and family planning—available within a specified distance or travel time. In terms of shelter, it would be the right to a basic dwelling (or a site for self-built premises) at affordable cost. The last could be defined as a percentage of the income of the poorest 20 per cent of households. In matters of the environment, the minimum might be specific thresholds of air- and water-quality, and access to green spaces measured in travel times. In family life, a minimum would be freedom from violence.

Targets and Timetables

It is not enough to set standards. The norm of universal primary education was set in the 1960s via the ICESCR, but today there are still more than thirty countries where this has not been achieved. To avoid indefinite postponement, the international community must set firm schedules for meeting the standards.

Working within established time-frames, governments should set concrete targets and timetables for achievement of the minimal standards *within a reasonable period*. 'Reasonable' time will vary, depending upon starting levels; a country with 40 per cent primary-school enrolment will take longer to reach universal primary education than one with 80 per cent enrolment.

At the international level, inconsistencies and incompatibilities in targets and timetables must be ended. The Commission recommends that all targets and schedules regarding social and economic rights adopted by UN conferences be reconciled and consolidated. Once agreed, it should not be for UN conferences to alter these; rather, the task of such meetings would then be to define and revise strategies required to reach targets already set.

As to the targets of each government, they should achieve measurable and verifiable improvement within successive decades—not exceeding, in most cases, two decades. Deadlines set at more than ten years later are not likely to energize the necessary effort, especially where there are multiple pressing demands on governmental resources and time.

The 'front line' of this approach must be the individual nations: their governments, citizens, and NGOs. In most matters the ultimate real provider of quality of life will be the individual, family, local community, or enterprise. The State would be the *enabler* or catalyst, the sustainer of the capacities of people; it would create the favourable framework of policy/essential services/processes within which citizens themselves could achieve an acceptable quality of life.

For poor countries, national-level commitments should be backed by an international compact through which foreign aid gives top priority to supplementing national resources so as to reach internationally defined minimal standards. This should be an aim of co-ordinated foreign aid (see the last chapter of this book).

For nations functioning above the minimum, governments should be held accountable for developing programmes meant to raise the levels of social groups still unaffected by the minima. Governments should aim, furthermore, at constant, equitable, and sustainable improvements in quality of life. This implies paying attention to 'targets arising', each with its own timetable.

Authorities at district and local levels may also select targets and set timetables for those matters falling within their purview: education, health, housing, public infrastructure, and many aspects of the environment.

The targets should not be arbitrary averages for the entire country. They should be, instead, minimal floor-levels above which everyone in the nation could be raised. This means that *disaggregated indicators*—broken down by gender, ethnic or income groups, or regions—would be needed in order to be sure that every group is raised above the minima, thereby eradicating poverty.

Even after basic minimal quality-of-life rights have been assured for all, sustainable improvement in the quality of life should continue to be an essential policy goal. The process is ongoing, permanent.

As the world's poorer countries achieve minimal quality of life, an equally important concern must be to strive for equity among nations. The Commission rejects what could become an implicit notion of a double standard of goals: minimal norms for the poor and rising target-levels for the rich, whether within or between two (or more) nations. *All* countries and classes, generations and genders, have the right to *all* minima as well as to *equity*.

The Indicators

The targets for the realization of the right to sustainable improvement in the quality of life needs to be converted into the form of *indicators*, measurable and verifiable parameters relating to society, economy, and environment.

Indicators serve many purposes. They take us beyond the sphere of targets as rhetoric, into the arena of concrete action and accountability. They allow us to set precise goals for future action. They enable governments and civil society to monitor progress towards the goals set, and they give warning signals of emerging problems that need correction.

Indicators do not serve governments only. If they are formulated with the citizenry and widely publicized, indicators can empower civil society and the public as a whole. They inform everyone about 'how things are'. They provide the public with a yardstick to measure progress towards existing objectives—a basis upon which to press for improvement when targets are not being met. Indicators also raise awareness and induce people themselves to change lifestyles, to improve their health and that of the environment.

Indicators should be readily available, measurable, easy to understand, springing from common-sense definitions by people of their quality of life. They must also be comparable among differing geographical areas and time-periods.

Negative indicators, like crimes or violence, especially against vulnerable groups (children, girls, the disabled, the elderly, minorities) are important today in identifying social forces that contribute to unsustainability in the quality of life. They serve, at the same time, to provoke a sense of outrage and motivation for social action by elements of society capable of laying the foundations to make quality of life sustainable in the future.

～

The formulation of indicators should be spearheaded by governments or local authorities with the active participation of civil society, academic institutions included. The indicators selected could make concrete, for instance, the 'national social development policies and strategies' called for by the Copenhagen Summit in March 1995.

Indicators should measure, primarily, the outcomes constituting the definition of each target for action. They should provide feedback, too, and the basis upon which citizens can later monitor progress. Indicators may thus become powerful tools for the 'grass roots' to follow developments in the quality of their own lives, thereby building through the same device a solid foundation on which the media, NGOs, and population organizations can hold government accountable.

Progress should be reported to the public, therefore, on a regular basis. The Commission recommends that such reporting be done by a body independent of the government of the day in order to prevent manipulation—or even suppression—of unwelcome results: a sort of ombudsman of quality of life. Assessing and reporting progress on quality of life could become the *Quality of Life Audit*.

While indicators measure outcome and reflect progress (or not) in the attainment of targets, they rely ultimately on two interrelated enabling conditions: policy and process. Policy, together with the programmes and services it serves to install, provide the systemic framework within which the attainment of goals can be pursued. Agricultural or reproductive-health programmes designed without the participation of their beneficiaries, for example, often do not achieve their aims. On the contrary, the efforts may sometimes be harmful.

Targets and indicators not only concretize various aspects of the quality of life; they also constitute the major mechanisms for (a) governments to commit themselves to change, and (b) civil society to hold its government(s) accountable. Such strategy, moreover, implies:

- the fulfilment of needs;
- the assertion of rights;
- a statement of responsibilities and accountabilities of both State and civil society.

Several organizations have developed indices giving an idea, here and there, of the *overall* quality of life. An *index* is a composite of several indicators; it seeks to represent the real welfare of people in broad terms. Indices can 'grab' the headlines in the mass media, solidifying public opinion, and mobilizing political leaders. In some cases indices can encourage an entire country to perform better. Indices cannot, however, and should not be used as guides in the formulation of detailed policy.

One of the earliest indices devised was the Physical Quality of Life Index (PQLI).[13] This index was based on three factors: infant mortality rate, life-expectancy at the age of 1 year, and the literacy rate of adults. Each factor was indexed on a scale of 0 to 100—0 being the worst performance recorded among the nations of 1950, and 100 the best performance to be expected anywhere by the year 2000. The Overseas Development Council, however, ceased publication of the PQLI in 1990.

The torch was immediately taken up by the UN Development Programme, which has published its Human Development Index annually since 1990. In its version for 1994, HDI used life-expectancy at birth as its health component. The educational element was a combination of adult literacy (given a weight of two-thirds) and the mean number of years of schooling received (a weight of one-third). Income was measured by the real, gross domestic product (or GDP) per person, adjusted for local differences in the cost of living. Because excess consumption brings little benefit in terms of welfare, income differences above $5,120 were heavily scaled down.[14]

The HDI has become, in international headlines, a figure for progress, although public interest tends to focus more on relative rank than on absolute score. It has served, nevertheless, to stimulate national debates over priorities and the distribution of resources.

As concern for the environment has mounted, there have been attempts made to draw up an index to measure the ecological aspects of quality of life. The New Economics Foundation in London developed a *Green League of Nations* index for twenty-one countries. This is calculated from eleven environmental indicators that range from gas emissions through threatened species to energy efficiency.[15]

Indices present drawbacks and dangers. Quality of life comprises disparate elements, never to be summed up satisfactorily so as to produce an overall score. They also contain a large measure of subjectivity. The choice of constituent items and the weight awarded to each are very much value-judgements, making the results far less objective than their numerical form makes them appear.

Reforming National Economic Accounts

In most countries there already exists 'government by targets and indicators', but these are overwhelmingly macroeconomic: low inflation, balanced budgets, growth of gross national product (GNP), and so on. It is essential, however, to place the right indicators at the heart of economic policy. Currently GNP and its growth are the touchstone of progress, nationally and internationally. Because it offers a massive summary of economic life, GNP has been mistaken for a comprehensive guide to a nation's welfare. It is often, as a consequence, taken to be the leading expression of quality of life and the prime standard for comparing welfare among nations.

GNP proves to be an inadequate road-map for the quality of life, however, because it does not sum up national welfare and fails to tell us if this welfare is sustainable. Nor do international comparisons reflect the current *relative* quality of life.[16] Only recently has the relative value of income, in terms of purchasing power, been introduced as a more meaningful yardstick in lieu of the traditional measurements comprising GNP.

GNP omits a great deal of indispensable activity, without which individual and collective life could not be sustained. It fails to cover the value of unpaid work (most of it by women) in the home or community; child care; and caring for the ill, the old, and the disabled. The non-monetized economy accounts for at least as many hours of work as *all* agriculture, industry, trade, and official services taken together. Most studies value this work at between 30 and 50 per cent of the GDP in industrialized and developing economies alike.[17]

Omitting unpaid labour from the accounts has serious consequences. The crucial roles of unpaid women and of unpaid care in the welfare of nations are thereby overlooked. 'If you're invisible in the national accounts, then you're absent when public policy is made.'[18] The 1993 version of the System of National Accounts, recommended by the UN Statistical Office, *includes* the unpaid production of goods intended for one's own consumption—such as subsistence food or do-it-yourself construction. It does not yet include, however, such self-provided services as domestic work or child care.[19] This system also includes the depletion of 'unproduced' natural assets: forests, national fishery stocks, groundwater, and mineral reserves.

So, as a first step in the right direction, the reformed System of National Accounts should be adopted by all countries as a matter of urgency.

⌒

But more must be done, and done quickly. The Commission strongly recommends that steps be taken to measure the unpaid caring services in the home as well as voluntary work in the community, and to value them in parallel accounts to be established for each country. This could be done by using the census and sample surveys, with the results updated and widely publicized on a regular basis.[20] Unless this is done, key policy decisions will continue to be made on the basis of erroneous information.

Such adjustments and additional information would make societies realize the cost of replacing unpaid care of the disadvantaged with professional (paid) care. While they would raise the status of women, they would provide a basis on which governments could recognize the social-security status and pension rights of unpaid care-providers. Such changes would encourage governments to support unpaid care-providers and volunteers for the work they accomplish in behalf of society and, if their burden became intolerable, the work of the care-providers would have to be done at higher expense—and of probably lower quality—by the State.[21]

Beyond that, parallel accounts should also be established—as soon as possible—that reflect environmental costs and depreciation of natural capital. The present measure of GNP tells us nothing about whether or not the incomes it adds up are sustainable. GNP counts the depletion of irreplaceable resources or sinks as *income*. Unadjusted, GNP not only misleads; it encourages us to live unsustainably. In its current form, GNP includes the value of corrective or preventive activities that merely compensate social and environmental costs—or else it forestalls them.

When Indonesia's economic growth was adjusted for depletion of petroleum reserves, forests, and soil fertility, the value of her GDP in 1983 was lowered by 22 per cent. Indonesia's economic growth rate between 1971 and 1984, 7 per cent by conventional accounting, dropped to 4 per cent when environmental losses were calculated. In Costa Rica the depletion of forests, soils, and fisheries came to 9 per cent of GDP in 1989, four times greater than depreciation of its conventional capital.[22]

We thus need to reflect on the estimated future costs of damage being done to the environment today, calling upon the best economic and scientific expertise available.[23]

Equity

The need for equity is deep-rooted in each of us. Once our sense of fairness and justice is violated, feelings of resentment may spoil the enjoyment of any level of quality of life; they may even trigger unrest. The Commission is convinced that equity is the basic principle to be respected by every individual, community, institution, and State.

Equity goes further than equality. A number of international conventions emphasize discrimination, stating (for example) that rights should be applied 'without discrimination of any kind as to race, colour, sex, language, religion, political or other opinion, national or social origin, property, birth or other status'.[24] The UN Declaration on the Right to Development (1986) affirms that States should 'ensure equality of opportunity for all in their access to basic resources, education, health services, food, housing, employment and the fair distribution of income'.

Conflicts are often provoked by perceived or real gross inequalities of wealth or power between social and ethnic groups or regions, by lack of democracy or direct participation, or by the failure of leaders to pay attention to popular demands. In these cases greater participation and equity would reduce the causes of conflict. Deep down, what is at stake is the indivisibility of reality: we cannot compartmentalize reality, whether it is a reality of wealth or power. It is the inequality that exists within nations or among them, in terms of wealth, power, and so forth, that lies at the root of antagonism: inequality among *all* the actors.

Equity is not merely equal rights, or equality before the law. The Commission holds that true equity denotes real equality of opportunity, and it is possible only with an improved degree of equality in the distribution of incomes, wealth, and access to services. Equity may thus, at times, require affirmative action—a certain inequality, weighted in favour of individuals or groups until now excluded, in order to redress past injustices.

Equity is not an issue to be deferred until a later stage of development. Nor is it an issue that will cease to matter once a country has grown richer. It is an essential part of policy, at every stage of its evolution. Countries dealing effectively with equity will be rewarded—as long as their policies are sound—with faster economic growth, higher human security, longer life-expectancy, and environmental sustainability. Above all, by applying equity measures countries redress thereby the quality of life for all and strengthen the cohesion of their people and of their different social groups.

➤ *Income distribution wherein the top 20 per cent of the country earns thirty-two times what the rest earns cannot continue. The task of social policy in a context of such profound inequality is Sisyphean.*

Vilmar Faria, Brazil
Latin America Public Hearing

➤ *If you look through the State budget of Russia, you will not find a separate item on social protection. Even at*

*the State level . . . social protection has not been singled
out.*

Yuri Mitev, Russia
Eastern Europe Public Hearing

*Some concerned people are too obsessed with tech-
niques of measurement, yet they are unable to measure
suffering. It is this unmeasurable side of suffering that
is awakening us to the realities. And what kind of society is it that remains indifferent to the abuse of a child?
We need to clear both our minds and our souls.*

Surchal Wun'Gaeo, Thailand
South Asia Public Hearing

References and Notes

1. Detailed exposition of this concept is found in UN Development Programme, *Human Development Report 1994* (Oxford, Oxford University Press, 1994).
2. Ibid.
3. Stockholm International Peace Research Institute, *SIPRI Yearbook 1994* (Oxford, Oxford University Press, 1994).
4. See Ruth Sivard Leger, *World Military and Social Expenditures 1993* (World Priorities, Washington, 1993).
5. *Human Development Report 1994*.
6. Calculated from data in *Human Development Report 1994*, and Sivard Leger, *World Military and Social Expenditures*.
7. Cf. UN Draft Optional Protocol Providing for Consideration of Communications, Committee on Economic, Social and Cultural Rights (doc. E/C.12/1994/12), New York, 1994.
8. Convention on the Rights of the Child, 4, 28; International Covenant on Economic, Social and Cultural Rights, 2.1. It should be noted that the clause in question (ICESCR 2.1) states 'to the maximum', and therefore requires that the very highest priority to be given to application of the rights.
9. Committee on Economic, Social and Cultural Rights, Fifth Session, *General Comment No. 3* (doc. E1991/23), New York, UN, 1990.
10. Ibid.; see also *Limburg Principles on the Implementation of the International Covenant on Economic, Social and Cultural Rights* (doc. E/CN.4/1987/17), New York, UN, 1987.
11. Ibid. 27; 28.
12. FIAN, *Economic Human Rights—Their Time Has Come* (Heidelberg, 1995).

13. John Sewell, *The United States and World Development: Agenda 1977* (New York, Praeger, 1977); Morris David Morris, *Measuring the Condition of the World's Poor* (New York, Pergamon Press, 1979).

14. *Human Development Report 1994*.

15. Alex MacGillivray, *A Green League of Nations* (London, New Economics Foundation, 1993). The indicators are emissions of nitrogen oxide, and of carbon dioxide and sulphur dioxide; water abstraction per person; per cent of total population served by sewage treatment; protected natural areas as per cent of land area; threatened bird and mammal species as per cent of totals; municipal solid waste per person; energy supply per unit of GDP; passenger km./person in private vehicles; nitrate fertilizers used per sq. km. of cropland.

16. Critique of GNP is found in many studies of environmental and alternative economics, e.g. Paul Ekins and Manfred Max-Neef (eds.), *Real Life Economics* (London, Routledge, 1992).

17. Luisella Goldschmidt-Clermont, *Economic Evaluations of Unpaid Household Work* (Women, Work and Development Series, No. 14; Geneva, ILO, 1987).

18. Marilyn Waring, *If Women Counted* (London, Macmillan, 1988).

19. Inter-Secretariat Working Group on National Accounts, *System of National Accounts 1993* (New York, UN, 1993).

20. There are sound reasons for keeping these figures out of the main national accounts. Since outputs have also to be recorded as incomes, they would have the effect—for example—of making unemployment non-existent.

21. *Report of the Committee on Women's Rights on the Assessment of Women's Unwaged Work* (doc. A3-0197/93), Strasbourg, European Parliament, 1993.

22. Roberto Repetto *et al.*, *Wasting Assets* (Washington, World Resources Institute, 1989); concerning Costa Rica, Raul Solorzano *et al.*, *Accounts Overdue* (Washington, 1991).

23. One of the most ambitious attempts to expand and 'green' the GNP is the US Genuine Progress Indicator (GPI), produced by the Redefining Progress Institute. This sets out to measure sustainable economic welfare, i.e. GNP per capita together with unpaid domestic and voluntary labour, but less environmental and social costs associated with 'progress'. See Herman Daly and John Cobb, *For the Common Good* (London, Greenprint, 1989); Clifford and John Cobb (eds.), *The Green National Product* (Lanham, University Press of America, 1994); Clifford Cobb and Ted Halstead, *The Genuine Progress Indicator* (San Francisco, Redefining Progress Institute, 1994).

The GPI includes consumer expenditure (adjusted for income distribution), capital formation, beneficial public expenditure, and the value of unpaid domestic work. It deducts loss of leisure time (which, in the USA, has diminished despite labour-saving devices), the costs of commuting, and under-employment. It deducts the cost of water, air, and noise pollution, and personal spending to defend against these. It deducts the loss of wetlands, farmland, forests, and from soil erosion. It deducts the cost of climate change and ozone depletion, and the cost of replacing non-renewable energy resources with renewable energy.

The GPI does not show *current* real economic welfare. It does not indicate whether people 'feel' better or worse off, but it tries to measure the amount of economic welfare today that is sustainable over the long term. The results suggest that, while sustainable welfare in the USA improved from 1950 until the late 1960s, it peaked in the early 1970s. It has been on a downward trend since 1976, and in 1992 was lower than at any time since 1956. A recent study in the UK traced the same pattern, showing that sustainable economic welfare peaked in 1974, falling thereafter. By 1990 the sustainable welfare level was half that in 1974, lower than at any time since 1958: Tim Jackson and Nick Marks, *Measuring Sustainable Economic Welfare* (New Economics Foundation and Stockholm Environment Institute, 1994).

The difficulty with these studies is that some of their assumptions, material included, and material excluded are questionable. The assumed cost of replacing depleted petroleum with renewable-energy sources ($75/barrel in 1988) is much higher than most current estimates. The treatment of consumer durables is also questionable; their benefits are assumed to be 22.5 per cent of the cost price (making $403 billion in 1992), but the whole of spending on consumer durables ($443 billion in 1992) is treated as a negative item. The result is that consumer durables are treated as a net cost in 1992 of $40 billion, leaving a 'minus' benefit for welfare.

24. International Covenant on Economic, Social and Cultural Rights, 2.2.

6 Respecting the Limits

The Carrying Capacity of the Earth

> In the wealthy world we feed our consumption with the
> natural resources of countries that will need them, if
> they are going to make a step forward to a better quality
> of life. We shall have to learn to share . . . to learn wis-
> dom.
>
> Phyllis Creighton, Canada
> North America Public Hearing

> We cannot go on living in a world . . . that prizes only
> individual rights. The basis of [our] life is the com-
> munity; without it, we have no life. The quality of life
> cannot be assured solely by the food that a person eats,
> but also by the environment, by collective co-existence,
> by having public responsibilities.
>
> Rigoberta Menchu, Guatemala
> Latin America Public Hearing

The Concept of Carrying Capacity

Given the economic challenge that we have just passed in review,
we have to look survival squarely in the face.

Has the world, or have individual countries, sufficient resources
to provide future populations with food, energy, and minerals? Can
the world's climate, rivers, and oceans sustain present and future
patterns of production and consumption without catastrophic collapse? Are we on a course to trespass Nature's limits and, if so, what
can we do to draw back within them? The issues concern both

North and South, and finding solutions is a shared responsibility—a sharing of the vision.

At first, our major concern over the interactions between environment and population were for the depletion and future availability of non-renewable resources (minerals, fossil fuels). Other severe problems then became evident: the pollution of air, fresh water and fish stocks; deforestation and loss of biodiversity. Phenomena such as mounting wastes discharged into the oceans, marine over-fishing, and accumulating atmospheric contamination leading to climate change are the new problems at global level.

These go to the heart of Earth and Nature's *carrying capacity*. This term was first used in the context of determining the maximal population of a given species that its environment can support indefinitely.[1] This is a disputable notion that the Commission does not share. The Commission proposes, instead, that *carrying capacity* be defined as the *maximal sustainable load that humankind can impose on the environment before it loses its capacity to support human activity*.

This means that we must avoid embarking on the irreversible processes of deterioration and destruction. We humans may cross boundaries at our peril—at the peril of the planet as a whole—but Nature will not be fooled. We need to find ways of living within such confines by adjusting and controlling demand.

The use of resources and our output of wastes will not depend on population numbers alone. They result now from the combined impact of the population, its prevailing production schemes, and its consumption patterns. Because different combinations of these may produce the same environmental impact, we can remain (in theory) within the limits of the environment's carrying capacity via permutations of the population–technology–consumption combination.

Advances in research and technology are sure to have significant impact in this respect, as should the advent of new market mechanisms. But into the effect of these advances will have to be factored the full environmental and social costs—hitherto treated as externalities, and thus a difficult calculation. The principle of 'the polluter pays' may prove inadequate, irrespective of the level of repayment made, because it may not be able to rectify all the damage done to Nature.

Carrying capacity may have different meanings, too. In the case of renewable resources (groundwater, timber and other plants, fish and animals) the term refers to the maximal sustainable yield indefinitely supplied without jeopardizing future stock. In the case of pollution (liquid and gaseous discharges into rivers, lakes, ocean, and atmosphere) carrying capacity refers to the critical load of contaminants that these sinks can absorb before irreversible change occurs.[2]

The reserves of metallic and other mineral resources are not static. While they are depleted through use, new exploration adds to the reserves. As technologies and prices shift, larger portions of the known reserves may become economical to extract, or synthetic substitutes may be introduced. Rather than the availability of such resources, however, it is the mounting volume of solid, liquid, and gaseous wastes generated by their processing and consumption that becomes crucial in the encroachment upon sustainability.

Mining, for example, was responsible for nearly 46 per cent of the solid wastes produced in Western Europe and North America in 1990: 2,951 billion tonnes of mining refuse dwarfed the 344 million tonnes of household wastes.[3] The problem should become more serious as both population and consumption grow.

Various attempts to estimate the carrying capacity for varying levels of global population have been made, based on selected elements: food, energy, minerals, the global commons of air, fresh water, the oceans, and solar radiation. They range from a low of 2 billion population through 7.7 and 11.4 billions to a high of 50–60 billions.[4]

The Commission sustains the view that, in scientific terms, it is impossible to calculate population ceilings for either the world or individual countries because they are based on existing knowledge and technological conditions as well as on present patterns of production and consumption. In reality, the existing parameters are time-bound and may vary with the passage of time. Societies have proved capable, thus far, of adjusting within a short time to the demands of war, famine, and other disasters. In any case, each resource, each waste sink, should be considered to have its own carrying capacity of human activity.

The quality of life of present and future generations will be affected by the prospects for food security, clean fresh water, unpolluted air, and biodiversity.

Feeding the World, Sustainably

Food supply is crucial to survival. Although our population has grown dramatically, global food production has usually kept in step with this growth and average nutritional standards have improved. With the world's population doubling between 1950 and 1988, food supply kept up with demand. Some analysts suggest, however, that we may be approaching the outer limits of sustainable food production.[5] The challenge is daunting indeed.

While we do not appear to be nearing a food crisis, pressure is mounting on the availability and security of food in many countries because of several trends. There is a maldistribution in global availability; and, as people are lifted from poverty, there is more demand for food supplies. There are other worrying signs of supply. Rice- and wheat-yields continue to rise, but more slowly than recently. And spending on agricultural research, especially in Africa, has fallen precipitously.

The maldistribution of food aggravates existing inequalities between North and South; it makes developing countries dependent on food imports or other aid—with all the attendant negative consequences on local production and self-sufficiency.

The 'green revolution', based on increased productivity using high-yield cereals, may have run its course—but not without having conveyed a false sense of security. Many countries are failing to raise food production as their populations grow: between 1980 and 1990 food production per person fell in no less than seventy-two of 113 developing nations. In thirty-seven developing countries calorie consumption diminished during the same period.[6] In many countries land and water are expected to become limiting factors for agriculture. There are signs, indeed, that we may be nearing the frontiers of easily cultivable land. Good farmland is constantly taken to build roads, housing, and factories. In industrialized countries and densely populated developing countries such as China, Egypt, and Bangladesh farm area is shrinking.[7]

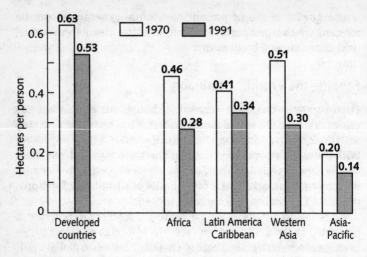

Fig. 6.1. Arable area per person (in hectares), 1970–91.
Source: Food and Agriculture Organization (1993).

The availability of arable land per capita is fast declining in the developing world (see Fig. 6.1). In 1991 there were 0.53 hectares of arable or permanent crop-land under cultivation per person in the developed countries, but even land-rich Latin America had only 0.34 hectares available per person. Africa—wrongly believed to have much land—had only 0.28 hectares/person, down sharply from 0.46 hectares/person in 1970. In East Asia the figure was 0.19 hectares, although a much higher share of this was irrigated soil.

Twenty-five developing countries (most in Asia and the Middle East) now farm more than 80 per cent of crop-suitable land. This means that they are farming marginal land, essentially unsuitable for long-term food production.[8] Fourteen sub-Saharan countries are already farming more than half their cultivable ground, as most countries' populations are expected to multiply between two-and-a-half and four times from 1995 until 2050.[9]

Even if land expansion does not slow any further below its levels during the 1980s, by 2050 there will be only 0.11 hectares/person of arable land in developing countries—using the medium projection of demographic growth. Developed countries, in the meantime, will enjoy about 0.51 hectares/person, or four-and-a-half times as much.[10]

∽

The application of inputs is not keeping up, either; world use of fertilizer began to fall after 1988. All developing regions saw a drop in irrigated areas per person. Land fertility, too, is giving way to erosion, salinization, and the failure to replace nutrients (micronutrients included). Seventeen per cent of the globe's vegetated land has been degraded since 1945; of this, 11 per cent has suffered a significant loss in productivity and would require major land-use changes or costly measures to restore.[11]

There are contrary signals, too. In some countries the prices of staples have been falling in real terms; yields are increasing (although falteringly); and average calorie and protein intakes have been rising in developing countries.[12]

Since we face a minimal increase in population of some 4 billion people, keeping food production even with the growth in population and consumption is a crucial matter, especially in terms of the growing ranks of the poor. This will mean a constant effort on all fronts, beginning with sound economic policies at the national level and ensuring market prices for farmers. Also of utmost importance will be raising the incomes of the poorest through employment, or else through improved access to land by agrarian reform and making available capital and technology therefor.

The operation of national agricultural research centres—and of extension services in order to diffuse the results among farmers—should command high priority, especially in low-income countries with deficits in food supply. In fact, however, agricultural aid in general has been cut back: its share of development aid of 20 per cent in 1980 slid to 12 per cent by 1992. Donor governments and other bodies should maintain a high level of assistance to agriculture, providing funds for research and extension service to small landholders, helping set research priorities and develop extension methods (including organization)—as much as possible in partnership with poor farmers.[13]

Because many nations are likely to fail in this respect, international efforts must be accelerated to ensure food security for all by relying on a redistribution of available farm supplies and of crops (possibly through increased imports and food aid) and a boost in agricultural research.

Agricultural research has been central to increased food production; it is sure to be more important in the future, as crops and methods will have to adapt to changing climate. But the effort should not be concentrated in high-potential areas or on methods that only the more affluent farmers can exploit. Research should be expected to produce new biological varieties and technologies (e.g. biofertilizers, biopesticides) suitable for poor and women farmers, and for marginal districts. The work should be done with the participation of those who know best their conditions, traditions, and possibilities: the cultivators themselves.

The international centres funded by the Consultative Group on International Agricultural Research (CGIAR) have proved essential to agriculture in the developing world. These centres drove the green revolution, and they continue to push the development of improved seeds and innovative techniques; their work is critical for poor countries unable to afford research or short of qualified personnel. Yet even the funding for these CGIAR centres dropped in constant dollars from $275 million in 1990 to $215 in 1994, lower than at any time since 1979. Given the enormity of the food challenge, funding for CGIAR centres must be ensured at much higher levels than at present, and placed on a stable and secure basis.[14]

Sustainability concerning food is vital. We need to move towards a more sustainable use of inputs to agriculture, towards more sustainable management practices. Subsidies encouraging over-use of water, fertilizer, and fossil fuels should be stopped. Organic wastes, currently being burned or flushed into water-courses (especially near towns and cities), should be restored to the soil.

Soil- and water-conservation are therefore indispensable to sustainable agriculture. Increasing crop production and conserving soil, water, and tree cover have been considered largely as separate, or conflicting, tasks. They should now be fused into a 'double green' revolution, aimed at both sustainability and a rise in production. Ways of raising yields should be sought that also improve the conservation of water, soil, and wood resources. Conservation methods, conversely speaking, need to be developed to improve food, feed, and fuel production.

Another dimension of the availability of food supplies is fish production. Until 1970 the total marine-fish catch rose faster than human population, allowing a gradual increase in the production of fish per capita. But this production actually peaked in 1970, at 14.3 kg/person. By 1991 production was at 12.6 kg/person. The raising in 1988 of per-capita catches was accomplished only by a constant rise in fishery efforts, with shiftings of the different species taken from different seas. This production pattern in the fishing industry proved to be detrimental because it encouraged *over-fishing* (mainly by the use of drift nets) that endangered future stocks of fish.

The growth of population and consumption in the future will raise massively the demand for food from the sea. Total production reached 98 million tonnes in 1990, and if current consumption in both developing and developed countries remains constant, then by 2050 there would be needed 142 million tonnes—exceeding the sustainable levels by far.[15]

Battling Water Stress and Scarcity

We underscore, here and elsewhere in this book, the crucial character of water for both the quality of life and sheer human survival. Water to drink, to grow and cook our food, to bathe and to wash our possessions, to make available to industry, to cool or heat. Land is productive only if there is sufficient water for crops. Industrial countries, in particular, have been profligate in the use of water for industry and for households.

The growth of population has a direct effect on the availability of fresh water. Since the resource is naturally limited, all demographic increase means an immediately lower availability per person. Given the population dynamics of the world, there is bound to be growing competition between rural and urban areas for scarcer water supplies.

Water shortage does not mean, however, that people are bound to die of thirst or starvation. But beneath certain thresholds the lack of water may limit agriculture, industry, home cleanliness or convenience, or else involve high costs for desalinizing or otherwise treating water for reuse.

According to the Swedish hydrologist Malin Falkenmark, there is *water stress* when supplies are less than 1,700 cubic metres/person annually. She notes that this may imply the need for long-distance transfers of water or the reuse of treated waste water, or cause interruptions in supply during dry periods. Where supplies fall below 1,000 cubic metres/person/year, the area is in a situation of *water scarcity*—when difficult choices must be made whether to serve first agriculture, industry, the people's health, or common convenience. Rationing or fixed periods of water-cuts may occur, because, already in 1990, 338 million people in twenty-eight countries experienced water stress.

On the UN's medium projection of demographic growth, the numbers to be affected by water scarcity will soar to 3,324 millions in 2025 and 4,386 millions by 2050.[16] Countries like Ethiopia, Somalia, Kenya, Rwanda, Burundi, Malawi, and South Africa will encounter extreme situations of water scarcity similar to those in Jordan and Israel today.[17] A number of African countries will see their situation transformed from abundance to acute scarcity over the next half-century. For example: in 1990 Nigerians enjoyed a supply of 3,200 cubic metres/person, but by 2050 (using the medium projection) they can expect to be down to 910 cubic metres each.

The future consumption levels of water will depend on the efficiency of its supply and use. In today's households over-use abounds. Conservation measures must be complemented by economy-oriented redesign of appliances using water.

Because many industrial processes require significant inputs of water, or use it as cooling agent or as pollutant disposal, technical solutions to water shortages should be aggressively pursued: research priorities that emphasize new harvesting techniques (capturing and exploiting rainwater), desalinization, using biofertilizers, plastic mulches, and drip irrigation in agriculture.

An impending global crisis with water cannot be solved without major policy changes. Recycling must become part of national policy, for example, using waste water after treatment for agricultural irrigation—thereby reducing the problem of sewage discharge into the ocean. Treated water can be used over and over.

Managing the Global Commons

The oceans and atmosphere contribute crucially to the planet's health and the survival of all species. Yet their use and abuse are a free-for-all, the absence of rules entailing a high risk of degradation of these commons—one not always immediately apparent. So the Commission believes that the global commons must be managed sustainably, this management being shared by both industrialized and developing countries. The over-users and abusers earn free benefits at others' expense—and at the future's expense—and they will wish to continue their 'free ride' as long as possible. Reaching agreement on sustainable and equitable use is, in our estimate, the most difficult step forward.

But the task cannot be shirked: it must be faced, and the longer we wait the more Draconian will be the ultimate measures to be taken. By not regulating adequately ocean fisheries now, there will be greater losses of employment later. If greenhouse-gas emissions are not checked today, there will be severe problems of economic and social disruption in the future.

Managing the commons requires rules and institutions with global reach. We see, today, some of these emerging slowly in regard to the seas and to climate. The Climate Convention presents a framework for world-wide controls on greenhouse gases, although we are far from agreement on even the most modest reductions. There is also a treaty in place to reduce the production of chlorofluorocarbons to zero. Faster progress is needed. The Commission, convinced that equity is essential to global agreements governing use of the global commons, is convinced that the only equitable rule is that each human being has the right to an equal amount of environmental space.

So it is incumbent, in the first instance, on the industrialized countries—principally responsible in the past for the use and abuse of the global commons—to reduce emission per person to an equitable level consonant with sustainability. The cuts will be deep in the cases of the United States, Canada, and Australia: reductions of about 90 per cent; in almost all the rich countries they will be around 70 per cent or more. These drastic drops are unlikely to be effected by preaching, or by simple, linear diminution. Rather, they will necessitate the introduction of environmentally sustainable technologies (including in the energy sector), together with adaptation of patterns of settlement and of life-styles. The sooner this begins the smoother should be the inevitably turbulent process of transition.

Curbing Ocean Pollution and Over-fishing

The oceans are under attack. They receive sediment from erosion, fertilizers from farms, pollution from factories, sewage from cities and towns. Their fishing stocks are being depleted. Of the world's seventeen major fishing grounds, four are considered 'fished out' and another nine are in serious decline.[18] World-wide, there are some 3 million vessels engaged in fishery; of these, only a few thousand are high-technology, industrial craft—yet they account for a hugely disproportionate share of the world's catch.

Some 20 million people are estimated to work on fishing boats and ships, supporting some 100 million men, women, and children. Many more people depend on fish for a significant part of their nutrition.

Away from land, atmospheric pollution dissolves in the oceans. Oil spills from tankers, and ships dump other waste. The depleted ozone layer above lets in ultraviolet radiation, damaging plankton. We have seen that entire oceanic regions are over-fished: species once rejected or converted into fishmeal are now used as food for humans.

Aquaculture (including shrimp farming) is used to compensate for part of the deficit of the fish harvest. And each year fishing produces waste; between 18 and 40 million tonnes of catch—undersized or unwanted—are thrown back annually, the equivalent of between a quarter and nearly half the landed catch.[19] And we have but fragmentary knowledge of the impact of all this, but it is probable that humans are having a devastating impact on most ocean ecosystems.

The emergence of global players in fishery operations, not dependent on a single fish stock nor even one country and who do not operate on a long-term calculus, have added an unknown dimension to the problem of over-fishing. Their production technologies are sophisticated, and ever-more efficient. Increasing capitalization of the industry induces fishers to over-exploit existing stocks of fish and use factory-ships to process immediately their catch; this means the disappearance of fish-processing jobs on land.

The overriding challenge, then, is reducing the aggregate fishing effort: too many vessels, using too efficient technologies, are doing too much fishing. Thought might be given to a moratorium on certain technologies, tied to sanctions when their use is scientifically determined to be detrimental to sustainable fishery. (Drift-netting and bottom-trawling cause serious damage to non-target species and to the sea floor on which certain species are dependent.)

Solutions may include a variety of measures, including market mechanisms to combat over-fishing at sea. This might be done by creating fishery property rights, for example, titles granted to exploit fishery resources, and the allocation to countries or communities of tradeable quotas. Another measure could be the co-ordination of fishery at regional and global levels. And institutions should be developed to keep human exploitation of the seas inside the limits of their carrying capacity.

Responsibility for studying and resolving ocean problems is currently fragmented among different international bodies: FAO, the UN Development Programme, UNESCO on matters of oceanography. The time may be ripe for consolidation of these scattered activities, unifying the systematic study of the ocean and its problems, combining the design of new policies and institutions to deal with them. For many countries, the adoption of aquaculture may be part of the solution too, thus reconciling its agricultural, economic, and nutritional aspects with real social needs.

Atmosphere: Reversing the Trend of Global Warming

The overwhelming reliance of the world economy on fossil fuels is the principal cause of global warming and of pollution. In the 1980s the net annual carbon dioxide (CO_2) emissions averaged between 6 and 8.2 billion tonnes—and current estimates suggest the world's energy demand will rise another 50 per cent by the year 2020. According to the central scenario of the IPCC (Intergovernmental Panel on Climate Change; see Chapter 3), CO_2 emissions would rise to 11.8 billion tonnes by 2025, 14.5 billion tonnes by 2050, and 20.3 billion tonnes by 2100.[20] By contrast, current knowledge indicates that the sustainable level of these emissions should be no more than 3 billion tonnes annually.

Even if the world-wide emissions of CO_2 were halted at their present level, the atmospheric concentrations of heat-trapping gases and other emissions would increase for another two centuries, a rise well beyond the point at which the Earth's climate would be disrupted. To hold the concentration at *double* today's amount would require cutting the world's emission levels below what they were in 1990: too much gas is being spewed into the air because of the coal and petroleum products that we burn and because of forest destruction. (The remaining vegetation and the oceans now do the absorbing of emissions.) So stabilizing CO_2 concentration at safe atmospheric levels means the need for a drastic cut in emissions.

It is clear that, without radical changes, the atmosphere will no longer be able to support the ecosystems that are life. If we do not take the measures indicated, the survival of the planet, and therefore of *Homo sapiens*, is jeopardized. We say elsewhere in this volume that the peril can be avoided by opting for an entirely new, qualitatively different, industrialization: an age of renewable energies. The fossil fuels must be phased out, with the advent of energy-efficient production technologies, new consumption patterns, and a changed life-style.

The first steps should be the removal of fossil-fuel subsidies everywhere and the offering of incentives for adopting technologies functioning on renewable energy. While most developing countries will increase their use of fossil fuels in the foreseeable future, it is not in their interest to stimulate such a rise. New taxes on fossil fuels, or taxes based on the carbon content of these combustibles, should be an integral part of *ecological tax reform*.

Shifting from fossil fuels can be hastened if the price of renewable energy can be made cheaper. Clean-energy alternatives (solar, wind, ocean, and geothermal power) have, so far, cost more than fossil fuels, so moving towards the renewables has been painfully slow. In 1970 renewable energies accounted for 2.3 per cent of all energy use, and by 1991 this figure had risen to only 2.8 per cent.[21] The Commission urges, therefore, that a centralized policy priority must be a reduction in the costs of renewable technologies. This could be sponsored through ecological tax reform, whereby taxes on labour are gradually reduced while taxes on fossil-fuel energies and other non-renewable natural resources are raised.

Research is essential for the improvement of efficiency and to ensure the switching of large-scale applications of renewable energy to replace systems based on fossil combustibles. Funding for the purpose needs to be increased significantly, and may well require an international effort analogous, in its process, to the Manhattan Project of the 1940s.

It is ironic that between 1982 and 1993 spending on renewable-energy research in the OECD countries was reduced by 40 per cent. By 1993 this type of research commanded less than 9 per cent of OECD's energy-research budget (against 13 per cent spent on fossil fuels and 71 per cent made available to the nuclear domain). This is an almost incredible short-sightedness on the part of governmental decision-makers.[22] Large-scale funding is a pre-condition for progress, and the research priorities should be for solar, photovoltaic, thermal, and biomass technologies. Research on energy efficiency and conservation, and on nuclear fusion and safer storing of nuclear wastes, should also benefit from steeply increased funding.

This is a global undertaking, and a part of it should take the form of an international network of laboratories doing research on renewable energy similar to that of CGIAR and other consortia established specifically for nuclear fusion. Each centre should concentrate on a specific field, envisaging technologies suited to its immediate location. Funding should be international, permitting the resulting technologies to be made available to developing countries.

Another priority area is that of developing energy-related technologies intended to reduce the pollution of air indoors caused by smoke: partly by diffusing cheap, fuel-efficient stoves, designed in collaboration with their intended users.

Arresting Deforestation and Other Forest Degradation

The negative trends afflicting forests must also be halted and reversed. By the middle of the twenty-first century a shrunken forest area will need to deliver even more product in order to meet the demands of about twice as many people as today. National strategies must be devised and put in place to raise productivity, halt woodland degradation and deforestation, enhance all the benefits from forests, and provide incentives for the conservation and sustainable management of our forest treasure.

Forest management itself needs more balance, with objectives more broadly based than on timber harvesting. Forest ecosystems as a whole need better protection, and management of timbering must be attuned to the benefits due to local people.

Governmental policy, correcting and positively influencing market forces via the incentives mentioned, and by objectively reviewing current subsidies, should play a critical role in the overall effort to safeguard forest resources. Scientific research must aim, within this framework, at developing improved criteria and indicators of sustainable forest management—region by region.

Deforestation can be slowed by regulating market prices for logging and limiting the damage done by loggers, strengthening regulations concerning forest management itself, and promoting massive re-afforestation.[23] In agricultural zones, deforestation can be slowed by adopting agroforestry, a method that also reduces soil erosion, raises water tables, increases the availability of fuel, and lessens the burdens of women's labour in fetching fuel and water.

To arrive at more sustainable and responsible forest management in the boreal regions, governments should eliminate transport and timber-pricing subsidies that today encourage large-scale wasteful exploitation of these northern forestlands. Effective measures—restrictions, bans, and penalties—need to be taken to contain emissions and other pollution from industrial plants, effluvia that are particularly damaging to woodlands.

Loss of habitat is the major hazard for our endangered species. The best way to preserve diverse species, therefore, is to safeguard natural habitats by policies slowing their menace and destruction. These policies may include retarding the spread of farmland into virgin tracts, and sustainable management of natural areas already in use: besides forests, the rangelands, mangroves, and coral reefs of the world. This will merge their continued utility to humans with the preservation of an optimum of biodiversity.[24]

Responsible Stewardship

In such a deliberate approach, a system of environmental impact assessment of all economic activities must be introduced, combined too with a new culture of reflecting the environmental costs inherent in virtually all human activity.

To underpin concentration on the Earth's carrying capacity we need expansion of funding for all the environmental sciences and for the associated social sciences. Part of the task of the environmental disciplines should be to estimate the maximal sustainable yields and critical loads so that the population can remain within them—or rectify things once we have exceeded these bounds. Computations of these kinds can be made at any level, from the village that desires to conserve soil and forest, through the nation or region planning its use of fresh water, to the level of the entire race faced with climate change. And at the global level these appraisals should be made by international panels of scientists and other specialists, on the model of the IPCC.

Monitoring indicators, for easy management by stewards appointed at the grass roots, need to be developed. This step will ensure that environmental issues become *people's concerns* and, thereby, major political issues. This would also ensure that the balance between Nature and human beings becomes a preoccupation beyond policy levels, one that takes its place as an integral factor in the sustainable quality of life.

Politics still seems to leave environmental questions outside the mainstream of its concerns, something belonging to the 'realm of the ecologists'. But what is at stake, in fact, are key issues of governance. Nature has now to become a dominant factor in politics, and it is only political action that will provide the stewardship required. We mean a stewardship responding to Nature: its resources, its diversity, its spiritual significance, and its aesthetic value. All these must be renovated, and their equilibrium restored to Nature and protected.

> ❧ *The globalized economic apparatus remains patriarchal and . . . drives most other human institutions, policy, and activity. The industrial revolution's second-order effects [include] poverty, pollution, unsustainable levels of consumption, waste and resource depletion. Development imperatives for the future must focus on redirecting the rules of the world economic game, [even] changing its 'scorecards', such as the GNP/GDP to measure economic growth.*

> Hazel Henderson, United States
> North America Public Hearing

References and Notes

1. Our use of biological *carrying capacity* and *population cycle* is based on Michael Begon *et al.*, *Ecology* (Oxford, Blackwell Scientific, Oxford, 1990) and Robert Ricklefs, *Ecology* (New York, W. H. Freeman, 1990).

2. J.-P. Hettelingh *et al.*, *Mapping Critical Loads for Europe* (Bilthoven, National Institute of Public Health and Environment Protection, 1991).

3. OECD, *Environmental Data 1993* (Paris, 1993).

4. See David Pimentel *et al.*, 'Natural Resources and an Optimum Human Population', *Population and Environment*, 15: 2; Donella Meadows *et al.*, *The Limits to Growth* (London, Earth Island, 1972); Donella Meadows, *Beyond the Limits* (London, Earthscan, 1992); P. Vitousek *et al.*, 'Human Appropriation of the Products of Photosynthesis', *Bioscience*, 36: 6 (1986); Graham Higgins *et al.*, *Potential Population Supporting Capacities of Lands in the Developing World* (Roma, FAO, 1982).

5. Lester Brown and Hal Kane, *Full House* (New York, W. W. Norton, 1994).

6. FAO, *State of Food and Agriculture 1992* (Rome, 1992).

7. Calculated from FAO (Economic and Social Policy Department), *Country Tables 1993* (Rome, 1994).

8. Computed from data supplied by Nikos Alexandratos, Economic and Social Policy Department, FAO; see also N. Alexandratos, *Agriculture:*

Towards 2000 (Chichester and New York, John Wiley, 1995). (Marginal land categories AT5 and AT7 are excluded.)

9. Ibid.

10. These are the Commission's calculations, assuming land expansion at the rates of 1980–9; FAO, *Country Tables 1993*.

11. International Soil Reference and Information Centre, cited in World Resources Institute, *World Resources 1992–3* (Oxford, Oxford University Press, 1992).

12. FAO, *FAO Outlook* (Rome, 1994); FAO, *Production Yearbook 1992* (Rome, 1993); FAO, *State of Food and Agriculture 1993* (Rome, 1993).

13. Derek Tribe, *Feeding and Greening the World* (Oxford, CAB International, 1995); 1992 share from *Development Co-operation 1994* (Paris, OECD, 1995).

14. Montague Yudelman, *Feeding 10 Billion People in 2050* (Action Group on Food Security, 1994).

15. Calculations made from FAO, *Agriculture: Towards 2010*, and UN, *Long-Range World Population Projections*; it is assumed that fishmeal production will remain at the level of 1990, 28 million tonnes.

16. Robert Engelman and Pamela Leroy, *Sustaining Water* (Washington, Population Action International, 1993), with supplement, *Sustaining Water: An Update* (1995).

17. Ibid.; *cf.* notably Harvard University's Middle East Water Project and its joint management plan in regard to transborder planning, management, and use of common water resources.

18. Don Hinrichsen, *Our Common Seas* (London, Earthscan, 1990); UN Environment Programme, *The State of the Marine Environment* (UNEP Regional Seas Reports and Studies No. 115; Nairobi, 1990).

19. FAO, *The State of World Fisheries and Aquaculture* (Rome, 1995).

20. William Pepper *et al.*, *Emissions Scenarios for the IPCC: An Update*, n.d.; Mimeographed paper and data diskettes available from the author at telefax no. +1 703 934 9740.

21. World Resources Institute, *World Resources 1994–5* (Oxford, Oxford University Press, 1994).

22. International Energy Agency, *Energy Policies of IEA Countries, 1993 Review* (Paris, OECD, 1994).

23. A. S. Mather, *Global Forest Resources* (London, Belhaven Press, 1990).

24. World Conservation Monitoring Centre, *Global Biodiversity* (London, Chapman and Hall, 1992).

7 Responding to Needs
The Caring Capacity of Humankind

> 🥭 *Once I was asked why Filipinas find it so easy, com-*
> *pared with their Asian sisters, to leave the country to*
> *work. This is because—economic pressures quite*
> *apart—there is minimal cultural resistance in our fam-*
> *ilies if a young woman (even a mother) leaves home to*
> *work abroad. Female emancipation has, in some ways,*
> *worked against the interests of our women.*
>
> Rina Jimenez David, Philippines
South-East Asia Public Hearing

> 🥭 *Inflation hits pensioners hard, especially the war-*
> *disabled. For the 5,000 rubles that I used to have in my*
> *savings book—the price of a car—I was given 12,305*
> *new rubles in exchange (when a kilo of sausages was*
> *worth 16,000 rubles). And pensioners who had saved for*
> *their funerals now cannot even afford the price of a*
> *coffin; they should be shoved into sacks and taken to be*
> *cremated.*
>
> D. Sidorov, Russia
Eastern Europe Public Hearing

Where are the Reservoirs of Care?

The ultimate goal of a sustainable improvement in the quality of life can be realized only if we face squarely the challenges described so far. These challenges are complex, and they cannot be met by a play of mind or by wilful determination alone. Nor do the weight of ideas and proposals emerging from meetings of international experts, from studies and publications of all kinds, or through the policy declarations of world leaders seem to suffice. For social policy to be effective, we need a value system in which care for others is emphasized.

To move towards such sustainable improvement for all—lifting 1 billion people above the level of survival—and preparing the ground for sustainable living over the next five decades cannot be left to the intermittent generosity of the affluent. Reaching levels of sustainable environment cannot be made contingent on the insight and goodwill of others. And a new economic rationale, based on a respect for Nature and renewed efforts to establish equity, is not likely to be adopted only by concerned people committed to change. All these actions must be pursued, expressing as they do individual and group engagements. The world needs today more than voluntarism.

We have highlighted the perils of eroding the planet's *carrying* capacity. We shall now concentrate on the erosion of *care*, a basic dimension of life, without which we shall not be capable of coping with the challenges lying ahead.

The Commission believes that we must transcend the narrow approach to the material basis of survival and move to establish a psychological, spiritual, and political capacity to care for each other as one of the essential determinants of progress and survival. The ability to care, which defines us as human beings, is the cement of society. We need now to explore if and how our 'reservoirs' of care can sustain us. No vision becomes real, nor can it gain momentum, if there is not a main thread stitching together relationships at all levels of experience.

⤙

But care, as an ethic, requires a drastic change of paradigm. The rising domination of the market-based economy occurred at the expense of care. While it is true that economic development was never regarded as isolated from social development, our primary objective has been the improvement of the conditions of living. In practice, however, the growth of output took centre-stage. When scarcity of resources occurs, it is inevitably at the cost of social investment in education, health, and housing. The limits of the existing development models are apparent indeed, in the critical situation represented by the hundreds of millions of deprived people, by the social inequalities leading to suffering and the rupture of social cohesion.

Resource scarcity has come to mean that reaching (narrow) economic targets has priority over quality of life, security, equity, and the human community. Scarcity has also fostered excessive concentration on the self, visible in the forms of individual aspiration and the striving for success, the quest for profit, wealth, and the resulting prestige and status symbols. Scarcity has rid the most destitute of the symbolic position of privilege that some civilizations accorded them—placing, instead, power at the centre of many relationships. This complicated the prospects of resolving peacefully all sorts of difficulties and conflicts arising naturally in society.

Yet we know that the ethic of care transcends economic rationality; it is capable of countering the pull of sheer individualism, of greed. The notion of caring for ourselves, for each other, and for our environment is the foundation upon which the sustainable improvement of the quality of life must be founded.

We are paralysed today by the paradox that, on the one hand, we seem to have the ability to solve virtually all problems but, on the other hand, we are unable to do so. We have the knowledge and many of the means (technology, policy options, financial resources), in other words, but we haven't the commitment and will-power to act. There are, admittedly, many obstacles to decisive action—foremost among them the typical human failings of short-sightedness, selfishness, and inertia. Urgently needed is a new frame of mind, a rejection of self-centredness. We need an all-embracing ethic of caring for our fellow-beings and for our home on Earth.

Care Rediscovered

Care, a commonplace term, reflects simple thoughts and emotions, enabling humans to tend Nature, to be actively concerned for one another, to hold society together. It is care that describes attitudes and actions acknowledging that human beings and their communities and nations are interdependent—that no one is isolated but is aware of 'otherness'.

To care also means to value and to love; also, to attend to, to nurse, to nourish. *To care for* implies a commitment transcending emotion, passing into the arena of action beyond medical and charitable work. Caring complements rationality in defining behaviour. *Caring* is the opposite of *indifference*, and thus further implies communication and a give-and-receive partnership.

Care as a social value has been a component of behaviour at all stages of development. The care of mothers for their children (and often close female relatives); attention paid to the vulnerable, the sick, and the old. The great religions that emerged with the agrarian civilizations emphasized the core values of caring, charity, even alms, with special attention for the poor and destitute, the ill, and widows and orphans. Care generalized the manifestations of compassion and sharing, and some of the religions extended these sympathies beyond humans and into the whole of Nature.

And yet, somehow, the caring activities tend to be less respected and less rewarded than humankind's productive activity. Worse, they are often invisible: perhaps because they are most closely associated with women.

-๑-

The Commission believes, therefore, that care must be made 'visible'. Even when no money value is attached to care and caring, society should be aware of the *cost it would have to incur* if the application of such values had to be bought. This need to render care visible is not only an imperative of justice towards those who help keep others alive and thus absorb some of the pressures on the social fabric. If care is not taken as part and parcel of the human condition, readjustment of our different roles in society—in our family, professional, and civic capacities—will be most difficult. Unless boys and men are involved in caring for others as women are, permanent imbalances will remain.

The ethic of care needs to operate publicly as well as privately. Ending poverty, curbing the waste of resources, promoting the quality of life of others: these are the essence of care. And caring for the environment is central to quality of life and of survival, for other species as well as our own. So the Earth's *carrying* capacity depends on the *caring* concern of us humans.

The Importance of Being Caring

. . . a society that took caring seriously would engage in a discussion of the issues of public life from a vision not of autonomous, equal rational actors each pursuing separate ends but from a vision of interdependent actors, each of whom needs and provides care in a variety of ways and each of whom has other interests and pursuits that exist outside the realm of care.

(Joan Tronton, *Moral Boundaries*)

These considerations have important implications for democracy and its evolution. Human beings all go through periods when they are dependent, non-autonomous, with their rights apparently diminished. Thus confronted, whether as individuals or groups, they need recourse to more than a sense of justice, more than a formalistic respect for human rights. What is needed is a new humanism, promoting rights not only in terms of legal guarantees but in terms of overriding human dignity. Care can be, indeed, the foundation for such a humanism—because we all know that laws do not suffice for the safeguarding and promotion of human rights.

The consequences for democracy go further. Based as care is on constant interaction between people, it has in itself the capacity to reinforce egalitarian attitudes and practices. Care is the opposite of power and control. At the level of the State, care means promoting and protecting quality of life, providing a just framework for life. A State not respecting rights is, by the fact itself, a State devoid of caring.

Care as an Element in Moral Reasoning

Not long ago the ideal of care as a guiding principle in ethics might have been seen as soft and sentimental. But as we watch uncaring societies breed economic insecurity, violence, and breakdown of the family, community, and even environment, the idea of caring is regaining ground.[1] There are several reasons for this, ranging from a broadening of humanitarian activity within and across national boundaries to the philosophical probing of political moralists.

An event making the concept of care more poignant still is the academic debate in the women's movement since the 1980s, exacerbated by Carol Gilligan's book *In a Different Voice*. The debate developed on the growing awareness that it is women who are confined to the realm of care, as if Nature had entrusted to them alone the task of caring. Not only is it women who take on the attentive tasks that concern us here, it is also they to whom society most often assigns the institutional responsibilities of nurse, teacher, day-care worker, and the like.

Care has emerged, too, as a factor in many aspects of decision-making and governance. In addition to work done by the Club of Rome, two recent reports have highlighted the importance of care and caring:

- *Our Global Neighbourhood*, issued by the Commission on Global Governance, not only refers to caring as one of the 'core values' that 'humanity upholds' (together with respect for life, liberty, justice, and equity, mutual respect and integrity). It goes further, stating that, 'The task for governance is to encourage a sense of caring.'

- A Royal Commission of Canada, entrusted with studying ethical and political questions raised by the new reproductive technologies, chose the 'ethic of care' as its broad orientation. 'The ethic of care', declared the Commission, 'holds that moral reasoning is not solely, or even primarily, a matter of finding rules to arbitrate between conflicting interests', further pointing out that 'the priority ... is on helping human relationships to flourish by seeking to foster the dignity of the individual and welfare of the community'.

When Care is Absent

This absence manifests itself through indifference, short-termism, neglect. Neglect is a lack of concern for quality of life, demonstrating low priority for preventive health and human security. It translates itself by reducing first, when budgetary savings are demanded, the caring services of health and education. Neglect means, that is to say, closing one's eyes and ears to social problems—letting pressure build until it finds outlets in riots, violence, and crime.

Such an attitude is commonly found among authoritarian regimes, but the democracies are not immune. Their pursuit of highly focused macroeconomic goals (combating inflation, balancing budgets), with little regard for the repercussions on other fundamental goals, can be interpreted as lack of responsiveness in public policy.

Short time-horizons are a common failing among the democracies; they rarely extend beyond the forthcoming election. Unpleasant governmental measures are usually taken during the early years of a governing mandate, while the final period is likely to be devoted to the 'sweetening' of voters for the next election. Indeed, how to marry long time-horizons with four- or five-year electoral cycles is a problem not yet solved by the democracies.

On the environmental front, neglect has been the rule in most societies. This is shown by allowing problems to build up until a level is reached at which they can no longer be ignored: by allowing, for example, biological species to dwindle to tiny pockets of survival before measures of safeguard are taken.

*

The antithesis of care is a relationship of power and control, one that can also lead to abuse and aggression. When the latter take place in the family, violence instead of soothing nurture threatens children's security (sometimes even their lives). Instead of serving a child's needs, aggression is repressive. Abuse and violence perpetuate themselves; we know that the children of abusive or violent parents often visit such treatment on their own offspring—or against their spouses and other persons.

It is at family level, therefore, that we see the most vivid forms of neglect: the outcomes of lack of care, born of indifference instead of love. Neglect provides a minimum of nurturing, protecting children half-heartedly at best, and exposing them to unnecessary risks. Family neglect and violence have their societal parallels. The violent State, for instance, ignores or abuses its citizens' rights. Instead of making concessions, the State meets protest with repression. Its victims seek revenge, and violence becomes only more violence.

We see the consequences of social neglect all round us; newspapers and television report abuse daily, an abuse which is dividing society, worsening crime, haunting people with insecurity. Not only is the family weakened, but so is the entire community, with individuals more and more 'privatized'. No wonder that the environment suffers, to the point of reducing our biological reserves. On a global scale, neglect ensures the persistence of absolute poverty, malnutrition, ill health, illiteracy, the faltering of ecosystems, and the growing menace of climate change.

The casualty list could be considerable, but such consequences are *not* inevitable. Nor should they be universal. Commitment to their avoidance is feasible, thanks to governments with broad perspectives willing to measure time in decades. Today, more than governments, many members of civil society are working to inculcate care and caring all round them.

Caring Within the Community, Especially Within the Family

The notion of care that reveals itself in all living communities, notably in the family, is ideally a partnership among equals, a relationship of dignity enjoyable by all human beings regardless of age or sex. Care should imply equality, the sharing of functions even among the most diverse social roles. Caring is an unending cycle nurturing human factors such as self-actualization, building self-esteem, mutual physical and emotional support, protecting each other from abuse and fear.

In families where gender oppression prevails, we have seen the irony of those who traditionally provide care—women and girls—being the very ones least likely to receive care. They are also the usual objects of violence and those who suffer the curtailment of their own development. And in families that do not benefit from a generational partnership, the old and the very old are often at the mercy of those who have the power, whether in the family or in the State. Restoring social equilibrium connotes firm re-connection of the entire cycle that joins children to the aged, permitting children to understand that one day they will provide care to those now caring for them.

All this means commitment: the engagement of effort and time, of material resources, of willingness. The model exemplar is a loving parent's care for its child. Experience, as well as science, has shown how much a child's growth depends on care. Love and empathy ensure the child's development to maturity through prevention of illness and injury, and remedial protection if these should occur. These acts are not mechanical, as they also respond to the child's expectations.[2]

Parental care among humans is a long process, from the arduous, day-to-day living of the poor striving for child survival to the non-poor who safeguard their offspring for a good sixteen to twenty years. Many families, too, are forced to look upon their children as their security in old age.

The Care Provided by Society

The care that families can provide may be strongly affected by the care that society offers. Not paternalism—but the breeding of unhealthy dependence on the all-provident State, sometimes with no individual effort. Our real goal, it would seem, is a society that cares enough so that its members care for each other—which brings us back to an enabling, empowering society.

Each aspect of familial care has its analogue at the social level. Nurturing means, of course, providing the *context* within which a family can nurture its members: with food, shelter, security; by cultivating gender equality and family stability, encouraging training or education, preparing for future livelihood, and assuring sustainable improvement in the total quality of life.

Protection embraces health services and other forms of social welfare, and the surety of law and order. The caring State emphasizes prevention, as we have seen in the cases of clean water and other public sanitation, combating pollution and thwarting crime, giving thought and aid in family planning. Widespread attentiveness by the State is crucial in terms of freedom of assembly and speech, a free press. A strong civil society with non-governmental entities of all kinds is equally important to the democratic processes. Alas, not all governments are so responsive.

Societal care also implies real commitment, well beyond lip-service: the commitment of resources of various kinds over extended time. We have seen how well-defined targets and time-tables are instrumental in the achievement of concrete goals: they link targets and timetables to action that can be measured and judged. What many societies need now are clearly constructed frameworks for such action—so that everyone concerned may take part directly in the decisions affecting them most: repairing the street, building a new school, ensuring community services and good conditions of work and play. And we may even find totally new forms by which care may be fully alive in society.

꩜

The wide international acceptance of the Copenhagen Social Summit's action plan brings a major change in approach, that is, economic objectives and policy are no longer treated in exclusivity. Instead, by invoking the 'enabling economic environment', the economics are now seen as the means of pursuit of other, more comprehensive aims.

In the Copenhagen documents we find clear and frequent expression of the priority now accorded to *people*, together with the social policy, social development, and the economic conditions that will make such goals attainable. Governments, for instance, are committed 'to place people at the centre of development' and, in consequence, 'to direct the economies to meet human needs more effectively';[3] 'recognize that the achievement of sustained social development requires sound, broadly based economic policies';[4] 'for enabling people to achieve social development', governments are committed 'to create an economic, political, social, cultural and legal environment' that will make this possible;[5] in order 'to promote more equitable access for all to income, resources and social services', they must 'create an enabling economic environment'.[6]

This is a clear statement of the leading position of social development. It must be said that the final text at Copenhagen represented a retreat behind verbal positions and even compromises that had been considered as accomplished during the Summit's preparatory phase. (The changes account for the critical tone of the report prepared by the non-governmental organizations present in Copenhagen.)

Yet politicians remain inclined to make social development subordinate to economic goals. At the end of the nineteenth century and towards the beginning of the twentieth individual social measures were introduced as correctives to the total economic process. While industrialization evolved, in other words, social measures took their shape only years later as compensation for the socially disastrous consequences of unleashed economic evolution.

A similar attitude—treating social goals as a poor afterthought to the dominant economic objectives—is still apparent in recent international documents dealing with development. Analysis of the strategies applicable to the four UN Development Decades reveals that they followed, uncritically, the same rationale adopted at the turn of the century: social goals were not absent, but a persistent effort was required to have them made explicit and integrated within the strategies.

It is true that there were attempts to give place to social development, but these passages often followed rather detailed sets of economic policy—with clauses such as 'the ultimate purpose of development is to provide increasing opportunities to all people for a better life'.[7] The strategy for the Third Development Decade (1981–90) focused, in its last part,[8] on 'social development'. Particular emphasis was given to 'reduction of poverty', 'education policies', 'primary health care', and 'population policies'. But such policies were put in a context bound to undermine their implementation: 'The ultimate aim of development is the improvement of the well-being of the entire population on the basis of its full participation in the process of development and a fair distribution of the benefits therefrom.'[9] Two pitfalls appear. First, by including social policies in 'the ultimate purpose of development' they are made subordinate to economic growth. Secondly, the aim of 'a fair distribution of the benefits therefrom' suggests making social development contingent on economic development—allotting it a secondary position based on 'distribution' rather than on rights. This approach reappears throughout the text of the global development strategy, revealing that the international community was unable to position properly the social policies that were emerging.

The time has come for 'qualitative and structural changes in society', as even the second International Development Strategy recognized, going hand in glove with structural changes in the economic process—rather than being dependent on 'rapid economic growth'. There is need to fortify the emerging consensus, freeing social policies from the bondage of stifling economic policies. This has been clearly articulated by people in distress at the hearings organized by the Commission in different parts of the world.

The fact that the Welfare State in Europe is passing through a crisis does not invalidate the issue raised here. On the contrary, well aware that social rights must be defended and promoted on an equal footing with civic and political rights, European States seek to revise the mechanisms enabling the State to discharge itself from such obligations. New thinking is necessary so that the various steps by which the current Welfare State was shaped may lead to new foundations for the socially caring State.

The Commission is convinced that the concept of care, with all the attentiveness that it requires to the real needs of individuals and groups—and by the response it implies to meet such needs, and by the consistency of the commitment to which it leads—provides adequate basis for future societal activity of the kind. *Care*, that is to say, *overrides expediency*.

Industrialized and developing countries come together in this joint effort, which will help confirm that the State is a socially caring one.

Social Policy as Public Policy

Social policies are the visible, political expression of the socially caring State. Before industrialization social policy was absent from the State's functions. Education was the domain of a combination of cultural, religious, and philanthropic forces. Health care was the purview of humanitarian institutions and individuals.

With the Industrial Revolution, the liberal State left measures loosely identifiable as 'social' in the hands of various (often opposed) interest groups and private persons. The assumption on which these systems worked was that of individual initiative, taken in the context of a society that—collectively—minimized or simply ignored social challenges. Law, as the supreme arbiter in society, was entrusted with the confirmation of equality among human beings, albeit at an abstract level.

Social policies became integral to public policy as the twentieth century unfolded. The reconstruction that followed the First and Second World Wars provided a new context for the introduction of social policies. The institutionalization of social policy sprang, in fact, from a continuing effort to minimize the human costs of industrialization: improving the living and labour conditions of workers, devising compensation for the hazards of their plans. Little by little, the State stepped into the field of social benefits (e.g. unemployment compensation), its role complemented by the sustained pressure of interest groups such as trade unions. There also came along collective bargaining between employers and the unions.

Today's 'social policies' were at first referred to as responses to 'the social question', or social issues. Far from being a comprehensive set of measures meant to resolve a specific issue, the new policies were decided and pursued in response to emergent causes of unrest or confrontation; they were thus a reflection of a permanent tension in power relations. Social mobilization seems, indeed, most effective in times of sociopolitical pressure—when State and society are braced to face new frontiers grounded largely (as Boaventura Sousa Santos reminded us in a recent issue of *Revista Crítica de Ciências*) on a principle of redistribution of resources-as-equality.

The benefits secured by this process came in the wake of a mobilization of actors who felt left behind as the rest of their nation progressed economically. The system promoting social policy that emerged in this relationship between State, civil society, and the citizen is what we know as the Welfare State. It came about, however, largely as a consequence of the characteristics of the respective national societies.

The process is far from complete: in most countries social benefits remain to be wrested through strong social action. In some countries even education is not yet free of charge; in others, while adequate laws may have been voted, there is no funding for services such as primary health care.

It is paradoxical that the current transition experienced in central and eastern Europe has brought about a reversal of previous processes, manifested by social retrenchment and a phase of impoverishment. More disconcertingly, perhaps, the world of today seems at a loss to find an all-encompassing perspective in which to deal with poverty, unemployment and other urgent needs raised by the foreseeable growth in population.

The Commission suggests, as a growing number of countries embark on broad economic development through industrialization, that they pursue the caring State model—at least as a starting-point for developing the policies needed to deal with social deprivation, social security, and equity. In the Commission's understanding, the Welfare State model does not identify with the first periods of industrialization. An effective Welfare State is, rather, a caring State awarding the highest priority to social policy and finding the material means by which to put it into force.

The State's Commitment to Social Policy

We have just seen that the emergence of the nation-state coincided with the earliest social policies adopted by States to cope with the social tensions brought about by industrialization. So it is easy to understand why such policies have not been formulated in countries where the nation-state is taking shape, or where industrialization remains in its early stages. Other forms of social tension tend to emerge, furthermore, such as ethnic or religious conflicts, and these do not always lead to the State's promotion of social rights.

The questions confronting many countries are varied. How to give form to social policies intended to promote social rights (education, health, work, etc.) where the conditions are quite different to those that gave birth to the social protection already familiar to many of us? Should civil society take the initiative in this regard? Is it essential to stimulate a strong civil society? Or should it be assumed that, unless social tensions flare up, there would not be enough pressure on the State to act?

The Welfare State is, by its very definition, a caring State. It aids the enabling of families and communities to care for both themselves and their environments. The caring State provides services to extend the caring capacities of families and communities, services that strongly stress prevention, preparing people for self-help. The State must remain a caring one despite any material and managerial inadequacies.

The Welfare State has put at the heart of its policies, responding to the various social needs, a goal of de-commercializing certain goods and services. To accomplish this, the State early created large administrations and institutions supposed to organize, manage, and deliver these goods and services. The trend reversed itself during the 1980s in some European countries and North America, as some services theretofore in the public domain were privatized in a quest for efficiency and economy. It is recognized, more and more, that the State need not deliver services directly; instead, the State may act as enabler and facilitator but without relinquishing its normative and regulatory duties, as well as its accountability.

Changes in demographic composition have had an impact on social policy. Lower fertility rates and higher life-expectancy in the industrialized countries are swelling the over-65 age-group. This points to a need for structures delivering intensive (and costly) care and domestic aid, thus imparting new purpose in life after retirement. The shifting ratio between people working and people out of work jeopardizes, furthermore, the future viability of many of the accomplishments of the Welfare State.

The lessons of Eastern Europe show that the withdrawal of the State from some aspects of social policy and the dismantling of institutions entrusted with administering social policy came too soon, too abruptly, and randomly. As a result the welfare system was fragmented, dissolved, and sometimes destroyed.

⟶

The Commission maintains that social policy lies at the heart of the State's responsibility. This may be translated, depending on circumstances, by pro-active social programmes carried out by various State institutions or through private-initiative arrangements— for which the State nevertheless sets a regulatory framework that assures equity. If a central government should withdraw from the State's financing commitments, the responsibilities should then be committed to the next lower levels of government. This in keeping with the principle of subsidiarity, or downward devolution of work closest to where it has its effects.

Troublesome questions arise again. How to devote energy and resources to eradicate the curse of poverty? How to be motivated to spare the resources needed for the health and education measures that are essential during demographic transitions? How to find the just balance between deprivation and high consumption? How to summon the good sense to avoid waste, precluding environmental degradation?

In order to achieve sustainable improvement in the quality of life, social investment must be at the top of governmental priority lists. Indeed, this was the main message of the World Summit for Social Development. Commitment has been loudly voiced to eliminate unemployment, assure full employment and social integration, confirm equality and equity between the sexes, increase the resources allocated to social development, guarantee universal (and equitable) access to education and primary health care, accelerate the development of Africa and the least developed countries, and strengthen international co-operation in social development. Implementation of these is the paramount task of governance today.

Not all social policies will have the same impact on the processes of demographic transition. In education, health, and employment, urgent and creative action will directly accelerate things. And the speed at which all of this can be done will determine the very character of the transition itself.

The Copenhagen Summit provided a solid beginning, one now to be followed up earnestly. The Commission urges intensified efforts, therefore, to shift spending priorities and pursue new approaches in order to combat social exclusion—a phenomenon repugnant in all its dimensions and at whatever level.

The Commission also considers it imperative that the Copenhagen Agreement be implemented without delay. Under this Agreement, all countries are pledged to draft strategies to reduce poverty overall, and include measures to remove the structural barriers preventing people from escaping from poverty, both of these within time-limits appropriate to each national context.

Each country should produce, with the participation of civil society, a single, national social development plan; it would cover all the major facets of quality of life (women, children, poverty, work, food, housing, education, health, and reproductive rights), making explicit the strategies to be used on behalf of the poorest and most marginalized groups. Included should be targets and timetables, and a specification of the indicators to be used in monitoring progress. *Local* versions should be drawn up by *local* authorities, also with strong popular participation.

The international community has an enabling and empowering role in this effort. It would help remove obstacles, such as crippling debt, and provide key resources to help the countries involved achieve an appropriate effectiveness. This should help create an equitable framework attaching to the global economy and to sustainable use of the global commons (e.g. oceans and atmosphere).

  ❯ *My home area is no longer what it used to be . . . There came a time when people were deceived by new things, bright lights. The lights were set up for [commercial] purposes. Then, which way, my people? Oh! choices— choices that we made, for better or for worse. Capital has moved onto the land, and people make profit from trees. Where there was once forest there now loom very big deserts. Those who left the land, to venture to the city: what became of them?*

                              Iluba Elimnyama Group, Zimbabwe
                              Southern Africa Public Hearing

  ❯ *A feature characteristic of our politicians is an exceptionally quantitative approach to the problems of social protection. The main figure of all those debates is the pensioner. . . . The very notion of 'social policy' needs to be elaborated. Priorities are not singled out and determined. The transitional nature of the crisis gives birth to great uncertainty. This is the most important factor which cannot be removed by some specific social policy; it can be removed only by finding a way out of the crisis.*

                                Anatoly Vishnevsky, Moscow
                              Eastern Europe Public Hearing

References

1. Caring, for example, is mentioned as part of new ethics of governance in Commission on Global Governance, *Our Global Neighbourhood* (Oxford, Oxford University Press, 1995).
2. See Carol Gilligan, *In a Different Voice* (Cambridge, Mass., Harvard University Press, 1993); R. Myers, *The Twelve Who Survive* (London, Routledge, 1992).
3. John Bowlby, *Child Care and the Growth of Love*, 2nd edn. (Harmondsworth, Penguin Books, 1965).
4. *Report of the World Summit for Social Development* (Prelim. version), 19 April 1995.
5. Ibid.
6. Ibid.
7. Ibid.
8. *III International Development Strategy* (New York, United Nations, 1981).
9. Ibid.

Part III

From Vision to Policies

8 Attitudes towards Population Change

A Paradigm Shift

❧ *Today we citizens of Brazil want the economics and politics to obey us, because it is we who build democracy. Without democracy we are simply subjects, servants, slaves of the logic of the local apartheid.*

Herbert de Souza (Betinho), Brazil
Latin America Public Hearing

❧ *The people of southern Africa want to be full and active participants in developing and implementing population and quality-of-life programmes . . . not simply passive recipients.*

Marvellous Mhloyi, Zimbabwe
Southern Africa Public Hearing

A Change in Perspective

What took place at the UN Conference on Population and Development, held in September 1994 in Cairo, is seen increasingly as a paradigm shift away from how population policies have been understood in earlier decades: 'a new definition of population policy was advanced . . . the sense and tone of the aggregated recommendations are such that, if implemented, they presage a major change of emphasis, even a paradigm shift, in the international community's approach to population growth'.[1] In light of its own work and especially its seven public hearings, the Commission fully shares this perspective.

The view contrasts with the predominant orientation of population policies of the 1960s and 1970s, when they were seen principally as a tool meant to exercise population control and reduce the rate of population growth. This manifested itself in the concern for the impact of population growth on food supplies and in the belief that population growth was an obstacle to development.[2] For example, US President Lyndon B. Johnson suggested in a State of the Union address, 'next to the pursuit of peace, the really greatest challenge to the human family is the race between food supply and population increase'.[3]

Even before the first UN Population Conference (held in 1974 in Bucharest), the concerns of the young developing countries necessitated a more balanced view of the goals and actions to be pursued by population policies; yet its implementation fell short of its ambitions. The balance was lost when the issue of population policies was reduced to only family-planning activities,[4] which helped foster a climate of as-yet unknown intervention. 'Defining the population problem in terms of a lack of contraceptive supplies enabled the United States to intervene quickly, cheaply, and without much attention to local circumstances.'[5] Consequently, vigorous efforts by many developing countries to reduce population growth through family planning brought positive results in terms of population-as-numbers.[6]

The Commission notes a remarkable recent change in attitudes towards population change. The effective delivery of contraceptives and related informational and motivational services, which lowered fertility, was not accompanied by complementary or supportive measures drawing upon social and economic change.[7] The status of women in the 1970s emerged as a major determinant of fertility, but the choice of indicators defining status led to many debates. After the initial parameters relating to literacy, education, and nuptiality (marriage age) were developed, others such as economic participation, education, and health were added gradually.

⦿

A change occurred in the brief time between 1974 and 1994. On the one hand, in face of massive structural changes in the world economy and the onset of globalization, *development* reached an impasse. On the other hand, the women's movement emerged and became an influential and decisive force. A total reversal ensued: women's reproductive rights became the corner-stone of debate on population and development—of, in fact, population policies.

The affirmation of a woman's inviolable right to reproductive choice has put *population policies* in a new context, one nothing short of a paradigm shift. For the first time a social issue of global and paramount importance is now defined in terms of both individual and collective rights. It follows that States have the obligation to respect, protect, and promote the reproductive rights of their citizens as much as all other rights. Such recognition is bound to change drastically policies related to population.

The Commission wholeheartedly welcomes this development, nothing short of a social revolution world-wide. The empowerment of women and other improvements in their status has been, after decolonization, the significant revolution of the twentieth century. In attempting to present a fresh vision, our Commission sought to lay the groundwork for a shift of paradigm in population policies for the future, and their implementation at national and international levels.

The Commission believes that population studies need to make clear, to all citizens, the different demographic scenarios and their consequences at local, national, and global levels—without, however, attempting to impose size of family. The Commission emphasizes the right of individuals to choose their family size freely and responsibly. The use of coercion in applying population policies is a violation of human rights and should be abandoned.

At the same time, population policies should comprise public policy affecting fertility and rate of population growth—health, education, investment in behalf of women and children (especially girls)—as well as seeking to empower citizens to solicit the action required.

Population Policies and their Societal Context

The change that took place in Cairo cannot be understood unless it is seen in a comprehensive, societal context. Attempts to regulate population dynamics are as old as organized societies. To procure food, maintain security, and provide sustainably for the future of a community: these have been considered the basic responsibility of the community's leadership or government.

Once a society perceived limits to its expansion because it found no way to expand its productive capacity, practices and then customs were adopted to control society's numbers. This is why population policies are so linked with the basic cultural characteristics of a given society.

Reducing mortality, infant mortality in particular (which would be achieved through public-health policies and international co-operation), brought about a longer life-expectancy. In time, this became interpreted as the *cause* of the population problem. Neither the reduction of mortality nor the extension of life-expectancy, however, was a factor in the early debates on population policy (whether at the national or international levels). Even as late as the 1990s, some medical scientists and economic policy-makers accused UNICEF's child-survival strategy of having pushed many developing countries into a 'population trap'.

Another polemic has been the widespread assumption that it is only developing countries that need population policies because of increasing demographics. This argument overlooks the significance of a population's growth rate, structure, composition, and mobility—some determining factors behind public policy and national development. So it is only recently that attention has begun to be paid to serious population problems within industrialized countries: declining birth-rates, extended life-expectancy, changes in age-structure, and increasing immigration. Social policies pursued in response to these trends are seldom acknowledged as population *policy*, and they seldom figure prominently in international debate on overall population policy. This was perceived, during the Commission's public hearings, as a deliberate double standard.

Policy misrepresentations of this sort may complicate initiatives, continuing actions, and the spirit of co-operation that are so vital to dialogue regarding population policies. The Commission holds, therefore, that these policies must always be exposed in their full context, not only within the societies concerned but also in relation to the universal goal of sustainable improvement in our quality of life. This requires that:

- the present gap between demographic science and population policies be narrowed; and
- dialogue and public consultation be permanent.

At the Core of Population–Development Interaction

An increasing fragmentation of knowledge and expertise, combined with deepening specialization among professionals, has prevented the interweaving of population and development issues. The population–development debate has often suffered, too, from divergent views between scientists and politicians. While many scientists advocate broad understanding of the factors determining population growth, political leaders have taken, by and large, a more simplistic approach.

Population specialists have steadily widened the scope of their work so as to capture the full complexity of population dynamics. The core set of demographic determinants—fertility, mortality, composition and distribution of population—has been complemented by social, economic, political, technological, and cultural variables that influence the core factors. Development science likewise covered an ever-expanding range of constituents which were subordinated, however, to the quest for economic growth. The last was deemed to be exclusively within the realm of politics.

While population growth was reflected in international development strategies, the correlation established between population and development had been limited to annual growth rate and its implications for GDP per capita. As population policies were treated separately in international policy documents, so were the workers and experts in demography.

Among the specialists in development, there were 'welfare relief agents' coming from both official and humanitarian organizations within the country and from international agencies. There were also 'development workers', individuals or groups representing diversified communities drawn from among religious missionaries, and 'co-operation agents' operating in behalf of bilateral or multilateral agencies. On totally different paths, there were also agents of 'population programmes' or 'family-planning programmes', often directed by foreigners.

The Nexus that Joins Ethics and Politics

The Cairo Conference, in its quest to reconcile science and politics and create direct links between them, proved to be a milestone. The Commission encourages continuation of this trend, since it is clear that population policy is an integral part of social policy. The Commission suggests, in the same vein, that all population and development experts and workers active in developing countries strengthen their mutual understanding and co-operation. The link that we have established between population and the sustainable improvement of the quality of life makes it evident that 'population matters' can be tackled efficiently only in the context of other factors contributing to quality of life—namely, the development factors.

Controversy has surrounded the role of science and technology. To be sure, contraceptives have been well received by women and men. But emphasis on *effective*, *long-term*, or *permanent* solutions to fertility problems has not been matched by comparable concern for the health of users or for the capacity of health services to provide necessary monitoring and after-care. This had led some users to believe that they are being manipulated.

Women's organizations in both North and South have opposed 'provider-controlled', long-acting hormonal implants and anti-fertility vaccines. They have questioned why 'user-controlled' barrier methods failed to take hold, and why they were replaced on the market by products newer yet in technology. There *is* demand for user-controlled methods, as we ourselves saw in a successful example of South–South co-operation. In that case, Brazilian women's organizations assisted an Indian counterpart in popularizing the use of diaphragms in the hope of inducing demand that could lead to domestic production in India.

Protests concerning user-control received the support of many physicians, although not from the entire profession. Population policies have thus brought some lack of credibility in the ethical standards observed by the medical profession.

Conflicts sharpened with the arrival of new reproductive technologies (NRTs). In our regional hearings from North America to South Asia we heard strong criticism of the concentration of research, development, and production of invasive, 'provider-controlled' contraceptives for women, while at the same time male consciousness, responsibility, and user-friendly contraceptives were neglected.

Experts identified the virtual monopoly of this R&D and manufacture within a few industrialized countries as insensitivity (and, in some cases, corruption) among health professionals and administrators. Some doctors and administrators of family-planning services admitted that donor agencies occasionally insisted on the use of long-term hormonal contraceptives—invasive techniques—in the programmes financed by them. There are scientists who argued that indigenous development of cheaper, more user-friendly and culturally acceptable contraceptives has been hindered by the unethical practices of outside donors and firms that manufacture contraceptives. The Commission's regional hearings were told that, in many countries, there may be a monopoly of the field by companies having home offices in industrialized nations. These are seen as driven more by profit motives than by seeking to adapt their products to local cultural conditions.

The Commission therefore urges increased funding from the governmental, foundational, and private sectors for the R&D and production of safe, acceptable, and user-controlled contraceptives for men as well as for women.

↦

NRTs have brought a new dimension to the debate, a debate that we pursue more fully in Chapter 13. NRTs are relevant to *all* countries, but they belong more properly to the field of reproductive health. They allow medical assistance to reproduction, sought by couples or individuals, via interference with human—especially women's—fertility. The use of NRTs presupposes a system of primary health care that functions well; it also raises a host of ethical questions. Several countries, of both South and North, have therefore established national bioethical advisory bodies. At the international level, a Bioethics Council has been established under UNESCO's umbrella. The application of technology, especially for health and reproduction, must always be guided by the ethical principle that *what is scientifically possible and technologically feasible must also be socially acceptable.*

The Commission suggests that each country establish an independent body to advise on the social acceptability and introduction of new biotechnologies, including technologies meant to reduce fertility or overcome infertility. Such a body, interdisciplinary and multi-institutional, would be asked to concern itself with the full range of ethical and social questions involved. It should provide advice periodically to policy-makers and disseminate its findings, in order to encourage general dialogue, to the public at large.

The values underlying the use of NRTs resemble closely those regulating the application of 'old' reproductive techniques, specifically intended to reduce fertility: individual autonomy, equality, respect for life and dignity, protection of the vulnerable, the non-commercialization of reproduction itself, an appropriate use of resources, accountability, and balancing individual against collective interests. The Royal Canadian Commission on New Reproductive Technologies has developed excellent guide-lines in these matters.

NRTs should not be used as a privilege or means of discrimination. Instead, they need careful evaluation to ensure that society is fully capable of absorbing them. Assessment of NRTs, as is the case with other novel technologies concerning the reduction of fertility, involves a series of steps:

- identification ↓ → scientific evaluation ↓
- ↓ selection ↓ consultation
- ↓ experimentation → ↓ decision-making → dissemination of information •

Our little schematic highlights the problem: tension between scientific-technological development and power, on the one hand, and political power, control, and accountability, on the other. The human and ethical implications related to old and new technologies of reproduction are, in our belief, too profound to be left to self-regulation.

The Commission encountered during its hearings considerable misgivings about some of the NRTs. As a consequence the Commission strongly advocates that all technologies aimed at reducing fertility be submitted to the same control and the same ethical standards as those applying to new technologies intended o surmount infertility. The Commission also perceives the need, on the international plane, for a body to draw up standards for NRTs that would be gender-sensitive and fully cognizant of human rights: guide-lines, that is to say, for future scientific research and product development.

A Holistic Approach to Population Policies

In its work, the Commission proceeded on the basis that only a systemic approach to population, quality of life, and environment can provide the needed framework for the formulation of population policies. The Commission thus suggests a holistic approach whereby population policies must be seen as one element of a system embracing all aspects of society and the quality of life. Population policies should not be an afterthought, in other words, in contemporary governance—something handled separately from the discussions and decisions concerning overall policy.

Hence the Committee believes that effective population policies cannot be dealt with by isolated committees or councils operating outside the main, decision-making mechanisms. Population policy, whether explicit or implicit, should become a fundamental and collective responsibility of a country's entire machinery of governance—of both government and parliament, and not left to advisory bodies alone.

While the responsibilities for policy affecting population are divided among ministries and agencies, a combining approach will help overcome this division. The approach requires transparency (full disclosure) and public accountability, since population policies must find their rightful place within the broader political, socioeconomic and cultural debate. Population policy must be backed, indeed, by a collective political will in order to:

- identify policy coherence and conflicts;
- facilitate resource mobilization and allocation.

It will also be necessary, at the global level, to avoid counterproductive categorization of population issues. Problems associated with fertility control are considered by the North as 'soft', whereas the South perceives them as 'hard'. Issues related to immigration are considered 'hard' in the North, 'soft' by the South. Adopting a holistic view would eliminate this divergence by subsuming all such parameters within a single concept of the quality of life. Opposing points of view would then assume equal importance.

The degree and extent of public participation will determine, to a considerable extent, the effectiveness of population policies. Wide participation is essential because it prevents distortion of population policy via shortened time horizons and the party politics so familiar to modern democracies. Broad participation should also strengthen the public's ability to intervene effectively at different levels by synergizing individual interests, perceptions, and choices into collective goals.

From the local, national, multinational, and global levels, debate concerning population policies must be widened further and intensified. It needs to be complemented by 'education for governance': preparing population histories, and considering the changing needs of children (since they do not represent themselves among adult debaters) and the position of adolescents (also unrepresented, but with their own expectations, problems about lifestyle and sexuality), the diversity of family structures and cultures, and disaggregation of data on population dynamics.

> ❧ *My second pregnancy produced twins just when my husband lost his job. With the twins I would go from Banconi to Dibida market to beg. My children don't eat in the morning unless a neighbour gives us leftovers. Plagued by these worries, I have not been able to find someone to give me advice on family-planning.*
>
> A woman from Bamako, Mali
> West Africa Public Hearing

References

1. C. Allison McIntosh and Jason L. Finkle, 'The Cairo Conference on Population and Development: A New Paradigm?', *Population and Development Review* 21: 2 (1995).

2. Peter J. Donaldson, *Nature Against Us—The United States and the World Population Crisis, 1965–1980* (Chapel Hill and London, The University of North Carolina Press, 1990).
3. As cited in Donaldson, *Nature Against Us*.
4. Ibid.
5. Ibid.
6. McIntosh and Finkle, 'The Cairo Conference'.
7. Ibid.

9 Redefining Work

🔹 *All over the world the proportion of women among the employed grows, here it drops. Everywhere social legislation proceeds from a guarding, paternalistic one to legislation that grants equal opportunities for work. But our legislation makes things more difficult . . . Unemployment in Russia has a woman's face . . .*

Zoia Khotkina, Russia
Eastern Europe Public Hearing

🔹 *Our movement believes that strengthening small business is fundamental to generating employment and producing a new Brazil. It is the big that has produced misery here: big corporations, big landowners, big landed estates. I prefer everything divided up, decentralized, independent.*

Herbert de Souza, Brazil
Latin America Public Hearing

Work is Central to Quality of Life

Work is an end as well as a means. It is important not only for its material returns; it provides the individual with a sense of social identity and purpose, a feeling of being integrated in society.

Work is thus central to quality of life. Whether people are employed by others or by themselves, work creates food supply, clothing, and shelter, or it provides the income to buy them. Work is the chief means by which people try to satisfy quality-of-life needs: an adequate standard of living, sufficient food, adequate housing, clean water, and sanitation.

Work occupies at least half our waking hours, so the conditions of work (physical and psychological) are at the core of the life experience. Social recognition coming from others, as well as a sense of social belonging, is influenced by one's degree of success at work.

Throughout the process of industrialization, work has been identified and equated with employment. This explains why most economic and labour policies, legislation, and statistics have been dominated by the parameters of employment and a quest for full employment. In fact, employment has been a central policy concern throughout the twentieth century, reflected in the creation of the International Labour Organization, or ILO, of the UN, the pursuit of Keynesian economic policies in the wake of the economic Depression, and the Charter of the United Nations.

Article 55 of the last stipulates that the UN shall promote full employment. This was motivated by a desire to avoid a repetition of the mass unemployment of the 1930s and its consequences. In 1966 the International Covenant on Economic, Social and Cultural Rights recognized that everyone has the right to work, to have free choice of employment, just and favourable conditions of work, and protection against unemployment. More recently, the World Social Summit (1995) again brought the issue of employment and livelihood to the centre of the debate on national and international policy.

But to equate work with employment only would deny important aspects of social recognition, the sense of identity and purpose related to the invisible contribution by millions of people whose work does not enter into the definition of *employment*. The prevailing concept of employment ignores, for example, the expanding informal economic sector, one that provides a livelihood to significant numbers of people in both industrialized and developing countries. And work, of course, generates products, services, and riches—the distribution of which enhance the quality of life.

The Commission proposes, therefore, to redefine work in a broad sense that encompasses both employment and unpaid activities (almost overwhelmingly done by women) benefiting society as a whole, families as well as individuals, and ensuring equitable distribution of the wealth generated.

Unemployment: Facts and Trends

The current period of demographic transition coincides with a marked change in the type and nature of human activity. Each year, for example, an additional *43 million* people enter the labour market: 118,000 every day, more than the work-force of the largest firms.[1] The ILO estimates that between 1995 and 2025 the global work-force will swell from 2.5 to 3.7 billion people. Some 99.7 per cent of this growth will be in today's developing countries.[2] A key problem for the future, then, is whether livelihoods can be created to satisfy the needs of the present labour-force and accommodate an additional 1.2 billion livelihoods that will be needed over the years until 2025. Figure 9.1 shows the anticipated growth in the global work force by 2020. In 1995 there were an estimated 120 million people officially unemployed in the world. There are perhaps another 600–700 million underemployed, those seeking additional work in order to earn a minimal income.[3]

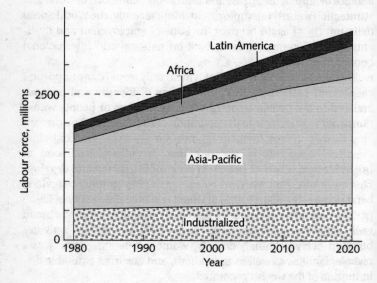

Fig. 9.1. Growth of the global labour-force, 1980–2020 (projected).

The economies of developing countries have not created work at a rhythm keeping pace with demographic growth. Most developing regions passed the peak growth rate of their labour-force in the early or mid-1980s, while Africa's should peak in 2010–20. The absolute numbers of people in search of livelihood is expected to rise dramatically, posing a daunting task—especially if further, serious surges in poverty are to be avoided. The societal organization of work and the impact of economic globalization, on the other hand, deny to an increasing percentage of people the means for a decent living.

All these developments affect the industrialized countries as well. There, the growth in numbers of jobs has not kept pace with the growth of the potential labour-force, mainly as a result of an increasing proportion of working women (although the labour-force as a whole grows more slowly as the population ages). In most parts of Europe the total labour-force will begin to decline from the year 2000.[4]

The present employment situation results from several trends. From 1973 the world's economy, struck by two 'oil shocks', entered a long wave of slower growth. Since 1980 a combination of debt, structural adjustment, transition away from communism, and deflationary governmental policies has reduced the growth of employment—or else exacerbated unemployment in most regions.[5] These trends have been accentuated by the pace of both technological advance and the revolution in knowledge/communication, creating in turn ever-more productive, capital-intensive, and automated production processes combined with their relocation to some low-wage countries.

In Asia the employment record has been largely positive. In most of East and South-East Asia unemployment in the early 1990s ranged between 1.8 and 2.7 per cent, although it was higher in Malaysia (6 per cent) and the Philippines (7 per cent). Real wages performed well, too: in manufacturing they rose an average of 5 per cent/year between 1980 and 1991. South Asia fared more modestly in the great regional boom, with unemployment rates ranging from 3 per cent in India to almost 15 per cent in Sri Lanka. Real wages in manufacturing, however, rose by only 1 per cent/year.[6]

In the industrialized countries of the OECD unemployment rose sevenfold, from 5 billion in 1966 to 35 million in 1994. The bulk of this rise occurred in Western Europe, where unemployment rates grew from 2–3 per cent in the 1950s and 1960s to 10–12 per cent by the early 1990s. In most countries there was a *rise in the total numbers employed* between 1983 and 1993.

The most disturbing employment trends were those of Central and Eastern Europe and the former Soviet Union, Latin America and the Caribbean, and Africa. All three regions underwent major shifts in their economic and trade structures, moving from protectionism and government-controlled markets to liberalization of both internal and external markets. Employment opportunities were reduced during this period by

- privatization and job losses in unviable State enterprises;
- cuts in governmental employment and subsidies; and
- the sudden opening of home markets to foreign competition.

In Eastern Europe and the disaggregated Soviet Union, the collapse of communism and the shock of a rapid transition to capitalism caused heavy unemployment—hitherto unknown in these economies. Only the Czech Republic weathered the storm, its unemployment remaining relatively low. In Russia unemployment in 1994 was officially declared to be 2 per cent; true unemployment was many times higher, since many workers were either laid off or left unpaid. In Poland, Bulgaria, Albania, Slovakia, and Slovenia unemployment rose from very low levels to 14–17 per cent by 1994.[7]

The countries of Latin America and Africa underwent their own forms of transition, shifting from regimes of import substitution and overvalued exchange rates to full exposure to the world's markets. At the same time, these countries grappled with unprecedented levels of debt.[8]

As formal employment opportunities declined in Latin America, people moved to the informal sector. Between 1980 and 1992 the proportion of non-farm workers earning their livelihoods in the informal sector rose from 25 to 32 per cent. Open unemployment remained moderate, except in the Caribbean where the rate in 1992 ranged between 16 and 23 per cent. Wages, at the same time, fell in the region. This decline varied between 5 per cent in industry and

20 per cent in agriculture. In the informal sector, however, income diminished 42 per cent.[9]

By 1995 there were signs in a number of Central and Eastern European and Latin American countries that their travails of transition and adjustment might be coming to an end. But Africa could look for no such light at the end of the tunnel. Although unemployment there ranged between 7 and 13 per cent in the mid-1980s, there was a steep decline in employment in the public sector and in factories; this became unviable once the overvalued exchange rates were slashed. Workers shifted *en masse* to the underpaid informal sector. During the years 1980–8 real wages in manufacturing tumbled by 12 per cent annually.[10]

But it would be simplistic to suggest a single causal relationship between unemployment and numbers of population. There is a variety of causes, as can be demonstrated for the industrialized nations and the former communist countries that register no population growth but suffer from the phenomenon of jobless economic growth. High levels of unemployment have come to be accepted as an almost inevitable feature of life. Even among the employed there is a widespread belief that secure, stable jobs are a thing of the past. Indeed, employment may have become the pre-eminent economic, social, and political issue of our time.

Apart from the naked figures, there has been a rise in inequality among nations. Asia's boom is a welcome development, since the region housed two-thirds of the world's poor in 1990. Recent trends have pushed Central and Eastern Europe and the former Soviet Union clearly into the ranks of the middle-income countries, now leaving Africa almost excluded from the world economy.[11]

There have also been increased inequalities within countries. The rise in long-term unemployment has created an expanding group of people virtually excluded from the labour market, demoralized and stigmatized. The very status of unemployment is aggravated by its duration: in 1993, in eight of the OECD countries, more than 40 per cent of the unemployed had been out of work for a year or longer.[12]

Exclusion from Work, Exclusion from Society

Excluding people from work has many damaging consequences, for both human security and equity. Exclusion reduces income and, therefore, everything that money can buy (especially food, shelter, and clothing); it undermines dignity and self-respect and deprives people of social interaction. Because of such pressures, unemployment makes family conflict and breakdown more likely.

Unemployment is also a threat to physical and mental health, among both children and parents, and it strikes some groups harder than others. Unemployment rates for youths aged 15–24 are usually two to three times greater than those for adults. In 1993 youth unemployment in Italy exceeded 30 per cent, in Spain it was over 40 per cent.[13] Older workers suffer, too. Companies in the process of downsizing have sacked older employees first, often pushing them to early retirement. And the effects of this type of retrenchment are more severe on women than men.

Although in most countries there has been a significant rise in female participation in the labour force since the Second World War, unemployment among women has become a permanent structural phenomenon. A striking example is the fact that in Central and Eastern Europe and the former Soviet Union, where women's participation was high under communism, women have been the hardest hit among the unemployed.[14]

Gaps have widened, in most countries, between people having valued skills or educational qualifications and those without. In many industrialized countries wage differentials between the highest and lowest 10 per cent deepened markedly between 1980 and 1991. Unemployment affected the least educated most of all.[15]

With the rise in unemployment and the lack of more flexible and just patterns of work, there has also been a decline in job security: a rise in part-time work, together with a trend towards shorter-term contracts—both of these tending to cut workers' rights and benefits. This has had spin-off effects on housing and other living conditions because those with work insecurity find it more difficult to obtain loans of any kind.

Work as a Continuum: The Emergence of an Active Society

The Commission is of the view that the nature of work as we have perceived it since the beginning of the Industrial Revolution is undergoing a most drastic change. Work can no longer be defined nationally, or internationally, by the concepts and variables of the past as new elements enter the equation.

The notion of the age of industrialization survives, but it must be supplemented today by facets of life that industrial activity cannot provide, for example, internalizing the externalities, or maintaining the social cohesion and the well-being of communities. Other changes have taken place in psychological and sociological terms as the perception of the role of work has changed during our lifetimes.

So future 'employment policies' cannot be elaborated on the basis of an equilibrium sought in the past. The Commission suggests, rather, that work be perceived as a continuum, to whose segments should be attached economic values: from jobs for mere survival to meaningful employment or significant roles (e.g. unpaid work as housewives or volunteers)—satisfying individual or societal needs, and ultimately empowering the people. The prevailing idea of 'productive work' should be expanded to include that growing portion of activities not considered hitherto as directly productive, such as research and development, or information and other services.

Structural reforms will be needed also, to enable society to cope with the structural causes of unemployment. If long-term 'structural unemployment' makes the livelihood (and the daily lives) of persons fully dependent on unemployment benefits, then human dignity may suffer. This is why proposals have been made to replace unemployment benefits by 'employment subsidies'.

The Commission embraces the idea of an 'active society', one that has been mooted to allow structural reforms to be made on the basis of three principles: diversity, flexibility, and mobility. There are other qualifications, too.

Diversity of work underlines the spectrum of activities to be performed. The diversity of activities is an expression of the *diversity of*

What is an Active Society?

An active society is characterized by opportunity and choice, cohesion, and solidarity. It is responsive to changing social and economic needs and enables its members to influence the direction of change. Enhancing 'parity' goes beyond attempts to achieve full employment or increased labour-force participation. It means taking bold steps to encourage economic and social participation by recognizing the multiple areas of activity—market and non-market—in which individuals are engaged, and acknowledging the growing interdependence between those areas of activity.

(A Group of Experts, OECD)[16]

choices at the disposal of an individual, both at a given moment and over his/her lifetime. This diversity is inadequately expressed by the one-dimensional, aggregate term of *labour-force*.

Flexibility in work encompasses both the concept of work as a continuum and the entitlements of those exercising an activity; it provides for the pursuing of individual interests and for a change of focus within an activity. Flexibility must be carefully evaluated, however, to avoid negative consequences for the enjoyment of social rights.

In order to consummate flexibility, a *mobility* that is both vertical and horizontal is fundamental among both employers and employees. Horizontal mobility, less well known in the past than vertical mobility within institution or sector, and dealing usually with geographic relocation, is itself undergoing pervasive change:

- as people move from one type of job to an entirely different one; and
- with the revolution in communication obviating the need for traditional central-office environments.

Changing Work Patterns

Creating Livelihoods in Rural Developing Areas

In developing countries the challenge is to create enough livelihoods to end poverty and absorb unemployment and underemployment, matching the future growth of the work-force.

Despite rapid urbanization, some 61 per cent of the workers in developing countries in 1990 still earned a living from agriculture.[17] So it is in rural districts (i.e. in farming and in non-farming employment in small towns) that much of the effort to create livelihoods should be concentrated. This approach can relieve poverty, boost food production, slow the migratory flows, and thereby ease pressure on cities.

Land reform is a pre-condition for the creation of a sufficient number of livelihoods. Redistributing agrarian land will increase rural employment and is a *conditio sine qua non* for eradicating rural unemployment. The Commission is convinced that land and agrarian reform is not only a requisite for equity and efficiency; reform will also help generate new jobs in developing countries and, in the process, boost food production. Farmers are often indirectly taxed through State-controlled prices and the State monopolies that purchase crops in many countries. Such reforms could create millions of new livelihoods.

Rural areas must also obtain a fair share of governmental expenditure, thus creating jobs directly.

The Role of the Informal Sector

Equal attention must be given to creating the means of livelihood in urban areas, by focusing anew on small enterprises and the informal sector. A large part of the informal sector in developing countries is part of the hidden economy, one expressing the desperate fight for survival and often intended to evade fiscal control and labour standards. This sector includes small-scale trades, services, and manufacture, usually operating beyond the scope of laws and regulations; it now accounts for as much as 40 per cent of all non-agricultural employment in Latin America, 55 per cent in Asia, and 70 per cent in African countries.[18]

Since the hurdles to entry in the informal sector are lower than for formal industry and trade, it is much easier for people to create their own livelihoods. Complying with official requirements concerning capital, education, or bureaucratic formalities can be costly and time-consuming.[19] In fact, small-scale enterprises and rural industries may be those most threatened by liberalization policies.

But the informal sector has disadvantages. Labour laws based on ILO conventions, including the right to unionize, are not applicable. Wages are often lower than the official minima. Health-and-safety regulations may be neglected or disregarded. Child labour may be employed, often in oppressive and dangerous conditions. And governments experience a loss of tax revenue.

But the answer is not harassment and persecution of the informal sector. The Commission believes that a solution is to upgrade the informal sector, along with other small businesses and crafts that *do* follow the rules. This means giving small, informal entities equal access to governmental credit or to foreign exchange (where this is regulated). Small enterprises can even flourish if they are given training in basic management, such as bookkeeping, quality control, and marketing. Aid from the government can be given on condition of compliance with the legal codes on health, safety, and child labour.

Developing countries should aim for a closer integration of their large-scale, smaller-scale, and micro-enterprises engaged in repairs, manufacturing components, and carrying out labour-intensive ancillary services such as cleaning, packing, and catering.[20]

The Commission also welcomes the growing international support for the creation of credit schemes for micro-enterprises. These benefit the poor, especially poor women. The Commission calls for further expansion of such programmes—thus far concentrated in Asia; it urges both bilateral and multilateral donors to provide the necessary funding. Governments of all developing countries must create the required political and legal environment, too, to enable 'micro-credit' structures to operate and flourish.

Traditional Labour Markets in Industrialized Environments

Unemployment in most industrialized countries is not a matter of shortage of work or of wealth: it is essentially a problem of the disribution of work opportunities and incomes. This requires a radical new approach to both time-sharing and profit-sharing.

The distribution of work opportunities is increasingly skewed. On the one hand, there is a growing minority of people who cannot find work, or cannot find as much as they need. On the other hand, there is a majority who, through the pressures of competition, are forced to work harder than they might prefer, even sacrificing family and leisure in order to keep a job.

Yet *there is no shortage of work*. Alongside the growing mass of unemployed is an increasing number of jobs that urgently need to be done. These are not being done because of a lack of public finance. *Nor is there a shortage of overall income*. Alongside a deepening poverty for an expanding minority, average national incomes per person continue to rise year after year in almost all the industrialized countries.

This suggests that the problem of livelihood in industrialized countries is soluble. Theoretically, there is enough income for everyone to enjoy a good standard of living; there is enough work that needs to be done for everyone to have a job, while still retaining time for family and leisure, for lifelong education, and for social commitments. The Commission is convinced that correcting the maldistribution of work and income is one of the greatest social challenges facing developed countries today. This will demand major

- changes in the regulation of work;
- increases in the availability of education and training throughout life; and
- shifts in the taxation and benefits systems.

Our approach would be to slow the elimination of jobs. Firms experiencing difficulties should be encouraged to put people on shortened working hours at reduced pay across the board—instead of laying them off. Governments can endorse this by allowing workers to claim partial unemployment benefits, thus making up for some of the workers' lost earnings while reducing the cost to government of full benefits for unemployment.

The long-term unemployed deserve special priority. Governments should provide subsidies to make more attractive the hiring of those long out of work, with a scale of rising subsidy for those who have been out of work the longest. While this may not increase the total number of jobs, the measure should forestall the creation of a permanent class of excluded people.

-ⵝ-

A second strategy is to improve the match between the patterns of work that people prefer and the jobs that are available. To encourage more people to take part-time jobs, part-time workers should benefit from rights similar to those covering job security, compensation, pensions, and so on for full-time employees. In the case of payment for work done, this would be in proportion to the number of hours worked. Innovative schemes such as job-sharing may also be encouraged.

Another approach would be a compulsory, nation-wide reduction in the total of hours worked. If this reduction were not accompanied by pay-cuts, competitiveness would be lost. Many full-time workers would prefer reduced hours, even if a pay-cut were entailed. A survey made in the United States in 1991 asked people if they would like to work one day a week less, with a corresponding drop in compensation. Of those earning $30,000 or more a year, 70 per cent said they would prefer this option. For those earning $20,000 the proportion was still high, at 48 per cent.[21]

Nation-wide reduction in hours worked would partly pay for

Part-time versus Full-time Work

A survey of European countries made in 1989 found that many people were unhappy with their working hours: 21 per cent of the full-time employees consulted would have preferred part-time work, while 30 per cent of part-time workers would have opted for full-time work. Because full-time workers were more numerous in the enquiry, the results meant that for each part-time worker who wished to work full-time, there were more than three full-time workers who preferred to work part-time.

(*The OECD Jobs Study* (Part II), 1994)

itself in increased motivation and productivity. This could be done by discouraging overtime work, granting longer holidays, reorganizing the work-week into four days, or granting longer parental leave at the time of the birth of a child. All these approaches would have benefits for both *caring* and *equity*: they would increase the amount of time to be spent with family or in caring for elderly or disabled dependants.

Hours could also be reduced by introducing sabbaticals (long periods of leave awarded after a number of years worked) or time for study or training-leaves. Such methods would also help improve the individual's knowledge and skill-levels for application to his or her work. Industrialized countries today need a new kind of labour flexibility whereby the skills of workers are constantly upgraded, both on and off the job. This will mean a substantial increase in employers' training schemes and in the number of vocational courses offered by colleges and universities.

Despite dramatic gains in productivity, weekly hours of work-per-employee in industry have not diminished appreciably in recent years—as had been the case during the earlier phases of industrialization. (This phenomenon has been interpreted as one of the causes of unabating unemployment.) Innovative schemes for sharing jobs, in firms such as Volkswagenwerk, highlight the possibly beneficial effects on unemployment: reduced weekly working hours per employee left openings for the creation of additional jobs.

The Commission proposes, therefore, that the potential of work-sharing be explored and adopted by a large number of enterprises, and even governments, as a means to relieve unemployment in the North as well as in the South. The Commission believes also that the sharing of work will eventually have to be complemented by plans to provide for profit-sharing. Rising unemployment rates sometimes contrast sharply with the realization of high profits, a paradox creating intolerable tensions within the labour–capital environment.

❦

Such redistribution of jobs will be only part of a new solution, however, so there remains the challenge of creating new work. Recent years have witnessed a political 'swing' in many countries against public employment. At the same time that private firms were downsizing in order to cope with tough competition, many governments were reducing their work-forces too. Therefore many of the new jobs required will have to be established in the private sector, for example, investing in infrastructure such as transport and communications, a move that should improve the entire economy's infrastructure.

There is also a category of employment where labour-intensiveness is the essence of quality; these are the caring and cultural professions, including education, health delivery, and the arts—areas where an increasing proportion of jobs will have to be created. The Commission believes, however, that while these possibilities offer considerable scope for innovative public–private sector partnerships, many of the jobs will also need to be created in the community-partnership area.

There is evidence that there will be much scope for expansion, especially in the caring professions: health and social workers, providers of care for children, the elderly, and the handicapped. The ageing of many Western societies should create growing demand for medical and other forms of individual care. The United States Bureau of Labour Statistics judges that between 1990 and 2005 the demand for registered nurses, nurses' aides, and health aides working in the home will increase by 40 per cent.

There will also be considerable scope for the expansion of employment in education and training, indispensable for the upgrading of skills in a fast-changing world. Still another area in which jobs can be established is in care for the environment. Conserving wildlife, restoring damaged habitats, cleaning polluted sites, recycling of all kinds: these are all labour-intensive.

Based on these suggestions, the Commission supports the concept of a *transitional labour market*, as suggested in recent research by Günter Schmidt.

A market of transitional labour would have four, central dimensions.

Organizational—a combination of gainful employment and other useful social activities not hitherto valued by the 'market': training, retraining, private care for dependent persons, education of children at home, unpaid cultural and political activities.

A Transitional Labour Market

is one characterized by diversity, flexibility, and mobility. Transitional employment can have many facets, specifically the:

- transition between part-time and full-time employment, or between work and training;
- transition between unemployment and employment;
- transition between education and employment;
- transition between private domestic work and employment; and
- transition from employment to retirement.

Income—a combination of wages or salaries with transfer payments, for example, if the wages of an individual are to be reduced in the wake of shortened work periods, this would be compensated by some form of unemployment benefits, or payments for hitherto unvalued activities.

Social policy—the possibility of transitional employment that is legally regulated or negotiated amongst the various social partners or at the level of the individual enterprise, for instance, part-time work during early parenthood.

Fiscal policy—the financing of employment or other socially useful activity from funds otherwise budgeted as unemployment benefits (tapping unemployment-insurance funds in order to pay for work done in structurally important areas such as environmental protection or needed social services).[22]

The Search for Livelihoods: Migration

The search for livelihood—physical and economic security, as well as a better quality of life—is a major factor driving migration, both within countries and across national frontiers. Today there are two competing trends affecting migration: (a) the rising migration flows themselves, while (b) many economies in both the North and the South experience a lessening in the employment to be offered.

Migration may be temporary or permanent. Temporary migrations, especially common among males in Africa, can split families, leaving women overburdened with the work of farm and household. Permanent migration, whether of young people or entire families, can uproot people from their culture, leaving communities bereft of inhabitants.

The major migration in developing countries is internal, from rural areas to cities and towns. A rise in poverty, landlessness, and environmental degradation is driving 20–30 million of the world's poorest people to urban areas.[23] Between 1950 and 1990 the world's towns and cities grew more than twice as fast as rural districts. In 1950 less than one person in three lived in cities, 737 million in all. By 1995 there were some 2,584 million city-dwellers, 45 per cent of the world's total population.[24]

In many countries urban expansion has not been well distributed. In 1980, for example, 36 per cent of Africa's urban population lived in the largest city of each country, a figure up from 28 per cent in 1960.[25] The number of cities with more than a million inhabitants grew from a total of eighty-three in 1960 to 325 in 1995.[26]

Rapid urban growth affects the quality of life for all city-dwellers. Migrants to the city frequently drift into crowded squatter settlements, often without sewage, clean water, electricity, or proper streets and roads. Recent studies in ten major cities in low-income countries found that the average family has only 6.1 square metres of floor space and that 44 per cent of the families lack immediate access to drinking water.[27]

The Commission is persuaded that sustainable improvement in the quality of life of people everywhere will bring about a reduction in all types of migrational flow and its related pressures.

⤙

The Commission opines further that, unless the balance of investment in rural development changes for the better or the tensions and insecurity of life in towns begin to affect people's life choices, the future will be an urban one only. The number of cities with more than a million inhabitants each rose four times within thirty-five years, so that by 2025 the UN expects that the population of the world's towns and cities will have expanded to 5,065 millions. This is to say that at least two out of three persons everywhere will be living in an urban ambience.[28]

Urban growth presents an enormous challenge to municipal management which, in turn, must be given the means and assistance to cope with problems, sometimes of apocalyptic weight. The Commission proposes, therefore, that rural areas be provided with a fair share of governmental expenditures, in direct proportion to their populations. This would help create jobs. The provision of a sounder social infrastructure and better services would also help reduce poverty, and create more livelihoods in transport, commerce, and other sectors. Studies in Bangladesh have shown that improved infrastructure has significantly reduced poverty.[29] The promotion of new human-settlement structures and a geographic reorganization of the territory, including urban reform, furthermore, might remove excessive pressures from urban areas.

But there also exists rural-to-rural migration in developing countries, driven (again) by the search for work or land. A large part of this movement is seasonal, affecting men and women and small children usually involved in agricultural labour in multiple-cropping areas or in construction or other manual work in regions better off than their own.

This type of search, by landless peasants or those displaced by 'mega-dams', mining, or manufacturing projects (or by urban expansion) sometimes occurs in newly irrigated zones where the migrants are given first preference; or sometimes they are given land which is not so well developed, but is offered by governments in compensation for what the migrants have lost. Sometimes the displacements are towards ecologically fragile, but still available areas. In the tropics, it is sometimes the rain-forest that is the destination, whereas in Africa unrelenting hunger drives people into semi-arid pastoral districts not suitable for farming.

These massive internal flows dwarf, in fact, international migration—although these flows attract more public attention at the global level. Early in 1995 about 100 million people were thought to be living outside their countries of birth.[30] There were large migrant flows between developing countries and, during the 1980s, about 1.25 million people migrated yearly from developing to industrialized countries.[31] The proportion of *refugees* among international migrants has been growing steadily too, as a result of both proliferating conflicts within countries and the tightening of immigration rules—forcing many to choose to declare themselves refugees or political asylum-seekers.

The world had about 23 million refugees in 1994. Of these, Africa had 7.4 million, Asia 5.7 million, Europe 6 million, the former Soviet Union 2.3 million, and North America 1.3 million. Besides these refugees there are now large numbers of asylum-seekers whose applications are being processed. Total applications in Europe and North America grew at a startling rate, rising from 100,000 in 1983 to 346,000 in 1988 and 700,000 by 1991. Since then the rules have been tightened, and the flow has lessened.[32]

The pressures of migration in one or the other form seem set to increase in the foreseeable future, as the income gaps grow between rich and poor countries. Demographic trends will boost this pressure. In northern and western Europe, for example, the labour-force is expected to diminish from 114 million in 1995 to 101 million by 2025. The supply of new entrants to the European working-force will drop even faster during the same period.

By 2025 western European males aged between 20 and 24 years will number 33 per cent fewer than today. In North Africa, on the other hand, the employable population will rise from 46.4 million in 1995 to 96.4 million by 2025. It is inevitable that many of the latter group will seek their fortunes amongst their more northerly neighbours.[33]

Migrant workers pose special problems as to their status, legal protection, and rights in the countries of immigration. In recent years the migration (both legal and illegal) of women has increased, many of the migrants assuming functions in households and in other care-related settings. Some women have migrated under the guise of entertainers, this being the only legitimate way to enter some countries.

It is clear that migration, immigration, and refugees, and the relationship of these to livelihood, must receive priority attention at the international level. So the Commission calls on the United Nations, regional organizations, and informal groupings of countries (e.g.

the Group of Seven, G7) to address these issues in an effort to devise appropriate, humane, and workable solutions in this age of global-ization.

Employment in the Globalized Economy

The universalization of employment and the rapid spread of new technologies are having a significant impact on the future of work and its world-wide distribution.

Deregulation and market liberalization in Asia and Latin America have attracted massive international investment, especially in the manufacturing industries. The proportion of manufactures in developing-country exports rose from 33 per cent in 1970 to 66 per cent by 1992.[34] This expansion has raised fears that jobs are being lost, fleeing industrialized nations to go to the newly industrializing countries—mostly because of significant differentials in labour costs.

The hourly cost in 1994 of employing a production worker was $25 in Germany and $16 in the United States. But in the Republic of Korea it was $5, in Mexico $2.40, in Poland $1.40, and in China, India, and Indonesia the rate can be $0.50 or less.[35] Globalization has been a major factor, moreover, in a declining demand for unskilled and less-educated workers among the industrialized countries. Many low-skilled, labour-intensive jobs will continue to be transferred to developing countries.

Technology and globalization tend to overlap in a new trend: the shift to the South of many service jobs of the North, thanks to advances in telecommunications. While Europe and North America sleep, low-paid women in Asia key in data that are then retransmitted via satellite. The computerized booking system of British Airways is maintained by a round-the-clock team of system analysts and programmers working in India. Air France's ticketing system is handled similarly.

The Commission believes that the transfer of jobs should not occur at the cost of working conditions or safety. Some transna-tional corporations have shown that profitability and responsible employment practices go hand in hand. Other companies must adopt similar standards—possibly according to a voluntary code of conduct—that should also lessen growing pressures in the industrialized countries to raise non-tariff barriers in order to exclude goods produced under exploitative conditions. This could complement ILO conventions that suffer, in fact, from lack of enforcement.

Liberalization of world trade is bound to continue. Most estimates of the benefits of the GATT Uruguay round show, however, that the expected benefits to the industrial countries are running at two to ten times higher than those accruing to the developing nations. Africa, in the process, is a net loser.

The Commission proposes that, under the auspices of the newly created World Trade Organization, negotiations should resume without delay, with the aim of facilitating further access of products from developing countries to the markets of the industrialized ones. More of the benefits of freer global trade accumulate in favour of developing countries.

The Impact of Technical Advances and New Technologies

Most economists argue that new technologies create as many jobs as they destroy. In the past this has been a truism, but the rapid and simultaneous diffusion of computers, other information technology, and robotics represents a shift with few precedents in history. In the past job-losses in manufacturing were absorbed by growth in the service industries. But the service (or tertiary) sector is now being computerized. Indeed, it has been estimated that three-quarters of the workers in industrial countries today perform tasks that could be automated.[36]

Inevitably these trends will be at the expense of the old jobs, and it is possible that they will stimulate growth, creating new jobs in other sectors. But at the moment no one can safely predict what the overall, consolidated effect will be at national and global levels.

The knowledge revolution, in particular, should have a significant impact on the way that societies operate, companies produce, and people interact; it will lead to the emergence of new, well-paid jobs, while other employment will disappear. The pace of development in computer technology and other information fields will create a growing gap between industrialized and developing countries. The latter are being excluded from access to the new technologies pending the proper training of human resources, the creation of supporting institutions, and the provision of requisite financing. And the issues related to the access and control of the new technologies are likely to prove the source of new tensions— perhaps *the* economic and social issue of the twenty-first century.

The Commission calls on international organizations and the private economic sector to examine the implications of these trends, and to take energetic action to prevent the emergence of new cleavages between the rich and the poor of the world.

> ✒ *We have two types of educational system, one catering for the élite, the other non-existent. Our foreign-educated youth has perspectives ranging from jobs in multinationals to regional banks. Otherwise, our youth has not gone beyond primary schooling and its future depends on lack of opportunity: carpet-making from the age of 5, working as domestic help, begging. What kind of quality of life is this for a population now 45 per cent below the age of 14?*
>
> Shagufta Alizai, Pakistan
> South Asia Public Hearing

> ✒ *With 300,000 high school graduates each year, Zimbabwe is only able to create a little over 30,000 new jobs annually. What happens to the rest?*
>
> Godwin Hlatshwayo, Zimbabwe
> Southern Africa Public Hearing

> ✒ *The contradiction between high rates of education entry even into college education and the difficulties they face once they begin to look for work has led to the feminization of local and overseas migration and what we have called the deskilling of the female population—teachers working as domestics, doctors working as nurses, nurses working as orderlies, down the line.*
>
> Rina Jimenez David, Philippines
> South-East Asia Public Hearing

References

1. International Labour Organization, *World Labour Report 1994* (Geneva, 1994).
2. ILO, *Employment and Population: An Inseparable Duo* (Geneva, 1994).
3. World Bank, *World Development Report 1995* (Oxford, Oxford University Press, 1995); UN Development Programme, *Human Development Report 1992* (Oxford, Oxford University Press, 1992).
4. ILO, *Employment and Population*.
5. OECD, *The OECD Jobs Study, Evidence and Explanation* (Paris, 1994).
6. ILO, the *World Labour Reports* for the years 1993, 1994, 1995 (Geneva, 1993–5); ILO, *World Employment 1995* (Geneva, 1995).
7. ILO, *World Labour Reports* for the years 1993 and 1994 (Geneva, 1993–4); 'A Puzzling Job', *The Economist*, 18 Feb. 1995; Marcia Greenberg, *Removing the Barriers* (New York, Institute for East–West Studies, 1994).
8. World Bank, *World Development Report 1995*.
9. ILO, *World Labour Report 1994*; ILO, *World Employment 1995*.
10. Ibid.
11. World Bank, *World Development Reports* for 1992 and 1995 (Washington, 1992, 1995).
12. OECD, *OECD in Figures* (Paris, 1995).
13. OECD, *Unemployment Outlook* (Paris, 1994).
14. Zdzislawa Janowska *et al.*, *Female Unemployment in Poland* (Warsaw, Friedrich Ebert Foundation, 1992).
15. OECD, *The OECD Jobs Study*.
16. 'Shaping Structural Change—The Role of Women', report prepared by a group of high-level experts for the Secretary General of OECD (Paris, 1991).
17. ILO, *World Employment 1995*.
18. ILO, *World Labour Report 1995*.
19. Hernan de Soto, *The Other Path: The Invisible Revolution in The Third World* (New York, Harper and Row, 1989).
20. Paul Streeten, *Strategies for Human Development: Global Poverty and Unemployment* (Copenhagen, Handelshøjskolens Verlag, 1994).
21. Judith B. Schor, 'Can the North Stop Consumption Growth?', in V. Bhaskar and Andrew Glyn (eds.), *The North and the South and the Environment* (Tokyo and London, UN University and Earthscan, 1995).
22. We cite the ideas of Günter Schmidt, *Is Full Employment Still Possible? Transition Labour Markets as a New Strategy of Labour-Market Policy* (Mimeographed report, Berlin, 1995).

23. UNFPA, *The State of the World Population* (New York, 1993).
24. UN, Population Division, *World Urbanization Prospects* (New York, 1995).
25. Calculated from World Bank, *World Development Report 1990* (Washington, 1990).
26. UN, Population Division, *World Urbanization Prospects*.
27. Alan Gilbert, *Human Resources: Work, Housing and Migration* (paper prepared for the Independent Commission on Population and Quality of Life, Mimeographed, Paris, 1994).
28. See n. 26.
29. Raisuddin Ahmed and Mahabub Hossain, *Development Impact of Rural Infrastructure in Bangladesh*, IFPRI Research Report 83 (Washington, International Family Planning Research Institute, 1990).
30. Population Action International, *Global Migration: People on the Move* (Washington, 1994).
31. Peter Stalker, *The Work of Strangers: A Survey of International Labour Migration*, (Geneva, ILO, 1995).
32. UN High Commission for Refugees, *UNHCR at a Glance*, Fact Sheet 34 (Geneva, 1995).
33. UN, *World Demographic Estimates and Projections, 1950–2025* (New York, 1988).
34. World Bank, *World Development Report 1994*.
35. 'Working Man's Dread', *The Economist*, 11 Feb. 1995.
36. 'A World without Jobs?', *The Economist*, 11 Feb. 1995.

10 Towards an Alternative Educational Policy

❧ *For years, an illiterate and childless woman noticed that children in her village could not go to the nearest primary school because it is too far. Recently she came to ask for fifty school primers and a small sum of money each month. An educated relative had moved to her village and agreed to teach the children. This disadvantaged woman is more responsible than the State.*

Narayan Banerjee, India
South Asia Public Hearing

❧ *You want to be able to educate your children and bring them a life of quality. A 'quality life' means good schools with good, well-trained staff. All this is investment; all this is development.*

Marvellous Mhloyi, Zimbabwe
Southern Africa Public Hearing

❧ *The more we gravitate around sectoral issues like education, health and violence, the more we return to the problem of poverty as the fundamental point of attack . . .*

Rosiska Darcy de Oliveira, Brazil
Latin America Public Hearing

The Roles of Education and Knowledge

Education is one of the keys to social development, and to virtually every aspect of the quality of life. First and foremost, however, education is about developing intellectual curiosity and enquiry. Education improves the quality of life and empowers people to solve all kinds of social and environmental problems; it spreads values in both official and hidden curricula.

In a globalized world—where technology reigns—knowledge is a powerful factor in production, essential for nations in pursuit of economic growth and for individuals to acquire the skills they need to find employment or succeed as self-employed.

Education also equips people to participate effectively in democracy and to assert their political and legal rights. In a world confronted by many complex challenges and conflicts, education becomes more and more critical in the development of skills and attitudes in order to analyse problems and find solutions.

Education is often seen as a fixed stage in life, beginning at about age 5, continuing through primary, secondary, and possibly tertiary levels; it ends once employment begins. But if we are to reach the full potential of education in order to solve economic, social, and environmental problems, we must free ourselves of this limited view.

The full potential of education is today far from being realized in almost all countries. In developing nations the right to basic education has not been met for 1.3 billion adults and children.[1] The primary challenge for the next two decades, then, is to fulfil the right to education for all those who have not had access to it (including those who failed the first time round). Meeting the challenge will require a profound transformation of educational systems and approaches so as to adapt them to the rapidly changing needs of societies as well as to the opportunities offered by technological advances.

Today educational systems are still treading the traditional paths, often oblivious to the different circumstances applying in individual countries. Education may be the only man-made system that has remained inert, and only marginally affected by the technological and information revolutions.

The Commission is convinced that massive resort to educational technologies can help introduce a high degree of flexibility in response to societal needs. Flexible responsiveness would raise productivity, lower the cost of education, and improve the internal and external efficiencies of the schooling system.

The inertia of an educational system is usually explained by its labour-intensity. If new educational technologies are appropriately integrated, however, the role of the teacher is bound to change, meaning that teachers must be trained differently.

The gap between the requirements of real life and the insulation of an educational system diminishes its potential for educating people in terms of tomorrow's social and economic needs.

The Right to Education, a promise unfulfilled

Education is recognized as a fundamental human right in all of the three great international treaties on economic and social rights. Free, compulsory, and universal primary education for all is among the most clearly defined of these rights. (Figure 10.1 indicates the number of children not in school, 1990–2000.)

The Commission believes that education must be perceived and

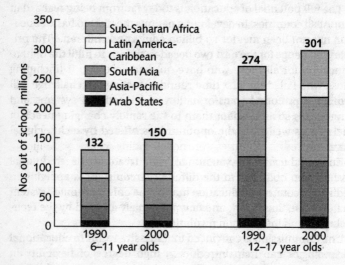

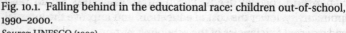

Fig. 10.1. Falling behind in the educational race: children out-of-school, 1990–2000.
Source: UNESCO (1993).

treated as a right that belongs, not to a specific age-group (confined to childhood and youth), but a lifelong right until old age, and whose realization can take many forms.

The right to education was promulgated in the International Covenant on Economic, Social and Cultural Rights (ICESCR, 1966); it was repeated in the Convention on the Rights of the Child (CRC, 1989). Both treaties provide that secondary and higher education should be made accessible to all, by the progressive introduction of free education. The ICESCR also recognizes the right of everyone who did not complete primary school to a basic 'second-chance' education.[2]

Impressive progress has been made towards realizing these rights. Adult literacy in developing countries rose from 46 per cent in 1970 to 69 per cent in 1992. Enrolment ratios at the primary level rose from an average 57.8 per cent for the group of 6–11 years in 1970 to 76.8 per cent in 1991. Secondary-school enrolment rose even more steeply, from 36 per cent in 1970 to 46.8 per cent by 1991.[3]

All the more impressive, these advances coincided with a massive growth in the school-age population. In developing countries the number of primary-school pupils rose from 310 million in 1970 to 514 million in 1992 while the number of secondary-school students climbed from 79 million to 224 million.[4]

These figures notwithstanding, the Commission is concerned that the right to education is still largely unfulfilled, the cause of educational deprivation. In 1990 more than 400 million school-age children in developing countries were not attending school: 132 million of primary-school age, 274 million of secondary-school age.[5]

Even more disconcertingly, UNESCO projected in 1993 that, in face of a growing population, the situation will not improve in the years to come. Enrolment rates for primary education in developing countries will remain stable for the next two decades. From 76.8 per cent in 1991, enrolment rates will peak at 77.7 per cent in 2000 and then diminish slowly to 76.8 per cent in 2015, then to 75.4 per cent by 2025. These figures are based on UN projections of overall population growth. Should these scenarios prove too optimistic, then enrolment ratios will drop even more.

Educational deprivation is even more widespread among adults. In the industrialized countries the adult beyond 25 years of age had ten years of schooling in 1992. In the developing world the comparable average was only 3.9 years; in thirty countries—twenty-five of them in Africa—the average was less than two years.[6] These figures virtually shout out: hundreds of millions of adults missed the chance of schooling, or else dropped out before acquiring basic literacy and numeracy.

The Commission is extremely concerned about the present state of affairs: almost 1.5 billion children and adults are either illiterates or on the way to becoming so. Surveys in developed countries suggest that 5 to 10 per cent of the population has difficulty reading or writing. This figure would be higher if one applied a more rigorous definition of illiteracy. Experts consider that a minimum of six years of primary education—as opposed to the currently used four to five years—are required to make literacy irreversible.

Dropping out before completing these five or six years of primary school means that the cost of education is almost completely wasted, for the family as well as for the nation. Applying current population dynamics, *we foresee that the situation is unlikely to change before 2025*. Unabated poverty, furthermore, will cause an even greater increase in the number of absolute illiterates and a reduced rate of children enrolling in primary education.

What is it Like to be Illiterate?

Literate people find it hard to grasp the full impact of illiteracy. In a world operating on written laws, rules, and instructions, being illiterate is a severe handicap when participating in decisions affecting life: it is tantamount to disability, affecting every aspect of living. It confines job opportunities to the most menial and low-paid tasks. It means being unable to read instructions on a packet of seed, a tin of powdered milk, or an oral contraceptive. It means being unable to read newspapers, street signs, *warning* signs. It means the inability to check legal rights, an inability to check if a title or deed is faulty. And it means being exposed to fraud and expropriation.

An important dimension of schooling is its external efficacy, by which we mean how well the educational system adapts itself to the needs of society—although we admit that society rarely articulates its requirements and expectations to the educational system with any degree of precision. Indeed, reviews of school curricula suggest a considerable discrepancy between *what is taught* and *what should be taught* in terms of evident social needs.

Recognizing the right to education is, paramountly, a matter of equity. Unfulfilled educational rights entail various consequences. They affect females more than males, rural people more than urban, the poor more than the rich, and ethnic minorities more than dominant majorities. Ensuring educational rights for all is synonymous, therefore, with ensuring equity in education. If the local school has not been completed, the rural child may continue its education only by travelling—often long distances, often in places with no public transport at all. It is clear that additional schools must be built in rural areas, relying on local materials assembled by local labour.

Targets and Timetables

Education needs a more committed approach to progressive standards, norms that are based on clear targets and timetables at national and international levels. Because the Commission is convinced that achieving primary education for all should be of top priority for all countries, it strongly endorses all proposals made in various international fora in regard to a relentless effort in the eradication of illiteracy and the promotion of literacy at primary level.

But serious slippage has occurred with respect to targets and commitments set earlier by the international community to ensure universal, primary education. According to the Second UN Development Strategy adopted in 1971, for example, universal enrolment was to be achieved by 1980. By the time of the World Conference on Education for All (in Jomtien, 1990) the deadline had been pushed to 2000—although this referred to *completion* of schooling. The World Summit for Children (1990) adopted a more formal target for universal enrolment by 2000, but reduced completion of target to 80 per cent. The International Conference on

Population and Development (1994) then rolled back the target another fifteen years (2015).[7] This confusion in targets clearly begs an authoritative reconciliation.

⤙

Projections now available, which naturally take population growth into account, forecast that the enrolment rate at primary level (which was 79.2 per cent in 1991) would slip to 77.6 per cent in 2025. The corresponding figures for Africa (49.7 per cent in 1991) will dip to 48.9 per cent in 2025—leaving, by that date, 546 million children in the age-group of 6 to 17 years out of school.

The target year for equalizing male and female enrolment in primary and secondary education is 2025. The goal is feasible, but it should be approached with urgency, and its progress rigorously monitored.

The Commission recommends that UNESCO and other qualified organizations jointly adopt, as soon as possible, an effective Strategy of Education for All by the Year 2010. The adoption of such a strategy will be conditioned, of course, by the introduction of any alternative educational policy, one complementing or supplementing the efforts of the formal educational system. Preparations should begin immediately, by naming the decade 2001–10 the Decade of Universal Basic Education.

The strategy should have two central goals. First, to provide all children, male and female, with at least six years of primary education. Secondly, to provide all adults with access—within less than one hour's travel—to a course in basic education. This would cover literacy and numeracy, together with the essentials of nutrition and health, child-rearing, environmental care, and community organization. The goal in numbers would be to achieve literacy at 80 per cent among adult men and women by 2010. There would be intermediate targets, too, to ensure that countries move steadily towards the objectives.

The Population Factor in Primary Education

Governments often find it difficult to keep the educational processes abreast (or even ahead) of fast growth of population.

Over the decade of the 1980s, sub-Saharan Africa (for instance) registered an increase in the total number of children in primary school, from 48 million to 58 million. Population growth boosted the numbers at the primary-education level even faster, in fact, so that the percentage of enrolment fell from 78 to 68 per cent.[8]

A growing number of school-age children will make the task of achieving universal primary education even more difficult. An extreme case is that of Ethiopia, where the number of pupils enrolled in primary school rose on average by 57,000 annually in the three decades beginning with 1960. Between 1990 and 2000 the number of children of primary-school age should increase by more than 1 million per year. To achieve universal enrolment, any future effort would have to be eighteen times greater than in the past.[9]

Countries with slower rates of population growth will face less-daunting tasks. India, as one illustration, increased enrolment by more than 2 million per year between 1960 and 1990. Between 1990 and 2000 India will need a growth of 1.25 million annually to make primary education universal. By contrast, Pakistan would need to raise the level of enrolment to 1.46 million (compared with an average annual increase of 170,000 between 1960 and 1990).[10]

The school-age group accounts for a high proportion of the census when compared with the working-age group (this is the 'school-dependency ratio'), the group that must pay the costs of education. This ratio will rise in Africa, while in the Arab States and South Asia the figure will fall slowly. In East Asia, Latin America, and the Caribbean—where the rates of population growth have slowed considerably—the school-dependency ratio has dropped rapidly. In East Asia, in fact, the ratio is little more than half that in Africa.[11]

High rates of population growth mean that countries would have to spend ever-higher proportions of the public budget merely to stay abreast of growing school populations—disregarding the need for more textbooks, improving the teacher–pupil ratio, or the introduction of new educational technologies.

Family size, too, influences educational achievement. Children from small families do better at school and stay there longer than those from larger families. In a major recent study of data concerning the United States, Judith Blake found that the difference between small and large families amounted to two years of extra schooling for children (after verifying factors related to parental background).[12]

Funding for Education

If we are to assure to everyone the right to basic education, we shall need increased resources. And if developing countries are to attain better educational standards, they must find ways to increase funding for basic education—essentially through budgetary reallocations. Sub-Saharan Africa spent 4.6 per cent of its GNP on education in 1991, a larger share than any other developing region except the Arab States but still less than the industrialized countries (5.5 per cent, on average). Yet Africa had only 68 per cent of its primary-age pupils and 18 per cent of secondary-age children enrolled in school.[13]

Poor countries will have difficulty achieving universal primary education (let alone the secondary level) with their own resources, and there is strong correlation between national poverty and educational levels. In 1992 there was no country with a real average income (at purchasing-power parity) below $1,900 that managed to graduate more than 80 per cent of its children from the fifth year of school.

As poverty deepens, educational advances may be lost. In Africa, troubled by debt crisis and structural adjustment despite a number of debt-reductions or cancellations decided by financing institutions or foreign countries, primary-school enrolment fell in twenty-two nations during the 1980s. Indebted countries suffered much more, of course, than the non-indebted. But at the same time 75 per cent of the non-indebted countries in Africa had primary-school enrolment ratios rising faster than in the 1970s. The figure for the severely indebted nations of Africa was only 10 per cent.

In the poorest countries and those most in debt, therefore, additional resources for education pose serious problems. For this reason, all future programmes of structural adjustment should contain provisions to ensure that spending levels for education (and health) are maintained. To accomplish this budgets may have to be reduced, while at the same time striving for greater efficiency and more flexibility and 'fluidity' of the educational systems. The reduction of public deficits simply demands doing more with less.

There is a great deal that a country can do with its own resources. At any given level of income we find great variations among countries' educational achievements. China, whose real income at purchasing-power parity was $1,910 in 1992, managed to graduate in the same year 88 per cent of its children at the end of primary fifth year. Pakistan, with an income of $2,130, managed only 37 per cent. Sri Lanka recorded 91 per cent, while Guatemala and the Dominican Republic—with incomes $500 higher—graduated only 41 per cent.[14] National income levels are more decisive for the secondary level, but there remain huge differences. India had 44 per cent of its secondary-school children in school in 1990, while Sri Lanka (with the same real income per capita) had only 19 per cent.

Increased budgets for education in many industrialized countries, on the other hand, may be an unrealistic expectation. Additional resources will need to be generated through internal reforms, reallocation, and improvements in both the internal and external efficiencies of the educative processes.

-ᴥ-

Higher education has a pivotal role of its own to play because institutions of higher learning influence the entire system and, through it (whether directly or not), all of society. The training and retraining of teachers needed for expanded educational systems, for example, takes place in tertiary institutions. The quest for national development thus necessitates a well-developed system of higher education. But many poor countries are desperately short of qualified personnel for planning, R&D, and managerial functions.

The tertiary sector, however, often swallows a disproportionate share of educational budgets; it is indeed expensive, requiring more books and equipment and enjoying low student-to-teacher ratios. In some of Asia's most successful expanding economies (Japan, the Republic of Korea, Thailand), spending per tertiary student is seldom three times more than that per primary pupil.[15] These ratios are more pronounced in many developing countries: in India, eight times higher in 1990, in Pakistan, twelve times, during the same year. In ten of the African countries, university-level education consumes more than 25 per cent of the educational budget.[16]

Imbalance of this kind is further aggravated by the high

proportion of tertiary students coming from high-income families, while a low proportion comes from the poor. When funds are short, subsidies for students enrolled in higher education should be reduced; a higher share of the costs can be raised through student loans and 'means-tested' (verified) parental contributions. And to counter brain-drain motivations, developing countries would do well to require that graduates spend a minimum number of years in their own countries after schooling in the effort to retrieve some of the cost of educating them.

Another way to make limited funds stretch further is to reduce the per-graduate costs at each educational level. Community empowerment, for example, can limit expenses if communities provide land, labour, and cash for the building and upkeep of schools.

Shortages of teachers and buildings may be mitigated by increasing class-size (but not beyond forty students), or introducing morning and afternoon shifts of classes. But the strategy should not be pushed to the point of overloading teachers. Older children and educated volunteers can be used as monitors to teach younger children, siblings still at home, and children out-of-school[17]—without diminishing the State's accountability for education.

Attaining all these targets will require expansion and redeployment. Foreign aid for education, expressed in real terms, has stagnated in recent years: lower in 1989 than in 1975, for instance. As a proportion of the ODA (Official Development Assistance) of the Organization for Economic Co-operation and Development (OECD), the level of aid fell during these years from 17.3 per cent to 10 per cent and by 1992 had reached 8.4 per cent of all bilateral aid.

The Commission holds that the international community, in its seriousness about influencing demographic growth rates, has a moral obligation (and a material self-interest) to help developing countries arrive at the goal of universal literacy and primary education. In Chapter 15 we shall discuss various schemes for the mobilization of additional funds. The Commission believes that the downward trend in the ODA figures just cited should be reversed as quickly a possible. Targeting the aid should be co-ordinated for those countries unlikely to reach their targets without external assistance.[18]

The Burden of Drop-outs and Repeaters

In 1991 forty-six countries had less than 100 per cent of their children of primary-school age enrolled; seventy countries had less than 75 per cent;[19] and in 1990, less than four out of five children in all of these countries completed five years at the primary level. To what extent is the school system, as currently conceived, succeeding in making children literate?[20] There is little doubt that completing high school is more important than merely being enrolled.

Success is measured by educational achievement, whereas *enrolment rate* is indicative of administrative reality at a given moment. The internal efficiency of the inputs and outputs of the formal educational system is, indeed, one of its worrisome features. What would happen, by way of comparison, if 50 per cent of the bridges built collapsed the day after their opening, or if more than 50 per cent of all persons admitted to hospital were to leave in coffins?

Somehow, when education is at stake—and more specifically primary education, with its dismal record of repeaters and drop-outs—society accepts slippage and failure. The latest data show that 50 per cent of the children who enter the first year of school in Latin America complete the primary level. This compares with 51 per cent in South Asia, 67 per cent in sub-Saharan Africa, 69 per cent in the Arab States and North America, and 85 per cent in East Asia. If data concerning repeaters are added, the picture is even grimmer: in French-speaking Africa 26 per cent of the children repeated each year, while English-speaking Africa registered 15 per cent.

The Commission believes that educational waste in the form of drop-outs and repeaters calls for action because, taken together, students not learning raise the cost of education. In 1990 twenty-five sub-Saharan countries out of thirty-nine invested at least 50 per cent more on each primary-school 'graduate' than would have been necessary were there no repeaters or drop-outs.[21]

❧

Reducing drop-out rates demands careful study of the reasons therefor—perhaps the same reasons why children are not enrolled in the first place. In developing countries students leave school prematurely to earn wages or work in the family's fields, yet in all of Asia more than 80 per cent of children complete primary school. In Africa the drop-out rates are high: in 1994 only 67 per cent of the children enrolled in primary education managed to finish a four-year cycle.

Repetition as a form of waste was represented in 1994 by 24 million children world-wide, or 9 per cent of total enrolment, in the primary years of school. Here again Africa had the highest rate of repetition, with more than 25 per cent repeating. Repetition is admittedly one way to ensure that a student can take his or her place in secondary school, but the process easily adds one or more years of 'cost of education' to both family and national budgets and occupies classroom space that could otherwise be allotted to out-of-school children.[22]

The key to reducing repetition is the adoption of early remediation: strategies to monitor performance regularly, targeting additional help for children falling behind. Reforms of longer term are also needed, such as curricular reform and better training and upgrading of teachers.

Reducing drop-outs, increasing enrolment: while these have socio-economic implications, they have much to do with the need to make schooling more and more relevant and challenging to students. Besides changes in curricula and teaching methods, corrective measures should include eventual abolition of fees at primary-school level, and compensating for losses through higher fees charged at the tertiary level.

School hours and length of terms in rural areas should be altered to fit closely the rhythm of family needs for youthful labour at home and in the fields. And where malnutrition is high, schools should be in a position to (a) offer nutritious meals and thus lower familial food costs, and thereby (b) improve students' learning performance.

Providing a Second Chance

The billion illiterates in developing countries, the rising number of adults marking time as illiterates in both industrialized and developing countries, the 400 million children not attending school—all these should not be abandoned to stigma and disadvantage, handicaps likely to be passed to their children. All these human beings have the right to a second chance.

Even in countries with fairly well-developed educational systems there are always citizens who have failed in school, or *whom the schools failed*. In the new, globalized, high-technology economy it is precisely such people who are excluded from work and often from society.

Some teaching programmes are especially geared to giving a second chance to children aged between 9 and 15 who are too old to begin primary school. Typical are the Djamaa centres in Conakry (Guinea), where unemployed secondary-school graduates are recruited to serve as instructors. In Bangladesh, non-formal primary schools provide two to three hours of schooling daily for those who have missed or dropped out from primary education.

Older people who are illiterate, or missed school altogether, need attention too. Adult-literacy and adult-education programmes have been notably useful in countries where they are part of a broad-based movement of national uplift or even revolution. Elsewhere, their results are frankly disappointing. A nation's further-education scheme needs substantial personnel and equipment, and thus funding, and it will succeed only when there is political commitment at the highest level—not to speak of students' commitment, since adults and working children have other demands on their time. They need strong motivation to attend classes and to retain what they are taught. Hence, basic educational programmes for adults must be closely geared to the community's real needs.

Literacy courses, for example, will be much better attended and far more useful if they combine literacy with other essential knowledge and skills, as we have already pointed out. Students should also be induced to stimulate other children (including their own) to want to learn: for example, how to make labour-saving devices (such as fuel-efficient stoves); in rural areas, basic agroforestry; and everywhere, environmental conservation.

Out-of-school education will help citizens learn, besides their rights, how to form community organizations. The Tostan project in Senegal has done this admirably well.[23] Depending on the setting, such instruction may also include improved agricultural and craft methods, simple bookkeeping, setting up a small enterprise, and the like.

Gender Inequality

The most pervasive inequality in education is that between men and women. At the world level in 1990 enrolment ratios in primary school of children aged 6 to 11 were 74.6 for girls against 88.3 for boys. These ratios in developed countries were, respectively, 91.8 and 92.2, in developing countries 71.3 and 81.5. In Africa the percentages were 52.4 and 61.5. The imbalance was worse at secondary level, where the totals were 48.3 per cent girls, 57.3 per cent boys.[24]

The legacy of discrimination has left a heavy burden on adult women. In 1992 there were forty-seven countries whose women of 25 years or older had less than an average of two years of schooling, while the men of twenty-one countries had as little instruction. In forty-two countries the women had less than half the schooling received by men. All these countries were in Africa, or South-Western or South Asia.[25] Women made up more than 60 per cent of the world's billion illiterates in 1990, and 44 per cent of the adult females in developing countries could not read—almost twice the figure for males.[26]

Why are there fewer girls than boys in school? First, because girls traditionally share with their mothers much of the responsibility of family maintenance. Among the world's poor families, women must also engage in earning activities besides doing housework. When this induces mothers to work outside the home, teenage or younger daughters often become 'little mothers' in their place. Apart from the care they provide for siblings, girls do far more work in the family than boys. In Burkina Faso, for instance, most girls do household chores by the age of 7, whereas boys seldom begin before 11 years. These responsibilities mean that girls tend to be kept away from classes. Advocates of women's education familiar with grass-root realities persistently demand child-care services in order to support the sustained enrolment of girls in school—in addition to reducing the time of females spent in fetching water, food, fuel, and fodder.

A second reason is cost. Even where education is nominally free, parents usually expect to pay for school-books, stationery, and (often) uniforms. In Kenya these costs can amount to 2,000 Kenyan shillings/year: US$70, almost a quarter of the average income per person.[27] Poor parents must then choose which children 'to invest in', and it is inevitably the girls who are excluded. Boys are more likely than their sisters to find paid jobs after their schooling, and more likely to leave the family domicile.

Other reasons include distance from school, lack of transport, fear of insecurity—all obstacles to learning by girls of the secondary-school category. These factors have grown in importance in urban areas, where there has been a rise in sexual violence against girls. In agriculture, a high demand for female labour in Asia and Africa is the reason why girls must learn manual skills early, when their hands and bodies are still flexible. Possession of these skills is considered important for marriage into families engaged in rural-agricultural occupations.

Cultural sensitivity, too, keeps girls away from school. In strict Muslim societies it is unacceptable for girls to be taught by male teachers, and these are the societies with the fewest women teachers. Women in Yemen constitute only one-tenth of the teaching staff in primary schools. The continuation of child marriage in South Asian communities, of various religions, is another barrier to female education. School-age pregnancy in Africa and Latin America is a major reason why girls are likely to leave secondary school. The daughters of teenage mothers insufficiently educated often become, in their turn, teenage mothers.[28]

Besides the *quantity* of exposure to education, the content of schooling also prevents girls from getting ahead in the world. Growing girls are urged to study subjects that educational planners believe lie within woman's traditional domain. Yet the generations-old lore of animal husbandry, agriculture, and forestry have become increasingly male preserves in education—despite the fact that boys and young men lack the experience of peasant women.

The use of herbs and the regulation of diet, critical in primary health care, have been for centuries the realm of the woman. But they are now supplanted by formal education, systematically and contemptuously destroying the ancient knowledge passed on by women—without even testing the validity of the new. This results in removing the inherited cultural base for primary health care.

A consequence of such policy is the reintroduction by the International Development Research Centre, UNICEF, WHO, and the Population Council (at substantial cost) of remedies such as rice gruel to combat diarrhoea in rural Bangladesh and India. Knowledge of old remedies had been passed down, through generations of mothers inhabiting the eastern part of the subcontinent and the coastal areas of the Bay of Bengal, until its rejection by educated members of their families.

Deprived of their traditional area of expertise, girls are also denied entry to modern sectors of knowledge to which they are entitled by non-discrimination policies. India adopted this policy at the time of independence in 1947, and the country now has a record performance of girls in mathematics and general science at the tertiary level. Yet the same country has failed, unfortunately, to provide opportunities in science education in girls' schools. Women gained admittance to agricultural and veterinary sciences and technological institutions only in the 1980s, mainly through feminist movements. At the same period, in countries as different as Ghana and Denmark, the vast majority of girls entering technical colleges continue to enrol in three 'pink collar' specialities: textile design, the clothing trade, and catering.[29]

Such disadvantages to the female come with a heavy cost, and not only to the women involved. There is, first, loss of income to their families and to the nation. Literate, numerate women are more likely to adopt improved farming methods,[30] and educated women are more productive than those not so favoured. In Morocco each additional year of a girl's education corresponds to a rise of 15.8 per cent in her earnings when she leaves school. In Thailand this increase is of 26 per cent.[31]

In second place comes a powerful effect on fertility: educating women is one of the best ways to slow population growth. Educated females are more likely than others to use family planning and are less inclined to have large families. It is estimated that between 40 and 60 per cent of the decline of fertility in four Latin American countries is attributable to higher levels of education for girls.[32]

Only secondary education, it was once believed, could reduce fertility. Recent surveys have shown that even five or six years of formal education has a strong effect, reducing fertility in some cases by as much as 3.7 children. Even uncompleted secondary education has reduced fertility in most cases, although there were five countries where this was accompanied by a slight increase.[33]

The Commission is persuaded that women's education has a *very strong effect* on the health and education of their children, who are healthier and more likely to be educated in their turn. Data from thirty-three developing countries suggest that each extra year of a mother's schooling is related to a drop in infant mortality of 7–9 per cent.[34] A study of four Latin American countries showed that educated women were more likely than others to attend pre-natal clinics, have their births supervised by trained persons, and have their babies immunized.[35]

The Commission believes that women's education may also be the most effective way to empower women, boosting their confidence so that they can demand better treatment from their husbands and society—all of which may, in itself, constitute a human right. Research in Bangladesh, Mexico, and Nigeria has found that educated women communicate more with their husbands and play a greater role in family decisions.[36] In Nigeria, Nepal, and India literate women were discovered to expect—and receive—better treatment in clinics and hospitals.[37]

Taking into account all the benefits accruable to women, children, and the societies they live in, the Commission suggests that women's education is probably the most important measure existing to improve the quality of life for the women and children of future generations.

The World Conference on Education for All (Jomtien) recommended a 'significant reduction' in the literacy gap between adult men and women by the year 2000. Closing the gap completely, therefore, should be a priority. Adult-education classes for women should be provided in literacy and numeracy, as well the knowledge and skills that will help females in their family and working lives.

Reducing wastage and increasing enrolment will, as indicated earlier, benefit girls and women as well as males. Even more specific measures may be needed, especially in secondary and tertiary education—although it is to be borne in mind that, in some societies, excessive feminization of teaching may have the disadvantage of devaluing the importance of education. Useful steps might include affirmative action in recruitment of new staff and enrolment for teaching training, combined with in-service retraining.

Child-care centres may enable parent-girls to stay in school longer and provide their own (limited) pre-school education to reduce the handicap suffered by children of non-literate backgrounds. This should also improve the later performance in class of these youngsters, and reduce drop-out rates.

A concerted effort is required to encourage girls, once in school, to study technical and scientific subjects normally considered studies for boys—because many of the best jobs in the future will require such qualifications. The subjects that boys study, too, will have to evolve to include knowledge and skills equipping them for a wider range of employment, including the 'pink-collar' occupations, and a more useful and involved family life. Revised teacher-training curricula should ensure guidance to reduce sexual stereotyping in school.

Harsh corporal punishment ought to be banned; it is not helpful to the pupil, and particularly humiliating and distressing for girls. In settings where girls are traditionally segregated, single-sex toilets, classrooms, and even separate buildings may be needed.

Efforts should be made to educate boys and girls in responsible sex in order to avoid teenage pregnancies, teaching complemented by responsible-sex programmes that are in harmony with the continuous schooling of girls. The practice of expelling pregnant schoolgirls should be halted and replaced by resorting to enabling facilities: special evening classes, making available crèche facilities at establishments of further education, and the like.

The Promise and Potential of New Technologies

The new technologies' time has come. A central aim is to educate illiterates and children beyond the reach of traditional educational systems. Nation-wide education demands effective machinery of dissemination, all that is offered by the modern technologies of radio, television, video-recorder, telephone, computer, cinema, satellite, and by global networking. As the information technologies become cheaper, they grow more versatile and durable. Electrification is no longer a requirement, the renewable energies being put to work—more and more—to replace current supplied by the national power grid. Interactive technologies, furthermore, have much potential for empowering people at any level of society through the use of such facilities.

Broadcasting media today reach farmers and nomads scattered through rain-forests and deserts. The standardized products of radio and TV place poor, remote villages on an equal footing with city or suburb. These media are used to train teachers and facilitators as well as students, and they can be combined with person-to-person contact to synergize their effect.

The *Télé pour tous* (TV for All) programme in Côte d'Ivoire, for example, has used battery-powered TV sets for broadcasting evening programmes about practical subjects ranging from building hygienic latrines or laying cement floors to obtaining governmental loans or organizing co-ops. During the daytime the same sets are used to televise school lessons.[38] A study by the Inter-American Development Bank showed that, in Haiti, TV education could be offered to all adults and children at a cost of only US$2 per person per year.

The knowledge revolution implies that a substantial portion of the work-force will be telecommuting, in one form or other, within a few years. It will thus be indispensable that the educational system prepare its students through both curriculum content and expanded use of the new media in the classroom.

Another objective in using the new technologies is increasingly evident as economies evolve: permeation of life's periods of work and retirement. If education is indeed a lifelong right, and as people change jobs and require retraining more frequently than in the past, periods of employment will be sandwiched with sequences of further education and training. Telecommuting will have an even more dramatic effect on these interspersed periods— all the more reason to change the curricula until now imposed 'from above' by administrators and teachers.

~~

Two other factors argue in favour of introducing new technologies to education. There is, first, the accelerated speed of the explosion of knowledge; this places growing pressure on learning capacities. Secondly, the spread of multicultural societies causes different sub- cultures to place conflicting demands on the educational system.

Educational systems need more flexibility, allowing certain benefits to unemployed persons taking courses, a flexibility offered by the new information technologies. The techniques used should include feedback processes for permanent adaptation of course content and be adaptable to mass use. All this allows people of any age (even without qualifications) to select from wide ranges of short modular courses.

In the use of the new technologies (television especially), care must be taken not to succumb to their drawbacks. Cinema and tele- vision films often contribute to the weakening of social values: pur- suing novelty and sensation, emphasizing conflict and violence, presenting sexuality without responsibility, showing rampant con- sumerism. Watching television often takes up as many waking hours as school, outweighing school many times over because of the diversity of vivid images presented—especially where schools themselves are not yet using TV or multimedia. Television can be, to be sure, the best or the worst of the media easily available.

But the world's poorest nations are not yet sharing in the telecommunications revolution; instead, the technology gap between poor and rich countries is widening. Most of the world has no experience in what readily accessible communications else- where could do for their society and economy. New funds will be required to help the poor nations build *effective* telephone net- works, and perhaps public–private partnerships will be the best way to generate the required investment in such opportunities.

The Commission is convinced that, given the decisive role of education in matters of population and quality of life, political will must be rallied to devise alternative educational approaches. New policies, funded globally and implemented nationally, will be especially concerned about making novel means accessible to the poor. Governments, pertinent intergovernmental organizations and NGOs, media and research institutions should urgently undertake studies as to how the immense potential of the new media can be best used for education, lifelong training, and social integration. The analyses will have to indicate the requirements to be met in terms of communication infrastructure for large-scale application.

The Commission considers it desirable also to undertake systematic study on issues in the media related to violence, sexuality, and consumerism.

Teaching Values, Teaching Care

As potentially the most powerful process in the socialization of the young, education traditionally has been acknowledged as a generator of values. The globalization of knowledge systems, the explosion of knowledge, and the increasing and often contradictory demands made by the processes of economic, political, and cultural change have affected this role of value-generator in education the most. In the world after the Second World War it became fashionable to talk about the value-free character of academic institutions. The wheel has since come full circle, as demand rises for the teaching of values as part of the educational method.

The Commission emphasizes the critical role of educational systems in promoting universal values essential to sustainable improvement in the quality of life.

The International Covenant on Economic, Social and Cultural Rights mentions a number of these values. Education should inculcate respect for human rights, for peace and tolerance between nations and ethnic or religious groups, and should prepare people to participate effectively in a society that begins with an awareness of rights and responsibilities and a more active view of participation through the ethic of care for humanity and Nature.

If education should promote the development of a caring society, then we have to stop thinking of it as a commodity only for self-advancement in life and only in economic terms. We need to concentrate on its unquestioned potential to teach everyone how to teach themselves, besides teaching the values of peace, tolerance, and justice. We believe that the specific values embodying an ethic of care must be taught at every stage of the educational system, from the earliest grades through secondary school to adult education. The notions of equality and equity, of rights and responsibilities, of protection of the vulnerable, of human dignity as well as the sense and importance of *interconnectedness between individuals*: these are some of the key components of the ethic of care.

Spreading awareness of such issues is increasingly seen as the responsibility of governments and NGOs. But universities and other centres of learning should not be exempt from this responsibility—for schoolteachers, adult educators, policy-makers, managers, media personnel, scientists, authors, artists, and bureaucrats (as well as initiators of NGOs) are most often products of higher education. The Commission has discovered many innovative and constructive examples of caring, of participatory activities by partnerships of university staff and peoples' organizations at the grass roots.

The Commission urges the community of educators, students, and scholars at all levels to extend their concerns beyond the classroom, using their institutional as well as human resources to promote sustainable improvement of everyone's quality of life.

> ✎ *Parents are more and more confronted with the necessity to pay for education as market relations penetrate the sphere of teaching. Often children have to give up classes because of poverty and social differentiation.*
>
> Natalia Rimachevskaya, Russia
> Eastern Europe Public Hearing

> ✎ *Today anything can be sold by using marketing techniques. What has to be sold are different ways of living and acting.*
>
> David Tejada, Peru
> Latin America Public Hearing

> ✎ *The children of the poor, the vast majority of the population, will remain poor because their parents are poor,*

*the State is poor, and the teachers too. Leaders think
education is the responsibility of welfare, but without
funds there is no welfare.*

N'golo Coulibaly, Mali
West Africa Public Hearing

❧ *For us young people the source of quality of life is education and our government needs to provide this education, because most of us cannot afford to pay school
fees. I think that the government should lower the
school fees. For a person to do anything, that person
must be educated.*

André Tioro, Mali
West Africa Public Hearing

❧ *The value of education today is the value of production,
because the scientific and technological revolution is
permanent. Training is no longer for specific knowledge.
A man is trained not for a specific job, but so as to have
a grounding which will enable him to adapt perman-
ently to a certain central body of know-how—language
as a first code, mathematics as a second major code; to
know how to situate himself in the world he lives in, so
as to understand social changes; sciences and foreign
languages, because in a globalized economy, multilin-
gual countries come to be schools for everyone.*

German Rama, Uruguay
Latin America Public Hearing

References

1. UNESCO, *World Education Report 1993* (Paris, 1993).
2. UCESCR, 13; CRC, 28.
3. 'Trends and Projections of Enrolment at Level of Education by Age and Sex (as assessed in 1993)', *Current Surveys and Research in Statistics* (doc. CBPF-94/WS.1-1994) (Paris, UNESCO, 1994).
4. UNESCO, *Statistical Yearbook 1994* (Paris, 1995).
5. UNESCO, *World Education Report 1993* (Paris, 1993).
6. UN Development Programme, *Human Development Report 1994* (Oxford, Oxford University Press, 1994).

7. *Second UN Strategy for Development*, 1970; International Conference on Population and Development, 1994.

8. When UNESCO adopted, in 1989, its *Plan of Action to Eradicate Illiteracy by the Year 2000*, its staff made it clear from the start that there was no possibility of *eradication*; the aim was rather 'encouraging, nurturing and instilling' the importance of literacy; UNESCO/ International Literacy Year, *Adult Education Information Notes No. 4*, 1989.

9. UNESCO, *Statistical Yearbook 1994*.

10. UNESCO, *Demographic Pressure on Primary Education (1993 Update)* (Paris, 1993).

11. UNESCO, *Education for All: Status and Trends 1994* (Paris, 1994).

12. UNESCO, *World Education Report 1993*.

13. UNICEF, *Progress of Nations 1995* (New York, 1995).

14. World Bank, *Social Indicators of Development 1994* (data diskettes) (Washington, 1994); D. Woodward, *Debt Adjustment and Poverty in Developing Countries*, Vol. II (London, Save the Children Fund, 1992).

15. World Bank, *World Development Report 1994* (Oxford, Oxford University Press, 1994); UNICEF, *Progress of Nations 1995*.

16. UNESCO, *World Education Report 1993*.

17. World Bank, *Priorities and Strategies for Education* (Washington, 1995).

18. Paul Harrison, *The Third Revolution* (London and New York, Penguin Books, 1993).

19. C. Colclough and W. Lewin, *Educating All the Children* (Oxford, Clarendon Press, 1993).

20. World Bank, *Social Indicators of Development 1994*.

21. Ibid., comprising countries with a coefficient of efficiency of 0.66 or less.

22. UNESCO, *World Education Report 1993*.

23. K. Fatema, *The BRAC Non-formal Primary Education Programme in Bangladesh* (New York, UNICEF, 1989).

24. D. Jacobs, *UNICEF Education Report of Activities* (New York, UNICEF, 1989).

25. UNESCO, *World Education Report 1993*.

26. UN Development Programme, *Human Development Report 1994*.

27. UNESCO, *World Education Report 1993*.

28. United Nations, *World Survey: Women in Agriculture*, paper presented at World Conference of the UN Decade for Women (Nairobi, July 1985).

29. UNICEF, *The Girl Child: An Investment in the Future* (New York, 1991).

30. UNICEF, *Strategies to Promote Girls' Education* (New York, 1990).

31. Nafis Sadik, *Investing in Women: Priority for the 1990s* (New York, UN Fund for Population Activities, 1990).

32. UN, *World Survey: Women in Industrial Development* (Nairobi, July 1985).

33. Ibid.

34. Debbie Taylor, 'Meeting the Need', *People and the Planet*, 2: 1 (1993).

35. M. B. Weinberger, C. Lloyd, and A. K. Blanc, *Women's Status and Fertility: A Decade of Change in Four Latin American Countries*, Oslo, Conference on Women's Position and Demographic Change in the Course of Development (1988).

36. J. G. Cleland and J. K. van Ginneken, *Maternal Education and Child Survival in Developing Countries* (Netherlands Institute of Preventive Health Care, 1989).

37. Weinberger *et al.*, *Women's Status and Fertility*.

38. A. K. Omideyi, 'Women's Position, Conjugal Relationships and Fertility Behaviour among the Yoruba'; K. O. Mason, 'The Impact of Women's Position on Demographic Change during the Course of Development'; S. Adnan, 'Birds in a Cage: Institutional Change and Women's Position in Bangladesh': papers presented at the Conference on Women's Position and Demographic Change in the Course of Development (Oslo, 1988).

11 From Medical to Health Care

> *In 1989 US$36 per inhabitant was applied to the health sector. In 1993, this figure had dropped to US$16 per inhabitant. More than 4,000 health-sector employees were dismissed. The number of medical consultations has plummeted, especially in reproductive health programmes.*
>
> Ana Maria Pizarro, Nicaragua
> Latin America Public Hearing

> *Our assessment of the elderly population as the main problem in health care [has changed] because today as many as 50 per cent of the newborn have some abnormalities—and the voice of children is not heard so much.*
>
> Marja Lauristin, Estonia
> Eastern Europe Public Hearing

> *Getting prevention on the [health] agenda will be done through more public participation.*
>
> Nancy Hall, Canada
> North America Public Hearing

Success Stories in the Health Sphere

For most people physical and mental health are the very core of what is meant by quality of life. When surveys ask people about the factors they rate highest for happiness, health usually comes at the top of the list, together with a happy family life. Health is the precondition of survival and enjoyment of life, and of full participation in economic and social life. Healthy mental and physical development affects attendance and success at school.

The achievements of the last three decades have been astonishing. Health has improved dramatically, and continues to do so in most countries. Between 1960 and 1992 average life-expectancy in developing countries rose from forty-six to sixty-three years. This extraordinary figure means that, during every calendar year, there was an increase of six months in life-expectancy. In the same period in these countries the proportion of children dying under the age of 5 fell by more than half: from 216 to 104 per 1,000 live births.[1]

Provision of the basic conditions necessary to health also improved, and the speed of this improvement increased markedly after 1975. The share of people with access to safe drinking-water in developing countries rose from 36 per cent in 1975–80 to 70 per cent in 1988–91. The number of people attended by a single physician fell from 7,600 in 1970 to 4,800 in 1991 (although there remain major problems in the distribution of doctors). Immunization coverage for the child-killing diseases rose from around 10 per cent late in the 1970s to 80 per cent by the early 1990s.[2]

Most of this success depended on a set of strategies that every other sector of human development can learn from:

- the primary health-care model, based on extending basic services and prevention to all (equity);
- community-level mobilization of local human resources;
- relying on a few high-impact, but low-cost, interventions; and
- international targeting and co-ordination.

Inspired by China's 'barefoot doctor' system, the primary health-care model (adopted under the motto 'Health for All' at a WHO-sponsored conference in Alma Ata in 1978) has come to serve as the corner-stone of all public policy. Unlike many models to be found in the field of development, Health for All has not lost its relevance.[3] Still, the question arises: Why, twenty years after its adoption, have not the main tenets of this policy been implemented in most world regions?

The premiss of primary health care is that everyone has the right to all basic preventive and curative services, financially accessible, and within easy reach of home. In this model, district and central

The Real Potential of Primary Health Care

In rural areas we train women without formal schooling for six months to a year. They become competent in care and prevention; they learn family planning, minor surgery, and how to handle a microscope. These workers have lowered our area's infant mortality rate to about 60 per 1,000 live births (compared with 106 for the country as a whole). While the national average of maternal mortality is 5 per 1,000 live births—and UN organizations speak of reducing it to 3 per 1,000—our ordinary village women have cut the rate to 2 per 1,000.

(Zaffrullah Choudhury, Bangladesh)

Western medicine has made illness a major industry, and most of the 6 per cent of GDP that India spends on health care goes for medicine to cure the 'diseases of the West' affecting our rich population. We have learnt from China that 'barefoot doctors' do not mean third-class care for third-class people. India would need about 2 million health-workers in this category—meaning 2 million jobs. The pre-condition is shifting power so that through the *panchayat* [local authority] the community's people will have control over the financial, administrative, and technical specialists involved.

(N. H. Antia, India)

hospitals are no longer the first and main providers; they are, instead, specialists backing up the primary level. Hospitals then have the role of training health-workers, ensuring reliable pharmaceutical and other medical supplies, and handling referrals of complicated, specialized cases. A few governments, together with many non-governmental organizations, have shown that such basic services can be brought to rural populations at low cost.

◆

Using the conventional approach, the high cost of medical training and technology was taken for granted; it dictated the pace at which services were offered. In the primary health-care models the right of everyone to health, on the other hand, is its driving-force. The levels of technology and expertise are chosen to ensure that, whatever the budgetary constraints, everyone has minimal service appropriate to the epidemiological realities of the area. This may mean the use of a limited list of inexpensive but essential drugs, or reliance on training courses for paramedics counted in weeks instead of years. Community-level care is dispensed by workers within the community. In the ideal model, one worker provides first-aid and essential drugs for the most common ailments, while another trained birth attendant provides family-planning services and both pre- and post-natal care (including safe delivery).

A second strategy underlying the success stories is that of the mobilization of the community. The community decides the priorities, selects health-workers, and monitors the quality of service— often supporting this service with contributions of land, labour, or cash. The approach works particularly well because such primary care is prevention-oriented, whether at the individual or family level, and at the community level as well. Health-workers are meant also to be monitors and enablers—helping the community obtain clean water, dig latrines, and improve hygiene and diet.

Community participation does not, however, develop automatically. As in the developed countries, there is serious opposition from the medical 'establishment' to any expansion of the outreach of health care services through people with fewer qualifications than this establishment has.

The various alternative models to established health delivery have put the emphasis on participation, development of local leaders, and instinctive dependence on women. The successful sustainability of those working in the alternative approaches has resulted from the decentralization of services to bring them under the control of local self-government. This has been found to make optimal use of available manpower and material resources.[4]

The situation in some Indian states (Kerala, Maharashtra, Karnataka) and in Bangladesh (Savar) has often been used as an exemplary illustration of what local participation can achieve in primary health care. And the case of Cuba underlines what political will can do to achieve a revolution in both rural and urban health:

Using Television to Improve Public Safety

We work with social communicators [including] authors of soap operas. Brazilian soap operas are enormously successful on television, even in Portugal. So we do 'health merchandising', using opportunities to introduce into the programme's theme subjects that are educational messages in health. We have an enormous number of traffic deaths, for example, so the simple use of a seat belt by a soap opera's hero means that an important image will be retained by people who are watching. If we do not use means outside those of the health services, we are not going to have results.

(Paolo Buss, Brazil)

free medical services, integrating public health and primary care, creating poly-clinics to deliver services, emphasizing sanitation, campaigning for public health, and reforming medical education. With leadership from the top and participation at the grass roots, Cuba has reached a remarkable level of health—where the gain in life-expectancy is still ahead of that in most developing countries.[5]

A third element in the strategy for achieving Health for All has been to rely on a limited number of selected interventions capable of producing high impact at low cost. UNICEF's slogan, GOBI-FF, has included such interventions by monitoring:

Growth of children to identify the malnourished, then focus help on those most in need;

Oral rehydration therapy, using a solution of salt and sugar to prevent dehydration caused by diarrhoea;

Breastfeeding;

Immunization against the major 'killer' diseases;

Family planning; and

Feeding supplements such as vitamin A or iodizing salt to prevent goitre.

The final element in this four-part strategy has been a sense of purpose and precision combined with public-health targeting in campaigns promoted or supported by international organizations, often under the leadership of WHO or UNICEF. Massive drives, such as the International Drinking Water Supply and Sanitation Decade (1981–90) and the Expanded Programme on Immunization have extended coverage dramatically (even if they did not always reach their ambitious targets). The health sector has also pioneered the use of indicators, targets, and timetables in order to reach clear and feasible objectives within a specified time.

Health Rights Unmet

Despite successes of these kinds, in the last decade of the twentieth century between 1 and 2 billion people are still denied *minimum rights* to health services. Most health problems do not require expensive, sophisticated equipment. Many illnesses are avoidable if there are available immunization and basic maternal care, and good preventive health around the home: breast-feeding,[6] clean water, hygiene and sanitation, and sound nutrition.

In the 1990s an estimated 1 to 2 billion people have no access to local health services or basic medication within a reasonable distance of home. Some 1.3 billion have no access to clean water, while 1.9 billion have no disposal facilities for human excreta.[7] The results of this denial are tragic: in 1990 almost 13 million children less than 5 years of age died. As many as half a million mothers died from the complications of childbirth, leaving orphans who had a greatly increased risk of early death, too.[8]

Denial of health rights has a much wider and lasting impact on nine of every ten children in developing countries who survive their fifth year. A combination of malnutrition, lack of maternal-care services, and exposure to disease means that the young may fail to reach their full physical and mental potential. They may frequently be left with mild or serious handicaps that blight the rest of their lives, reducing their chances in education and employment.

Nutrition, obviously, is an important ingredient of both health and education. Just as nutrition is one of the soundest foundations of lifelong health, so inadequate or unbalanced nutrition is a major cause of poor health and premature death. Malnutrition weakens resistance to disease, of course; conversely, many diseases reduce one's ability to take in and absorb food. Although energy intake in

> ## Measuring Progress by Height
>
> The height of children and adults is a good indicator of social progress. When society progresses normally—when food, nutritional level and overall health are adequate, each generation is taller than the preceding one. Among people who are economically well off, there is an increase of 4–5 cm in height in two generations. If mothers among the poor are 150 cm in height, the daughters will average 150 cm. This results not only from inadequate diet but also from the excessive expenditure of energy.
>
> (Veena Shatrughna, India)

developing countries has risen from only 1,940 calories/day in 1960 to almost 2,500 in 1988–90,[9] there are still some 55 per cent of children's deaths in developing countries linked to malnutrition.

Health problems are not confined to the developing nations. Recent studies in developed countries on the determinants of health show that there are strong links between socio-economic status and better health. Good housing, a safe environment, solid education, and secure employment are all elements of improved health. Adverse health is equally linked to unwise life-styles, at both individual and social levels.

The Determinants of Health

So the biological endowment of individuals and of populations, their physical environment, and their socio-economic milieu all shape individual responses to illness through complex interrelationships. They also point to the large differences in health status not only among individuals but among groups within a given society, not to speak of differences among countries. If work-surroundings and the broader physical environment have significant impact on health, so have education, income, social support, and one's place in the social fabric. Each of these factors affect both illness and the responses to disease.[10]

If most determinants of health are outside the reach of formal, national health-care systems, they are not beyond the reach of public policy. Although research has not fully mapped out the exact dynamics of this interplay, we know what integrated action can be—and ought to be—taken on several fronts. To that end, the Commission advocates the adoption of the primary health-care model, including the best of the traditional and alternative therapies, and developing in a balanced way medical and hospital care at the same time, accessible to all in both physical and financial terms. The Commission calls, further, for a concerted redistribution of public expenditures towards and within the larger social sector of education, housing, employment, and environmental policies.

For most developed countries the Commission proposes a shift of financial resources from the overdeveloped, curative, hospital-based model to primary-care community clinics, home-care programmes, and preventive initiatives. This will imply a new division of labour between health-care professionals, especially in regard to responsibilities and tasks assumed by physicians that could devolve to nurses, midwives, and community-health-workers. This means, briefly, the relative de-medicalization of life and de-institutionalization of care through the creation of innovative and less-expensive approaches to keeping populations healthy.

The gearing of international assistance in health delivery needs also to be oriented to basic, preventive health, especially since it influences health policy at the national level. In 1990 overall development assistance made up 2.8 per cent of the developing countries' total expenditures on health. The share was much higher in the poor countries where health rights are respected: in sub-Saharan Africa this share averaged 10.4 per cent, and in twelve countries it was 40 per cent or more.[11] Health budgets are distorted when international funds pay for the creation of hospitals or other medical institutions, required governments to find funds for daily operations and maintenance—again draining resources from preventive and primary care.

❧

One critical determinant of health is education, especially female education. Indeed, in poor countries female education is probably *the most effective health measure* known. Educated women may be less bound by certain harmful traditional ideas about health and the feeding of small children. They understand hygiene and first aid and are more likely to make use of modern health facilities. They have fewer, more widely spaced births, whose children are more likely to survive.[12]

Income is another factor facilitating self-help in health. In all countries the poor are much more likely to suffer from all types of ailments, have shorter live-expectancy, and experience higher mortality of infant and child.

In developing countries, as people become better off, they can more easily afford transport costs or time lost at work resulting from seeking curative care. In developed countries the poor are more likely to suffer the invisible poverty of inadequate diet or unhealthy housing. Hence raising incomes, especially of the poorest groups, is important to health. The link between poverty and health also applies between different national economies. There are sharp rises in life-expectancy, and sharp falls in under age-5 mortality—at least until a national average-income of $2,000/$3,000 per person/year, although income above the $8,000 level makes virtually no difference.[13]

Rising incomes, industrialization, and urbanization often lead to unhealthy life-styles. There is a shift in diet and a gradual decline in physical exercise as human energy is replaced by 'commercial' energy in transport and industry. The Commission notes, therefore, that life-style transitions produce a transition in health—one from acute and mainly communicable diseases to chronic and largely non-communicable ailments associated with a longer life. Prevention can greatly reduce the incidence of such anomalies.

In all these cases, while health professionals and research scientists must alert people to the risk incurred, it is the public policies outside the health domain that have the most impact. The Commission is convinced that prevention demands strong health-education campaigns and making health education a compulsory subject in school.

❧

The Commission concludes that the various determinants of health mean that health policy must be co-ordinated across a broad field and must be as holistic as population policy. While a health policy focused on curative intervention is bound to fail, one including public-health measures is more likely to succeed. Moreover, a policy capable of dealing with a variety of social factors has the best chance of success.

We also suggest that a comprehensive health policy for women must include nutrition (especially perinatal nutrition), safe motherhood, family planning, food-price policy, prevention of smoking by adolescent girls and young women, promotion of sports and exercise, and sound transport, planning and environmental measures. While such policy should include the de-medicalization of female health, from pregnancy through menopause to old age, it should also give medical attention to health problems more prevalent in, or unique to, women.

Health is thus more than a mere portfolio for health ministries; it is a societal challenge, and one requiring the objectives of governmental services that include agriculture, education, environment, food, industry, and transport.

An Unfinished Revolution

That the revolution in primary health care has not been realized in many cases is because the changes being made are often cosmetic instead of structural. Apart from drives for immunization and clean water, health services in poor communities have remained tokens of what they should be. The powers and privileges of physicians and hospitals remain largely intact, and in most developing countries health care is still an urban affair—depending far more on hospitals than health-care workers, and dispensed top–down. In almost all countries treatment is also more oriented to cure by professionals than to prevention within families and communities.

Of course the primary health-care concept was bound to arouse resistance from the groups whose privileges it threatened: the doctors in big city hospitals, and the country's élites, old and new, whose attachment to the medical and curative model of health is very strong and who prefer to be treated by doctors rather than nurses. In fact, the high-tech medical model being the dominant one, and being supported by powerful medical technology and pharmaceutical industries, it is not surprising that the ideal of the super-equipped, modern hospital, offering the team of specialists to back up one's family physician, has become the dream of most people in all countries. However, in developed or developing countries alike, this share-out is counterproductive: when people cannot get community help for simple conditions, they crowd into hospitals. Higher-level services are overburdened, and treatment costs many times more than it should.

The strong emphasis of the primary health-care model on prevention and self-help is far from becoming reality. Most ailments, everywhere, are preventable—whether by governmental action (immunization) or community campaigns (water and sanitation)—but most can be prevented by *people* via hygiene, healthy nutrition and practices such as breast-feeding.

One of the health-care priorities, therefore, is to bring both preventive and curative assistance within reach of those billions of the population who will profit from them today and tomorrow. So the Commission believes that measures are necessary to realize the most important goals, specifically:

- pursuing equity, favouring those most in need of health services;
- stressing prevention and self-help;
- increasing participation, devolving of powers and budgets; and
- changing the medical-care culture by focusing on the patient.

The Commission further suggests that targets be linked with timetables at both national and international levels, integrating at the same times principles such as equity and community action—prescribed by WHO at Alma Ata in 1978 and in the Ottawa Charter of 1986. For massive inequity persists.

In 1991, for example, only 28 per cent of health expenditures in developing countries reached local health services.[14] Of the $21 spent per person by developing countries on health services in 1990, only $1 went to public prevention: clean water and sanitation, vector control, health education. About $5 went to essential clinical services: safe maternity, family planning, treatment of sexually transmitted disease, infections and minor trauma, paediatrics, first-level assessment, health advice, and the alleviation of pain.[15]

Some Distortions in Health Priorities

There are 271 doctorless communities—yet the Philippines is the world's top exporter of doctors and nurses.

(Agnes Zenaida Camacho, Philippines)

In India about 3 per cent of the national budget goes to health, and more than half of that to management costs. A sub-centre is expected to serve 4–5 villages with a meagre budget of 2,000 rupees/year ($66) for essential, life-saving drugs.

(Prabeen Singh, India)

Discretionary clinical services (mostly in hospitals and clinics) took up about $14, more than twice that of the two basic levels combined.

We mentioned urban bias. In India the rural areas holding 70 per cent of the population must make do with 30 per cent of the country's physicians and 30 per cent of the health budget.[16] In many countries rural populations are simply beyond the reach of even emergency services. In Zimbabwe 33 per cent of rural women are more than an hour distant from the nearest health facility (against only 2 per cent of urban women). The average percentage of urban population with access to water was double that of the rural inhabitants; in Africa the ratio is 2.8 to 1.[17]

The Commission recommends that, in countries where imbalances exist, resources for discretionary clinical services be shifted into public-health and essential clinical services. Additional resources should be allocated to health and water budgets in order to expand service to rural and urban-squatter areas until equal access has been achieved.

The health sector needs, indeed, a sea-change in attitudes towards the treatment of patients. Required are major reforms in medical education and training, and the devising of quality-control systems to ensure that patients are given meaningful information about their condition and proposed treatment. They should be offered choices and treated with dignity and respect as partners in their own health care.

Professional Competence versus Cultural Non-communication

The doctor did not speak directly to me, and I was often given medication that I did not need or want. No one explained the benefits or side-effects of the medication.

(Jeannette McDonald, United States)

The patient must have the ability and flexibility to make appointments and to visit various health-care providers. Many immigrant and refugee populations do not have the tools to gain access to the system. There is a lack of culturally appropriate practices on the part of the provider. This is perpetuated by a system of medical education in which cultural awareness is almost entirely absent.

(Mary Chung, United States)

People of different culture and language are consistently discriminated against, and are being given delayed or dangerous treatment because of the lack of communication between provider and patient.

(Luz Alvarez Martinez, United States)

Such a change means major reforms in medical education, the restoration of ethical principles to the profession, and less biased but more scientific assessments of women's health, of alternative systems of medicines,[18] of the contribution to the healing process of the nursing theory of caring.

Resources for Health Care: Maintaining the Impetus

A new threat to health comes from overextending the free-market philosophy to the spheres of the caring services—though experience has shown time and again, in developed and developing countries, that health is not a market commodity and cannot be treated as such. In some countries, dogmatic views about so-called abusers of the health care system and neo-conservative economic philosophy are pushing the drive. But in many parts of the world, there are genuine concerns—and all sorts of initiatives to assist—about the shrinking resources available to the health care sector.

Structural adjustment programmes in many developing countries usually result in cuts in public spending, health included. An analysis prepared for the Save the Children Fund (United Kingdom) found that African countries receiving intensive adjustment lending reduced spending on health and education, whereas countries finding other sources of finance (or requiring none) raised their spending in these two key sectors.[19] It is often easier to cut spending on supplies than on salaries, so health-workers on the front-line often find themselves without bandages, medications, or the fuels to heat sterilizing pans to do their work, and family-planning workers without supplies of contraceptives.[20]

In ten African countries adjustment and economic crisis, coupled with the AIDS epidemic, have reduced life-expectancy (contrary to global trends). In Uganda, for example, expectancy fell from forty-eight years in 1987 to forty-three in 1992; in Zambia, from fifty-three to forty-eight during the same years.[21] Such data lead the Commission to recommend that structural adjustment programmes include explicit conditions requiring that spending on health (including preventive and reproductive health) be maintained.

Studies made in Ghana, Swaziland, Lesotho and Canada indicate sharp falls in the use of health services by the less privileged after the introduction of fees—in fact those most in need of the health care system.[22] Introducing market principles in the health service creates hazards and poses special problems, for example, 'cost recovery' charges for clean water or medical treatment. The impact of market intrusions into the health service will be felt long after the debt crisis is over. Paying for water or for medical services is not intrinsically wrong. People often buy water from vendors, or buy their own medicines from pharmacists, or seek private treatment from alternative practitioners. Moreover, the rich use the more expensive parts of water and health services much more intensively than the poor. In Tanzania, the richest 20 per cent are twice as likely to use even government subsidized hospitals as the poorest 20 per cent.[23] The Commission believes that such basic services should remain free of charge to all in order to avoid the formation of any sort of two-tiered system.

⸺

The struggle for public health cannot be won once and for all; it needs to be fought ceaselessly, and the growth of population makes the fight all the tougher. Clean water, for example, was brought to an additional 1,205 millions of people between 1980 and 1990, but the number of people not served with clean water fell by only 428 millions: population simply grew by 777 millions during the same period. The challenge during the 1990s is even greater, since clean water must be brought to another 831 millions in order to stop the number of the unserved population from rising.[24]

The immunization of children is a constant global requirement. The impetus in developing countries was not maintained during the early 1990s, coverage falling back somewhat. In some industrialized nations, immunization levels have fallen because of parental or governmental complacency. If the efforts continue to slip, epidemics may spread and the advances made thus far in child survival will be lost.[25]

Vigilance must also be maintained against new diseases such as AIDS or the Ebola virus (haemorrhagic fever), and the re-emergence of old ones like tuberculosis and malaria. The coming decades will witness a growing human resistance to antibiotics. While genetic engineering may offer new solutions, bacterial and insect vectors are likely to adapt quickly to innovative drugs. And there remains the risk that many medical advances may be neutralized by the over-use or abuse of antibiotics and pesticides.

There have been impressive successes in the health sphere from which other quality-of-life sectors can learn. But there is still much unfinished business. The right to health must be realized for the one to two billion people who do not yet enjoy it—and for the extra billions of people who will be added to the world's population over the coming decades. And this calls for both a significant shift in medical and other health services and for no less than a revolution in the culture and power structure of health care.

~ *Health policies are disease policies. A central health policy should combine information, education, and social communication with the individual and family as the fundamental resource.*

David Tejada, Peru
Latin America Public Hearing

~ *Perhaps family health-care is not basic enough as a priority, that it is really water and sanitation that count. The Chinese understand that dealing with such basic factors as health helps them avoid extreme poverty. We have to learn from them.*

Solita Monsod, Philippines
South-East Asia Public Hearing

References and Notes

1. UN Development Programme, *Human Development Report 1994* (Oxford, Oxford University Press, 1994); UNICEF, *State of the World's Children 1995* (Oxford, Oxford University Press, 1995).

2. UN Development Programme, *Human Development Report 1994*; World Bank, *World Development Report 1994* (Oxford, Oxford University Press, 1994); UNICEF, *State of the World's Children 1995*.

3. E. Tarimo and E. G. Webster, *Primary Health Care Concepts and Challenges in a Changing World: Alma-Ata Revisited* (Geneva, WHO, 1994).

4. D. Bandyopadhyay, *Powerlessness and Fertility*, paper presented to the Commission's Experts Group Meeting on Population and Governance, Bellagio (Sept. 1993).

5. Sergio Diaz-Briquets, *The Health Revolution in Cuba* (Austin, University of Texas Press, 1983); Larry R. Oberg, *Human Services in Postrevolutionary Cuba* (Westport and London, Greenwood Press, 1984).

6. The most current view of breast-feeding is that human milk contains special antibodies that extend the reach of the mother's immune responses to the infant's own defences: Jack Newman, 'How Breast Milk Protects Newborns', *Scientific American*, Dec. 1995.

7. *Human Development Report 1994*.

8. Ibid.

9. FAO, *Production Yearbook 1992* (Rome, 1993).

10. Premier's Council on Health Strategy, *Nurturing Health: A Framework on the Determinants of Health* (Toronto, Government of

Ontario, 1991); Robert G. Evans, Morris L. Barer, Theodore R. Marmor (eds.), *Why Are Some People Healthy and Others Not?* (New York, Aldine de Gruyter, 1994).

11. C. J. L. Murray and A. D. Lopez, *Global Comparative Assessments in the Health Sector* (Geneva, WHO, 1994).

12. Elizabeth M. King and M. Anne Hill, *Women's Education in Developing Countries* (Baltimore, Johns Hopkins University Press, 1993).

13. Ibid.

14. WHO, *Implementation of the Global Strategy for Health for All by the Year 2000* (Geneva, 1993).

15. *World Development Report 1994.*

16. Ibid.

17. World Bank, *Social Indicators of Development 1994* (data diskettes) (Washington, 1994).

18. These would benefit from scientific validation and should not become a part of cultural fundamentalism.

19. David Woodward, *Debt, Adjustment and Poverty in Developing Countries*, vol. 2 (London, Pinter, 1992).

20. Giovanni Cornea *et al.*, *Adjustment with a Human Face* (Oxford, Clarendon Press, 1988).

21. *World Development Report 1994.*

22. R. Tarimo, *The Prognosis of Health Care Services in Africa*, independent paper (Geneva, WHO, n.d.); P. Smithson, *Health Financing and Sustainability*, Working Paper 10 (London, Save the Children Fund, 1994); R. G. Beck and J. M. Horne, 'Study of User Charges in Saskatchewan 1968–71', in *User Charges for Health Services: A Report of the Ontario Council of Health* (Toronto, 1979); and American papers such as that of E. B. Keeler *et al.* published by *J. Amer. Medical Association* in 1985, 'How Free Care Reduced Hypertension in the Health Insurance Experiment'.

23. R. Paul Shaw and Charles Griffin, *Financing Health Care in Sub-Saharan Africa through User Fees and Insurance* (World Bank, Washington DC, 1995).

24. International Drinking Water Supply and Sanitation Decade, *End of Decade Review* (Geneva, WHO, 1992).

25. Expanded Programme on Immunization, *Programme Report 1993* (Geneva, WHO, 1994).

12 Reproductive Choices

❧ *Health policies only see women as reproducers and mothers. Existing programmes provide only prenatal care, institutional care during birth and nursing, post-natal care and care for the baby's development and growth. To these conceptual limitations is now added the structural crisis in the health system. In Nicaragua, in 1980, only 38 per cent of our women used contraception—and we know that the figure is still very low. Recent studies found that 74 per cent of women do not use any method, so the first cause of death among women is clandestine abortion in the cities and haemorrhage during childbirth in the countryside.*

Ana Maria Pizarro, Nicaragua
Latin America Public Hearing

❧ *Child prostitution is frequently organized, protected and vindictive, to silence its opponents. During the past twenty years my co-workers and I have felt the heavy boot of government officials and paedophile protectors as they tried to cover up the evil and protect their political careers and vested interests in the commercial sex industry in Olongapo. There syndicates systematically went about selling children as young as four to paedophiles. Instead of prosecuting the criminals, they persecuted, harassed and issued death threats to those of us working for the rights of children. . . . These unspeakable crimes against children and humanity are not only deadly threats to the life of Filipino children; they are the symptoms of an even greater evil—the unjust economic and social structures of the Philippines that have institutionalized poverty. A ruling élite, representing about fifty vastly wealthy families who own 70 per cent of the economy, controls the political processes and the distribution of the national wealth. Little goes to health, education and social services.*

Alex C. Hermoso, Preda Foundation, Manila
South-East Asia Public Hearing

~ *Some of the international agencies providing health care sometimes believe that nothing more than the setting up of numerous contraceptive distribution outlets is necessary. But health care cannot be handed down 'vertically'. Some women must first have some form of genuine contact with other women. There are other services offering prevention and care which are part of the health system. The sole function of health-care services must not be the reduction of fertility rates, because the quality of life of a population is global.*

Barbara Klugman
Southern Africa Public Hearing

~ *In Indonesia the birth rate has dropped from 2.4 per cent in the 1980s to 1.7 per cent today . . . a success story. But behind this success are overt and covert coercion, ranging from home visits by the wives of local authorities, visits by the police and military, to accusations of being Communist or threats of being moved to islands away from Java.*

Wardah Hafidz, Indonesia
South-East Asia Public Hearing

Personal and Social Dimensions of Reproductive Choice

The pattern of reproduction in a community is conditioned by historical circumstances, culture, and collective as well as individual values that develop as a function of the circumstances. Classical civilizations regarded reproduction as a natural obligation on the part of all—women and men—to ensure the group's continuity. Respect for ancestors, a characteristic of many cultures, strengthened this obligation by emphasizing one's debt to one's forebears. Continuation of the lineage was, in effect, repayment of this debt.

Since descent was matrilineal or patrilineal (sometimes both), there could be a divergence of views between men and women concerning the obligation. The woman in the matrilineal community provided the link between past and future; the man's role was subsidiary. In patrilineal groups, however, the primary responsibility for progeniture lay with the man: if the wife did not, or could not, bear children, the man was expected to take another woman. Here the wife's duty was not to her own lineage but to her husband's. The practices of adoption (of a child from within the kin group) and levirate (marriage with a brother's widow) offered alternatives to barrenness by one or the other spouse.

Perpetuation of the lineage was even more important when property was involved: livestock, land, inheritance of other kinds (feudal or religious rights and duties, occupational lore and skills). When land was owned communally, children were seen as the 'common good'—whose rearing and welfare were a collective responsibility rather than that of the parental couple. In the few communities of these types still surviving notions of illegitimacy or of children becoming orphans tend to develop slowly.

The instinct for group perpetuation is all-pervasive, whether or not we consider the possibly divergent views between men and women. In some communities found on the Indian subcontinent there exist female and male clans. Daughters belong to the mother's clan, sons to the father's.

It is important to keep these diversities in mind because the concept of choice relates closely to individual rights, and they carry an obligation of reciprocity—acknowledging that reproductive rights and choices of others may differ from one's own. Social institutions and cultural values, fluid as they have become, still exert considerable influence on individual choices. Much as we cherish an individual's autonomy within a given social context, some balancing of rights and responsibilities is inevitably called for.

-❧-

The concern for future generations has become coloured by our anguish for the world we shall leave to them. Standing at the crossroads of past and future, today's individual must 'decide' whether or not to have children, how many, and their spacing. The economic value of children has been argued *ad nauseam*, but the debate trivializes the complexity of a decision process that works differently between men and women. For their part, the men in most civilizations fear to procreate. On the other hand, however, women are perceived and valued by their capacity to give birth, even in societies where their direct participation in professional as well as social life is approved.

Child-bearing cannot be dealt with in isolation from the understanding of sexuality. Every individual perceives his or her existence in terms of all the dimensions of being. Sexuality is one of these dimensions, an expression of individual personality; it is also one of the most meaningful foundations of human bonding, through caring and other emotions that supply vitality to the most positive of social relations.

The obsession with sexuality that characterizes today's culture (one promoted actively by the mass media) affects the moment when sexuality manifests itself in youth, and it is a factor in its own banalization. The sexuality of young people also reflects the place that sex occupies in society as a whole. Adolescent pregnancies and sexual abuse of children and teenagers (even within the family) are world-wide signals not to be ignored.

Suffering, Exhilaration, Anguish, and Love

No matter how diverse the conditions of women's lives . . . their responses to pregnancy and childbirth are strikingly similar: the intense exhilaration, longing, fear or dejection associated with thoughts of becoming pregnant, depending on the circumstances; the desperate furtiveness often associated with extramarital pregnancies; the bonding with a newborn baby or, at times, its rejection; the anguish about one born too early or in poor health; and the blending of love and suffering when the birth of a child is welcomed by one parent but not the other.

(Sisela Bok,[1] United States)

The sexual behaviour of youth expresses, simultaneously, both the 'youth culture' and the culture that adults have created generally. The desire to explore all reality, to go as far as seems possible in togetherness these are powerful drives. These may be reinforced by other anxieties: insecurities about education and work, sex-as-commodity purveyed through pornography, the sensationalism of the tabloid press, and sex tourism. The pattern of 'always more' encountered in general consumption has permeated sexuality.

The family used to be the milieu for a child's early socialization. However diversified might have been the roles assigned to men and women, the family in most cultures prepared children for young adulthood. The family is where the young first experienced gender roles and the division of familial labour. But social change has transferred these roles increasingly from the family to the education system, or to peer-groups and gangs, or to the media. This has affected many children's basic perceptions of family life, child-bearing, and what society expects from the individual.

Old taboos have disappeared, and with them have vanished initiation rites through which the wisdom of many cultures helped young people learn to manage their sexuality. Today's all-knowing, blasé attitudes—displacing the 'magic' of initiation—conceal doubts and fears that inhibit self-knowledge. Societies may have to rethink and re-invent values and practices that will enable youth to mature in more harmony than at present.

Sexuality is thus situated within the mystery of the person, and therefore lies in the broad realm of personal freedom. Without a serious educational effort that encompasses the sexuality of children and adolescents, the human being of today risks failing to reach maturity with responsible attitudes towards sex. The Commission is of the opinion, therefore, that sexual education is essential in society. It may also help inculcate a true appreciation of the boundaries of personal freedom and its responsibilities. A special responsibility in this regard rests with both educational curricula and the media.

~ *Adolescents are becoming sexually active at younger ages . . . In our region 55 per cent of young men and 52 per cent of young women have had sex and are sexually*

*active before they leave secondary school. Yet we cannot
[distribute] condoms in our high schools. The problem
of our young people is not only protection against pregnancy. It is responsible sexuality and prevention of sexually transmitted diseases.*

Nancy Hall and Franca Bertoncin, Canada
North America Public Hearing

The concept of free choice in the context of reproduction policy
is conditioned (and constrained) by:

* the opportunities that society provides;
* the values influencing the whole personality;
* the individual's self-image; and
* self-esteem.

The autonomy offered to the individual by free choice, itself ana-
thema to coercion, needs balancing by the possible social consequences to others; it places in question the notion of absolute
freedom of action. The issue of reproductive choice cannot, therefore, be separated from the wider context of each individual's social
responsibilities.

The Commission points out that the idea of free choice carries
with it expectations that have been socially constructed. Society
contributes immensely to defining the identity of individuals, their
expected roles as mothers and parents, children or adolescents, as
citizens, workers, or artists. The process by which a person
becomes autonomous in regard to these identities will determine
his or her ability to choose freely from a medley of roles, often contradictory in themselves.

Reproductive Rights as Human Rights

The idea of reproductive rights is not really new. The rights result
from the integration of several universally accepted rights emerging from the domain of fundamental liberties and other guarantees
and from 'social rights'. Many national constitutions clearly provide for these, including (taken verbatim) the right to:

- protection of family, e.g. family planning;
- constitution of a family;
- education and support of children;
- special protection during and after pregnancy;
- parenthood as an eminent social value;
- health; and
- integrity of all persons.

Although the concept of reproductive rights emerged during the 1980s, most of their constituent elements were already recognized internationally. The Convention on the Elimination of All Forms of Discrimination against Women (1979) recognized the right to choose family size 'freely and responsibly', the right to family-planning education, information, and counselling services, and the right to safe pregnancy, delivery, and post-natal care. The right to health, accepted in all the international treaties on social rights, implies all the other rights.

The UN's Committee on Economic, Social and Cultural Rights (established in 1987) adopted the view that 'individual and collective interests are not in direct line with each other'. The Committee enquire regularly as to the status of 'infant-mortality rates and health-care facilities for pregnant women',[2] nation by nation.

Yet the concept of reproductive rights *appears* to be new. It reaffirms all the separate rights that tend to become blurred within the limited scope of the approaches to population control as well as within the clinical attitudes towards patients (as subjects, cases, or file numbers). The Commission suggests, as a consequence, that reproductive rights assume the new quality of human rights.

Inherent in the reproductive rights is the affirmation that women in all societies be treated as full citizens, on a par with men. Once values—such as the integrity of one's body, informed consent concerning all interventions on or in one's body, safe motherhood, freedom to decide as to how one enters the chain of successive generations—are recognized as rights, there is then further evolution: 'the elevation of these values to human-rights status means, as an absolute minimum, that they, and whatever measures are necessary to secure their realization, are not negotiable.'[3] The Commission suggests that the notion of the non-negotiability of reproductive rights as human rights equates with several fundamental principles: the dignity of the individual, equity and non-discrimination, and participation and solidarity.

The principle of the individual's *dignity* requires transcending motherhood, and its related issues, in order to address all of the circumstances afferent to the woman's reproductive system throughout the life-cycle. The Commission calls for urgent remedial measures with regard to a number of practices today impinging on the woman's reproductive rights. The Commission considers these to be massive violations of human rights:

- female infanticide, sex selection, or determination, sometimes followed by sex-specific abortion without medical justification;
- genital mutilation of young girls;
- an increase of sexual assaults, with impunity, on boys and girls and adolescents in almost all cultures;
- commerce in young girls from poor families in search of employment;
- luring young girls into domestic service or entertainment jobs as a mask for criminal prostitution, all over the globe;
- health- and family-planning workers who ignore the special rights of women during and after menopause;
- child marriage and enforced or induced sexual intercourse with minors (not yet acknowledged as rape by all legislation).

The principle of *equity and non-discrimination* requires that the lack of access of some women (in isolated villages, or marginal groups in urban settings) to reproductive health services be rectified as a matter of priority.

The *participation* principle refers to mobilization of the dynamic forces capable of translating reproductive rights into reality. This is a multiple process. All women should be provided with information and education in order to manage their own reproductive rights throughout life, and to serve as communicators of the same to others in the family, work-place, or community. Men and boys should be taught the validity of the reproductive rights of women. Communities, societies, and entire cultures should, furthermore, accept these rights and the responsibilities that they imply. The

State's role is to respect, protect, and promote reproductive rights as it would other rights, and not be party to violations. Participation by schools, universities, professional associations, trade unions, religious or cultural groups, and civil-society organizations of all kinds becomes, in turn, the expression of the all-embracing principle of *solidarity*.

The Commission affirms that reproductive rights are both a reflection of the quality of life as it is examined in this report and an integral part of this quality.

The Commission concurs in the idea, which has made its way throughout the UN Conferences of recent years, that reproductive health care is a critical part of health care. The Commission further believes that any call for choice must be balanced by the notion of *availability*, bearing in mind that many countries face critical constraints on resources intended to ensure reproductive services. Absolute priority accorded to an ever-growing range of choice in reproductive services might otherwise result in the neglect of other important sectors of health care.

The choice of family size poses a dilemma, given the conflicting precepts of *freedom* and *responsibility*. Most people decide on family size within the framework of their (a) desires and (b) present and future resources. What may appear advantageous to individuals may, in the aggregate, cause problems for a society as a whole. Here enters responsibility: when making their personal decisions, parents need also to take into account the impact of their choice on future generations and the likely consequences for our natural environment. Government, for its part, can help reconcile such conflicts by creating conditions in which individual choices coincide as closely as possible with social and environmental objectives.

Given the paramount importance of these issues for both the population and sustainable development, the Commission finds it desirable that a group of international leaders initiate the adoption of a declaration on reproductive rights. The declaration should affirm the rights to free choice and primary health care for reproductive needs, safeguarding user participation and quality of service. A statement of this kind should set the standards for a new culture to be respected by policy-makers and reproductive-health professionals—whose responsibilities could be included in a code of conduct. Counselling and other services should be provided from adolescence to old age, ensuring informed consent before any intervention, and outlawing coercive practices.

The Contentious Issue of Abortion

WHO estimates that about one in four pregnancies ends in abortion. Each year between 26 million and 31 million abortions are performed in countries where this is legal, under safe medical conditions. Some 20 million unsafe abortions are performed annually, resulting in one death for every 250 abortions. Most of the latter take place in developing countries. Unsafe abortions may also cause complications in the short or long term, even permanent infertility.[4] The victims are often adolescent girls denied access to sex education and contraception techniques. In Chile, after the government had offered free insertion of intra-uterine devices, deaths from unsafe abortion were halved between 1965 and 1976.[5] Figure 12.1 shows the relative prevalence of contraceptives in the world.

> ❧ *Russia was the first country to legalize abortion and commercialize it. The 'abortional culture' was banned in 1936, when it went underground. It was legalized again in 1955. Today . . . safe abortions do not exceed 30 per cent, and post-abortion lethality accounts for about 30 per cent of maternal mortality. A negative attitude towards patients is characteristic of the health services in post-Soviet Russia; the negative attitude of gynaecologists towards women having abortions [combines] with 70–80 per cent of abortions performed with relatively poor anaesthesia.*
>
> Andrei Popov, Russia
> Eastern Europe Public Hearing

> ❧ *In Pakistan family planning is considered not Islamic, so every measure taken by the State must be justified in*

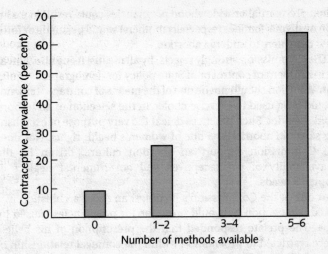

Fig. 12.1. Contraceptives: more choice, more use. Graphs depict that the use of contraceptives rises as a function of the number of methods available.

Source: Ross and Frankenberg, The Population Council.

> the name of Islam. Pakistan calls its family-planning programme a population-welfare programme. We have women who have been deprived of the chance to exercise the choice of contraception.
>
> Hina Gilani, Pakistan
> South Asia Public Hearing

> ❧ I can hold down a job, thanks to family planning. But I need a note from my husband in order to procure supplies from the family-planning clinic. Once I appeared without a note, and I was sent home to obtain a note from him.
>
> A mother of two, Mali
> West Africa Public Hearing

Historically, women in all cultures were driven to seek abortions when their situation conflicted with the received social expectations.

When pre-marital or widowhood pregnancies could result in exclusion or stigma, families (especially mothers) would persuade or force their daughters to undergo abortion.

The Commission strongly rejects, by all means, using abortion as an instrument of control or of State policy for demographic regulation. Abortion should not be one of the means of contraception, nor should it be used to exercise choice in the selection of an unborn child's gender. Such practices defeat the very purpose of establishing safety in abortions as one of women's health rights. Nor does the Commission support an abortion culture, driven by the unavailability of contraceptives and governmental neglect of women's needs.

At one of the Commission's hearings, an Asian archbishop was asked what action he would prescribe for pregnancies caused by rape. The prelate responded that the prescription of his beliefs 'were restricted to procreation within the conjugal relationship of marriage'.

A troubling phenomenon is that of the rising number of cases of incest in many parts of the world. The victims are most often young girls, and they seek to terminate their pregnancies by abortion. The Commission believes that civil society, especially its cultural and religious leaders, cannot remain blind to such injustice—needs that some governments have already responded to.

The Commission believes further that all aspects of abortion, especially the related health hazards, must be exposed while debating on legislation. Social, cultural, and religious leaders bear special responsibility in weighing the entire range of arguments to be used to make recommendations to policy-makers. The Commission also recommends that abortion be decriminalized, although specific penal measures may be necessary in the case of sex-specific abortion in order to prevent abuse of the law.

Reproductive Health-Care Services

Women and men need ready, affordable access to reproductive health services that are culture-sensitive and meet their requirements at different stages of life. A choice of safe, convenient, and effective methods is advisable. And the services proffered should be just that, rather than expecting that the population is nothing more than regiments aligned to do battle to cut the birth rate, for example.

The Commission is convinced that the all-embracing concept of reproductive health is critical to the quality of life for men and children as well as women. It includes family planning, safe motherhood, prevention and treatment of sexually transmitted disease, and infertility. The four areas are closely interrelated in cause-and-effect cycles.

The Cairo and Beijing conferences recommended that reproductive health services be available through the general health-delivery system and, at the grass roots, via the primary care mechanism.[6] This becomes a double integration: family planning is absorbed into reproductive health, and reproductive health becomes part of general health.

The Commission fully endorses the proposal that reproductive health not be treated separately, fenced off from the rest of health delivery. This will require an understanding about the model of primary reproductive care to be offered. It should be limited to promoting prevention first, and emergency treatment for common complaints. Problems requiring more complex diagnosis and treatment would be referred to higher levels in the health service. Such problems would include problematic pregnancies, contraceptive clients seeking longer-lasting methods, or antibiotic treatment of infertility resulting from sexually transmitted anomalies.

The Commission recommends, therefore, that the UN Fund for Population Activities, in collaboration with institutions such as WHO and UNICEF, define a model of primary reproductive health care—one representing the minimal support to be brought within everyone's reach.

About one in five births in developing countries is unchosen.[7] In twenty-four of forty-two countries covered by demographic and health surveys, women report at least one unchosen birth on average.[8] Fifty-seven per cent of the world's married couples of reproductive age today use some form of contraception, a fivefold increase since the 1960s.[9] Yet there are an estimated 350 million couples world-wide who have not access to the full range of contemporary methods.[10] The number of reproductive-age couples is projected to grow by about 18 million each year during the 1990s.[11]

These figures do not include sexually active, unmarried individuals: a group at high risk of both unwanted pregnancies and diseases transmitted sexually.

Unmarried adolescents often have the greatest trouble to secure reproductive health services, especially family planning. In fact, demographic and health surveys of nineteen sub-Saharan African countries found that young women first have intercourse about a year-and-a-half before marriage. Surveys in Latin America determined a one-year gap between sexual initiation and marriage.[12]

Reducing distance and costs is critical. When Thailand began free distribution of the contraceptive pill in 1976 its use grew by more than 50 per cent within a year. Most of the women taking the pill were doing so for the first time.[13] Community-based distribution extends family-planning information and services to rural areas and urban slums. Community distributors are usually lay-workers who supply contraceptives taken from small depots during home visits. Often these workers are unpaid. A review of twenty-eight such projects found that the use of contraceptives doubled within two years of introduction.[14]

The Commission believes that priority must be given to extending reproductive health services to within distances accessible by population elements (men, adolescents, unmarried people) currently not serviced and to reducing charges to affordable levels. The range of services should be broadened as much as possible.

People at different stages of life have different contraceptive needs. In many countries the range of methods remains limited, although studies in seven Asian countries revealed that each new contraceptive method introduced attracts many new users.[15] Countries where only one or two contraceptive methods are available experience an average contraceptive use of about 25 per cent; in those where five or six methods are in use, the figure reaches 64 per cent.[16]

> ❧ *Women fear visiting medical institutions. Doctors resent doing pregnancy termination again and again, so they insist that women undergo sterilization. If a woman anticipates this, she will not seek a termination even if*

there is an official facility nearby. So she visits an
untrained practitioner, and trouble may follow.

(Imrana Qadeer, India)

➤ *Sterilization seems to be the inexorable fate of women in*
Brazil's Northeast where 19 per cent of the women are
sterilized before the age of 25 and where—by chance?—
the black population is concentrated.

(Edna Roland-Geledes, Brazil)

WHO estimates that, world-wide, between 60 million and 80 million couples are affected by infertility. As much as 96 per cent of this infertility results from sexually transmitted disease, infection of the reproductive tract subsequent to unhygienic delivery of the newborn baby, poorly performed abortion, or use of inappropriate contraceptives. In some sub-Saharan regions one couple in three is affected by such 'secondary sterility'. Only a small proportion of sterility is attributable to congenital anomalies.[17]

The Commission believes that prevention of infertility and basic treatment of curable sexually transmitted disease, thanks to universal access to services ensuring safe motherhood, must be integral to reproductive health services. The Commission suggests that an appropriate balance be found between fund allocation to primary services and to expensive, high-technology treatment (including research on primary sterility).

The Commission believes that counselling is essential to ensure that clients understand their options, the advantages and disadvantages of the methods available, and their correct use. In Nigeria, for example, clients of family planning who have been counselled by trained nurses are twice as likely as a control group to return for follow-up.[18]

When fertility declines through voluntary measures, its rate remains generally low. The Commission's hearings, however, uncovered many examples of direct or indirect coercion to use contraceptives or otherwise lower fertility. The Commission suggests that voluntary family-planning programmes are far more effective than those involving coercion to promote sustained use of contraceptives and small families.[19]

Human Rights and the Use of Coercion

Coercion may take many forms: from the (rare) occasions of physical coercion to many subtle, and less than subtle, forms of pressure: fines, withdrawal of benefits, outright violation of basic rights. Coercion is not only an abuse of a person's rights, it seldom attains its objective. A general pattern discernible is coercion from the top down through vertically administered family-planning or fertility-control services. This pressure from the top translates into targets—numbers—for use by the service-delivery system. The most favoured, and controversial, method to assure this is the offer of incentives or disincentives to the motivators (counselling staff). The approach is most evident when the services available are limited because of the inadequacy of the methods used or the personnel doing the counselling, and their overall quality of care. Using financial and other resources as incentives to field workers, paramedical staff, and other 'outreach' personnel leaves that much less for proper training of staff and generally improving the quality of service.

The Commission notes that incentive payments, promises of promotion, or threat of sanction if targets are not attained invite abuse by health-workers and reduce the funds available for the real needs. They are especially dangerous in the case of long-term treatment.

The Commission also learned, with interest, of successful approaches involving the use of *collective incentives* permitting local self-government to improve quality of life for adults and children—and an indirect influence on population trends. Presented by twelve women's organizations in India, the idea is to reward local bodies for eliminating child marriage and illiteracy, reducing infant mortality, achieving universal enrolment in primary school, and assuring primary health- and child-care centres for all villages and urban neighbourhoods.[20]

The Commission is convinced that community involvement is

particularly important to resolve socio-cultural resistance, mostly rooted in fear that reflects ignorance of the physiological processes. Opposition by husbands, older family members, and religious leaders has often been dissipated by the training of community leaders, members of youth organizations, and women's groups—expanding their knowledge and stimulating thought in the direction of broad social responsibilities.

Information, Education, and Counselling

Community development, building up demand, and innovative training offered to community-level workers are fundamental for the transmittal of reliable information. Yet such actions cannot be the sole communication-base for the transfer of reliable information (sometimes science-based and complex).

Some examples may illustrate the complexities involved. On the average, an unplanned pregnancy is twenty times more dangerous for the woman than the use of modern, contraceptive methods.[21] In Egypt there are 103 maternal deaths per 100,000 births annually, compared with 8 per 100,000 among users of the pill and 3 per 100,000 among users of intra-uterine devices.[22]

The Commission holds that improving the quality and credibility of information, education, and counselling in reproductive health care is critical for individuals making ethically and socially responsible choices concerning pregnancy and childbirth. There exist various innovative social-development models to these ends.

Accurate and unbiased information is of special importance in reproductive health care where the consequences of error or ignorance may have long-term effects. The critique made by many women's organizations of the quality of information about contraceptive drugs and techniques stems from the fact that many physicians and other care-providers depend on information supplied by manufacturers.

Not all doctors, whether private or in public health, will have access to the fast-changing findings of medical research in matters of reproductive health. The role of State agencies responsible for protecting the public from the dangers of new drugs and technologies is often criticized in this respect. The growing alliance between

Table 12.1. *Mortality risks in the United States related to contraceptive techniques*

Activity	Chance of death per year
[Driving an automobile: base]	[1 in 6,000]
Giving birth	1 in 11,000
Smoker using oral contraceptives	1 in 16,000
Contracting pelvic inflammatory disease from intercourse	1 in 50,000
Non-smoker using oral contraceptives	1 in 63,000
Having a tubal ligation (with laparoscopy*)	1 in 67,000
Using intra-uterine devices	1 in 100,000
Having a vasectomy	1 in 300,000

Note: * Intervention within the abdominal wall via a small, flexible fiberoptic instrument.
Source: Robert A. Hatcher *et al.*, *Contraceptive Technology*, 16th edn. (New York, Irvington Publishers, 1994).

the women's movement and ethically concerned sections of the medical community, however, is a positive development and one that needs reinforcement. Sustained involvement of research and teaching institutions to improve the quality of information, education, and counselling within the community is sure to have a positive effect on their basic functions.

> *It's time for a serious change. If we are supposed to be tomorrow's leaders, stop treating us like yesterday's babies. With the proper training teenagers are capable of educating other teenagers as well as or better than many adults. . . . Think about this, whom do teens talk to more—their peers or adults? Speaking for myself, as a teen I feel more comfortable talking to a friend or someone of my own age-range about sex or whatever the case may be. I can look at it this way also: I have noticed that my friends feel safer and more comfortable talking to me about HIV and condom use more so than they do when they went to the school nurse.*
>
> William Johnson, Teen Council, United States
> North America Public Hearing

❧ *Teaching human sexuality courses for undergraduates and medical students, I was often surprised by the level of ignorance about such things as human sexual response, pregnancy, birth and contraceptive effectiveness. When first-year medical students missed as many or more factual questions in this area as did undergraduate students, I knew that the so-called sexual revolution might have occurred in behaviour but not in knowledge.*

Eleanor Morrison, United States
North America Public Hearing

❧ *Family planning is an empowerment, I have no doubt about that, but this empowerment, when it is forced on the women, may not be an empowerment. In the name of family-planning services, women were given Norplant, not knowing what are their implications, or even a sterilization. They might have accepted sterilization, thinking it's going to help their family norm, but what about the other side-effects? When she bleeds more, when she has menorrhea, who looks after her?*

Zaffrullah Choudhury, Bangladesh
South Asia Public Hearing

❧ *I would like to mention an enormous problem, that of the unsatisfied requirements in family planning services in this country, the need for contraceptives and qualified assistance to people in the provinces, the need for a friendly attitude to patients and the need for qualified and cheap assistance for marginal strata of the population.*

Andrei Popov, Moscow
Eastern Europe Public Hearing

❧ *Having many children is no longer in style. In our mothers' time, the head of the family, even if he had four wives and several children, provided for all of them. Today, all the children are the mother's responsibility.*

Tinga Sow, Mali
West Africa Public Hearing

References

1. Sisela Bok, 'Population and Ethics: Expanding the Moral Space', in Germain and Chen Sen (eds.), *Population Politics Reconsidered* (Cambridge, Mass., Harvard University Press, 1994). The comment reflects an extraordinary span of literature over space and time, from classical Greece to medieval Europe, to Japan, India, and Zimbabwe.
2. UN document E/C.12/1987/SR.8.
3. Ibid.
4. WHO, Division of Family Health, *Abortion: A Tabulation of Available Data on the Frequency and Mortality of Unsafe Abortion* (2nd edn. Geneva, 1994).
5. G. Adriasole *et al.*, *Actualizacion del documento 'Evaluacion de 10 anos de planificacion familiar en Chile'* (Santiago, Asociacion Chilena de Proteccion de la Familiar (ACPF) (1970); ACPF, Memoria (Santiago, APROFA, 1986).
6. UN, *Report of the International Conference on Population and Development* (doc. A/CONF.171/13, New York, 1994).
7. John Bongaarts, W. Parker Mauldin and James F. Phillips, 'The Demographic Impact of Family Planning Programs', *Studies in Family Planning*, 21: 6 (1990).
8. Dara Carr and Ann Way, *Women's Lives and Experiences: A Decade of Research Findings from Demographic and Health Survey Programs* (Calverton, Md., Marco International, 1994).
9. World Bank, *Population and Development: Implications for the World Bank* (Washington, 1994).
10. UN, *Report of the International Conference on Population and Development*.
11. Ibid.
12. Carr and Way, *Women's Lives and Experiences*.
13. J. Knodel, T. Bennett and S. Panyadilok, 'Do Free Pills Make a Difference? Thailand's Experience', *International Family Planning Perspectives*, 10: 3 (1984).
14. John A. Ross and Elizabeth Frankenberg, *Findings from Two Decades of Family Planning Research* (New York, Population Council, 1993).
15. R. and D. Freedman, 'The Role of Family Planning Programmes as a Fertility Determinant', in J. F. Phillips and J. A. Ross (eds.) *Family Planning Programmes and Fertility* (Oxford, Clarendon Press, 1992).
16. Ross and Frankenberg, *Findings . . . of Family Planning Research*.
17. WHO, *Reproductive Health: A Key to a Brighter Future* (Geneva, 1992).
18. Young-Mi Kim et al., 'Improving the Quality of Service Delivery in Nigeria', *Studies in Family Planning*, 23: 2 (1992).
19. Steve W. Sinding, 'The Role of Government and Demographic

Change', paper presented to the Commission on Population and Quality of Life, Paris, Apr. 1993.

20. *A Positive Population Policy*, memorandum submitted to the Swaminathan Expert Group on Population Policy, 1993.

21. Dr Allen Rosenfield, cited in Ann Starrs, *Preventing the Tragedy of Maternal Deaths* (Nairobi and Washington, World Bank, 1987).

22. WHO, Division of Family Health, *Maternal Mortality Rates: A Tabulation of Available Information* (Geneva, 1985), as cited in Population Reference Bureau, *Contraceptive Safety: Rumours and Realities* (Washington, 1988).

13 Empowering Women

🔊 *Reproductive rights are linked to the empowerment of women. How could they ever function in the context of poverty, in the context of exclusion? How are reproductive rights to be exercised in the context of a health system which is bankrupt? I believe this to be a question we cannot evade without falling into a fallacy, of defending a world policy on reproductive rights and believing that it would be viable in societies which lack the minimum conditions necessary for a health response for all. The reform of the State in order to ensure the delivery of social services for all, combined with women's empowerment to play their irreplaceable role as guardians of family and community well-being, are pre-conditions for the effective safeguard of reproductive rights.*

Rosiska Darcy de Oliveira, Brazil
Latin America Public Hearing

🔊 *The question to be asked is whether it is possible for a woman whose control over herself has been 'traded' to be truly liberated, since payment of the bride price means that everything the bride represents (including her labour and reproductive system) is the total possession of her husband and his family. Can she be liberated when her actions are fully dependent upon her husband's approval; when once within the four walls of her home she has to exercise the greatest care to avoid impromptu punitive measures; when her health is exposed to grave danger due to her husband's sexual practices; and when she has no right to her own eco-*

nomic development? Herein then lies the premise for the true liberation of African women and their integration into national development efforts.

Judith Chikore, Zimbabwe
Southern Africa Public Hearing

✎ *In Nepal, the women participate in agriculture, say about 80 per cent of the women. In this world, the women of Nepal do not count. In practice, the women are far behind. The literacy rate is 18 per cent, in primary education the enrollment is 37 per cent, in the lower secondary is 31 per cent, in the high secondary is 39 per cent. In the higher education it is not even 1 per cent. In the health field, the female mortality rate in Nepal is very high: in 1981 it was 850 in a 100,000 people, now it is 550, infant mortality is 165 per 1,000, very high. And the life expectancy of women is very low, 52 years, whereas of men it is 56.*

Shahana Pradhan, Nepal
South Asia Public Hearing

Crowning a Century of Struggle

A major civilization transformation has taken place throughout the twentieth century: the evolving empowerment of women together with the recognition of women's rights as human rights. This quiet transformation has been achieved by a dogged, incessant effort. Its consequences are bound to change gender relations and specific conditions within every society; its impact on national and international political, economic, and social life will be fundamental.

The spotlight has often been on women as innocent but primary victims of conflicts among nations, as well as of violence within societies and families. Less visibly, it is women who have borne the brunt of innumerable economic and social inequalities within entire countries and societies. Fig. 13.1 shows the skewed distribution of women in power, world-wide. The real extent of the women's revolution, therefore, will manifest itself in a higher visibility of women as actors, direct participants, and leaders in all

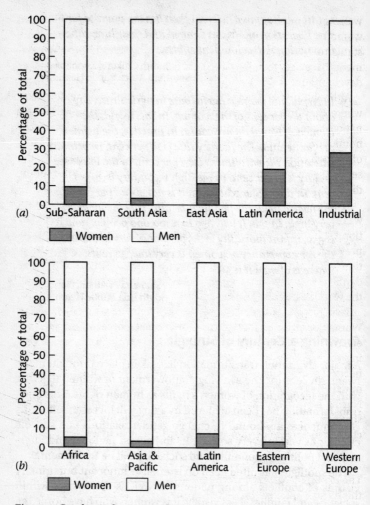

Fig. 13.1. Gender and power in the 1990s, (a) proportion of men in Third-World administrative or managerial jobs, with women occupying on average 13.5 per cent of those positions; (b) cabinet posts distributed by sex, with women in 6 per cent of the posts. These developing-world figures contrast with industrialized-world proportions of (a) 31 per cent, (b) about 5 per cent of the posts.
Source: UNDP, UNICEF (1995).

walks of life and in the international arena too. This will crown women's long and often frustrating transition from a subordinate status to one full of dignity, from being statistically invisible elements of society to being a recognized—and often pivotal—pillar of development.

Although it is only a century since women gained the vote anywhere, they now have the right to vote in all but five countries. Many nation-states have incorporated a stipulation of social and economic equality in their constitutions. This change began the process of women becoming more visible in the educated professions, the service sector, and the industrial labour-force, yet it left the subordinated social status of the majority of women untouched.

With a few exceptions, the first wave of the feminist movement was carried out essentially by the middle class; it focused on education. The second wave, beginning in the 1960s, resulted from the presence of a much larger percentage of women in higher education, and was truly a sexual revolution, a revolt against double standards in social morality, and a protest against the subordination of the woman at home and in society.

Two factors added strength to the way the process evolved. Women questioned so much the conventional organization of society, particularly in applied economics and politics, that, while feeling excluded from these fields, many asked themselves if the needed changes could be brought about only by their being co-opted (by men) into the system. The women's movement in the North, in fact, became fragmented because many based their struggle on rights while others sought to bring about societal change directly in certain key areas of human activity.

⟶

The experience of the South reinforced some of the dimensions of this effort. There the impact on women of industrialization, urbanization, and population growth was similar to the general effect experienced by the entirety of the industrial countries in the nineteenth century. Level of consciousness, emergence of successive generations of women at the forefront of knowledge, growing numbers of women with enough education to investigate the conditions, aspirations, and perspectives among the poor—all this was an impulsion to react to the need for change in societal patterns. These, in turn, would have great influence on the 'agenda' of the women's global movement.

The adoption of the Convention on the Elimination of Discrimination against Women (CEDAW), voted on by the UN General Assembly in 1980, precipitated the gathering of data on the status of women in many countries, North and South alike. The emergence of new perspectives for women's organizations on national and local levels was driven, too, by a changing consciousness and a struggle for solidarity across divisions by class, race, religion, and nationality. Other factors contributed to this process: the growth of women's studies in many universities throughout the world, supplemented by burgeoning networks of the cross-fertilization of ideas, approaches, tactics, and strategies. Added to these was the active role played by women in the struggle for democracy against oppressive regimes in Latin America, Africa, and Asia.

The United Nations conferences on women and other development and socio-economic issues, held since 1975, have helped to heighten the visibility of the role, the plight, and the potential of women on the international scene. These meetings exposed a theretofore unknown dimension of development: the systemic discrimination and marginalization of women (and their deprivation all over the world) that created a momentum for change.

While the right to vote of women broke a stubborn taboo that had prevailed in democratic systems, women's access to political power remained limited and, in some countries, only recently took hold. In cultural life, however, women had already gained a prominent place.

The *role* of women, as a separate issue of more than merely token significance, entered international debate at the first UN Conference on Population and Development, held in Bucharest (Romania) in 1974. Since then the dimensions of the problem have become more complex. Other conferences followed, with the contribution of rural women to agrarian economies acknowledged by the World Conference on Agrarian Reform and Rural Development (1979). The African famines of the time raised the question of whether they might have been caused, too, by the neglect of women's role as primary food-producers.

The events taking place inside the Planet Femina tent during the Environment and Development summit held in Rio de Janeiro in 1992 influenced the results of that important conference. The Conference on Human Rights held in Vienna (1993) agreed that 'women's rights are human rights'. At the Conference on Population and Development, held in Cairo (1994), thousands of women brought visible support and added strength to the now widely accepted concept of women's reproductive rights. (See Chapter 12, above.)

The position adopted at the Social Summit in Copenhagen (1995) made the empowerment of women part of the basic commitment of some 120 heads of State or government. Indeed, the summit at Copenhagen explicitly merged:

- women's rights into the broader covenant on human rights; and
- the central role of women into social development and thus into their own empowerment.

In the parallel fora organized by NGOs at each of these global meetings, new alliances were formed. By the 1980s a 'politically and ideologically less specific form' of women's consciousness spread among the masses of the women around the world—far beyond anything achieved by the first wave of feminism. Women as a social group became, what it was not before, a major political force.

The International Year of Women (1975), the Decade of Women (1975–85), and the strategies adopted during the three women's world conferences stimulated the establishment of national machineries for strengthening the empowerment of women. This brought about a higher degree of awareness of the overt and covert biases against women in all fields of activity.

Reinforcing the Visibility of Women

Women's existence in socio-political terms depends on their visibility, since most cultures tend to leave women invisible. The male-dominated society tends to 'veil' its women; they are comparatively little present in the news, in socio-economic or political analysis, even in projections of the future. The hard-won, spreading visibility of women should not be allowed to be veiled again. The global, trickle-down effect of women's rights, their visibility, and their participation must be accelerated and reinforced at all levels—to ensure success in their struggle for a better life, both for themselves and for others.

The visibility of women has led to a situation going far beyond equality of opportunity. As other equalities widen, gender equality for all remains a mirage. A few women manage to climb the ladder of success, but the majority remains excluded. Passively perceived subordination is unacceptable, in terms of both rights and quality of life.

The recognition of the dignity of all human beings had led to the acknowledgement of their equality, the universality of this equality constituting the core of basic human rights. Inequality, on the other hand, is the negation of human rights. In matters affecting women, *inequality* has often been replaced by the softer *discrimination*, a term disguising the denial of women's rights. At the very least, a wider acceptance and enforcement of the provisions of the International Convention on the Elimination of Discrimination against Women (CEDAW—already mentioned several times in this book) becomes critical.

The increased visibility of women notwithstanding, an appalling gap persists between agreed principles and the rights of women on the one hand, and reality and practice on the other hand. Principles agreed upon internationally and even those codified in national legislation often remain dead letters, or else the international instruments become meaningless in face of the numerous reservations expressed upon ratification. Taking advantage of the momentum of visibility, the drive for empowerment must have force, aiming initially at the realization of well-defined 'plateaus', such as *equal pay for equal work* (already codified for many years in ILO Convention 100).

⤙

Equal-pay legislation should be adopted and expanded in all countries so as to incorporate the principle of *equal pay for work of equal value*. This would allow for a re-evaluation of women's professional and 'pink-collar' occupations, with increases in both pay and status.

Affirmative action should be adopted, therefore, as policy until the persistent inequalities in women's pay and status are eliminated. Goals and timetables should be developed to this effect, implemented, and monitored. Affirmative-action measures might include the provision of day-care centres; flexible working-hours; women's quotas in recruitment, promotion, and retraining; and outlawing and prosecuting sexual harassment in the work-place.

Labour laws need also to be expanded to provide better conditions, benefits, and job security for domestic and agricultural workers, part-time, temporary, and miscellaneous workers in the home, and employees in export-processing zones. Women often predominate in these categories, leaving them particularly vulnerable to poor working conditions and other exploitation.

Women's productive activities tend to vanish as the national census is compiled, an invisibility that has serious consequences for development. A study made by FAO in 1979 found that African women made up 80 per cent of the food producers in some countries, yet they received less than 10 per cent of the visits made by agricultural advisers.

Thus, decades of struggle by the women's movement finally have brought recognition from the United Nations that the value of their unpaid, largely invisible work is a contribution to the global quality of life computable at $11 billion per year. Of the total burden of work, paid and unpaid, women carry 53 per cent in the developing countries and 51 per cent in the industrialized nations. Men's share is thus less in both. By calculating the unpaid activities as market transactions at prevailing wages, UNDP's *Human Development Report 1995* arrived at a figure of $16 billion annually, that is, 70 per cent of the officially estimated $23 billion annually for the value of all work performed. The woman's contribution accounts, therefore, for eleven-sixteenths or nearly three-fourths of the total.

The distribution between paid and unpaid labour gives much wider variations because in the industrial countries men spend two-thirds of their working time in paid status (and one-third unpaid). For women the situation is reversed. In the developing countries more than three-quarters of men's work is in market activities; the men enjoy the lion's share of income and recognition, although much of the market activity results from *joint production*, from which women glean neither recognition nor a just share of the revenue.

More research should be conducted, therefore, on the contribution of women's unpaid work to family and national economies—including work in subsistence agriculture, livestock husbandry, domestic work, child-care, and care for the elderly, the disabled, and the ill. This analysis should incorporate time-use data, and should be used in the design of future policy. All new development initiatives and economic and social planning should be subject to a 'gender audit' to assess their effects on women's quality of life as well as on the inequalities persisting between men and women.

Poverty and illiteracy, too, continue to have female faces. With differentiation continuing in wages, it also applies to participation in the formal labour-force (with consequent effects on maternity, child-care, and social security); to access to credit and other economic opportunities; and within political and administrative bodies of many kinds.

The Commission concurs in the conclusions of the *Human Development Report 1995* that 'the free workings of the economic and political processes are unlikely to deliver equality of opportunity' for women, the poor, or the powerless.

Concrete strategies, affirmative action, and investment in quality of life are all needed to improve our overall quality of life. But to summon the requisite political will requires continued pressure coming from the struggle by women.

The majority of the world's women are poor citizens of the poor countries: they are 'deprived' and 'backward'. About 40 per cent of females world-wide (and especially in the developing regions) are children under the age of 15. The *World Health Report 1995* highlighted the grim prospects facing a baby girl born in one of the least developed countries, where one-sixth of all births occur annually.

Equity demands that the conditions of such deprived infants and children be improved without delay. Programme initiatives for older women are nothing more than salvaging measures, and salvage is not always possible. Evidence of missed investment and lost opportunity is all too abundant. Low-birth-weight babies, illiteracy and the lack of primary education, poor skills and poor self-

Born in a Least Developed Country: A Baby Girl

This child will not share in the global, upward trend of increased life-expectancy. She can expect to live until (at most) age 44 if she clears early hurdles: a 1 in 3 chance of being malnourished and underweight all her life, a 1 in 10 prospect of dying before the end of her first year, a 1 in 5 chance of death by the age of five. In some African countries this baby's chance of being vaccinated and protected from diseases such as cholera and tuberculosis will be less than 1 in 2. Her chances of schooling (at least enough to learn to read and write) are 1 in 3. She will be chronically anaemic and overworked. Puberty will only add to her problems.

(*World Health Report 1995*)

reliance, self-denial within family and community, low social confidence, powerlessness: these are all *both* causes and effects.

The vulnerability of the girl-child is no longer only a poverty issue; it is a global affliction. Canada, the Netherlands, New Zealand, Norway, and the United States report sexual abuse during childhood and adolescence. An estimated 1 million girls and young women are forced into prostitution annually, with the largest share possibly in Asia.

The Commission believes that the formulation of a comprehensive global-action plan for girls and adolescent females is a critical component to redress many of the prevailing injustices suffered by women. The constituent elements of such action exist, although they are scattered among a host of international documents. They need pulling together within an over-arching, conceptual framework in order to articulate the political urgency of *action*—as well as recognition of subcategories by age. Such a plan should set the stage for changes truly needed.

The Meaning and Implications of Empowerment

Women are now proclaimed free and responsible in the very sphere from which, for centuries and even millennia, patriarchy derived its domination: the reproduction of the race. This is a colossal revolution—a turning-point in the understanding of women, their dignity as fully franchised human beings, no longer defined simply by their ability to procreate.

But free and responsible decisions are not made in a vacuum. They need a context of social, economic, and cultural conditions in which freedom and responsibility acquire concrete meaning. Hence the central role of women's rights must be acknowledged and fostered not only in the area of reproduction but in all societal processes. Acting to empower women supposes that not only rights are proclaimed but that social rights, too, are put at the forefront of the political agenda.

Women's empowerment as a means to strengthen women's participation in all facets of economic, social, and political life is based on the linkages between personal liberties—where no interference or coercion to affect individual conscience is permissible—and social entitlements. The latter requires affirmative action and guarantees by law and public authorities.[1]

Liberties and entitlements have to be reciprocal and responsible to avoid destruction of the social base of these rights, since rights and entitlements are relational—reflecting their social context. Uncharted, unlimited, personal liberty results in the alienation and isolation of the individual from society. From specific rights (especially concerning reproduction), women strive to have all their rights acknowledged in order to provide a framework for the shaping of their efforts to contribute to the 'shaping of life' at all levels, in all situations. Only then will visibility operate at the level of new thinking, new policies, new actions.

⟿

In the early stages of empowerment women compare the reality of their lives with the rights they have. Poor women, across all the cultures, are not familiar with the language of rights. It is *responsibilities* to which they have been socialized. Exposure to the concept of rights, and the legitimacy of rights within a given context, progressively energizes women to articulate their suppressed feelings of unfairness and injustice in a social order that does not enable them to put things right.

Through this process women assume their own identity, value themselves, increase their self-confidence and self-esteem, and then cross the threshold of fear of the feeling of powerlessness. The process does not transform women into individuals because collective needs remain their established responsibilities. Beginning with their children and the family, the responsibility easily extends to local groups and work-places with which they identify—a responsibility requiring, incidentally, some good management on their part.

Analysis of women's predicament gradually uncovers the structural questions on the power by which the status of discrimination is maintained. Women then see, from their immediate surroundings upwards to the national level, how often traditions, institutions, and decisions are built upon the power exercised on a few by the 'power' of an immense majority.

If this connection between one's own unjust situation and the structural inequalities existing in society is missed, women may benefit from different social features in their lives (e.g. better reproductive-health services) without, in fact, moving forward in their empowerment.[2] Instead of acquiring a capacity for self-determination, they will remain 'assisted' people.

When the connection is pursued, on the contrary, women discover the deep roots of discrimination and their marginalization. They are able to perceive that part of what happens to them is, in fact, the outcome of structural domination of ideological biases between the sexes. They understand that empowerment is incompatible with the down-grading of women, as it is expressed in so many different ways. Only then can women act together, trying to change the circumstances in which they live.

Once rights are proclaimed, the process of empowerment cannot stop: the rights move to the top of the political agenda. This is a radical change, and the women's movement is not likely to withdraw from this challenge.

There is a danger, of course, that empowerment may be sloganized without coming to realization—as has happened to other internationally accepted notions: *women's integration, women's participation*, and the like. There is even the danger that empowerment could become devoid of meaning.

Why, then, are so many national and international authorities ready to agree that women's empowerment should be placed at the centre of development? The only plausible reason is a dawning recognition that women are, indeed, becoming a political force, both nationally and internationally. Even those responsible for the strategies and institutions often criticized by women's groups are trying to initiate attitudes of 'genderization'. These usually translate into women-specific projects, for the economic empowerment of poor women in developing countries, as a response to the mounting evidence of the *feminization of poverty* that the growing visibility of women has brought in its wake.

When we speak of empowerment, however, we are not targeting specific groups of poor women in very difficult situations. Naturally, if such an effort had to be made these groups would receive absolute priority. But efforts made in specific directions of this kind must go hand in hand with parallel undertakings towards (and by) other groups in society. Women working in administration, in the liberal professions, in academia, and elsewhere—all these need to be mobilized for the processes of empowerment.

In society everyone is part of the structure, relating and depending upon other people. Even if small fractions of the overall society become empowered, gaining a sense of the action in their favour yet remaining isolated. Universal empowerment will not happen. The empowerment process, then, can be considered as *access to the collective identity and purposes of women in our time*. Once visible and empowered, women will be able to lay hands on the basic tools needed to shape a change in our civilization.

A New Status of Influence in the Decision-Making Processes

The sense of solidarity among women is, historically speaking, new. Women helped each other for centuries, but in ours women have shown an outstanding capacity for working together. In order to meet the challenges of the decades ahead, solidarity must now be erected upon the outcome of all the processes of empowerment.

Women no longer accept mere concessions offered by national or global power-structures. Women's organizations, formerly construing themselves as non-political, are today involved in analysing the world's political economy; they are prepared to identify, assess, and contribute to those strategies meant to sustain improvement of the quality of life. Therefore, across the spectrum of political power, women must achieve a certain status and level of influence in the making of decisions. 'More of the same will not do.'

The very process of the empowering of women will change the way in which the women themselves exercise power, for power is everywhere: from home to work-place to Cabinet to summit meetings. Power—based on competition, on 'either/or', on domination over others—produces the type of relationships and social conditions that many women reject. To become effective, the drive towards the empowerment of women must become manifest in the active promotion of global justice and the resolution of conflict by negotiation, and be driven through economic and political creativity on the part of women. The empowerment of women means, finally (as we have advocated throughout this report) *a totally new approach to the problem of population dynamics*:

- a new view of population policies, together with
- necessary changes in national structures and international institutions.

Both governments and financial institutions, as well as international agencies, must contribute to the empowerment of women by a radical shift in economic, and especially financial, policy—through shifts of priority within national budgets, extending credit to women's collective initiatives, and bringing changes to the conditions pertaining to international lending. If States and the international agencies act in a manner consistent with this recurring emphasis on the rights of women, then their priorities will have to move from a one-sided and technocratic economic balance of budgets to new policies capable of improving the social opportunities that will enable all women to exercise their proper rights.

In their turn, women will have to move away from a politics of recommendation to one of participation and *partnership*:

A New Voice, that of the Empowered Woman

Change will come about only if women, at all levels fully aware of their rights and responsibilities, express their convictions collectively. True, this will be a different voice: one seeking to integrate rather than exclude, one inciting convergence instead of separation, one abandoning abstract rights for *lived capacities*, one that places justice directly in the hands of the capacity to *care*.

partnership in managing society, the quality of life, and the fate of future generations.

Given the progress made to date as well as the perspectives opened, we believe that the world stands at the swelling of a new wave, a wave that will bring in its sweep the right and duty of women to add their experience and their culture to the organization of both society and economics. All means available should be deployed to support and make use of the women's world view that they bring to this goal.

❧ *We must formulate concepts of value and symbols allowing us to build civilizing change, a new way of living in society, moving away from the way that allows some to be better than others—in which some are allowed everything, others almost nothing.*

> Margarida Pisano, Chile
> Latin America Public Hearing

❧ *Please recommend the promotion of legal literacy, as a doorway to one's rights. We have been working in the area of legal literacy, making booklets that explain the law in simple terms to people who are literate, newly literate, and we often find even illiterate—mainly for women. These workshops not only are built around books, but also stories, songs, pictures and play acting. There was a case of a woman worker injured when working with a contractor. She injured her hand. The woman picked up the booklet which had the Workman's Compensation Act in it, and went around to*

*the rural contractor. The contractor was also a rural
man, he was just as ignorant, he had never paid compensation in his life, but they battled for two or three
days and finally he paid her a fairly large sum of money.
It is necessary for these people to be backed up by an
organization. If they have this knowledge by themselves
in isolation, they are not able to use it.*

Vasudha Dhagamwar, New Delhi
South Asia Public Hearing

*This was an approach that has us coming together and
sharing experiences. In black culture and African-
American culture, we tend not to air our dirty laundry
in public. And what we recognized as women, as we
began to share those stories, was that this conspiracy of
silence was killing us.*

*So we use many of these circles to grieve and to weep,
but we also use them to move beyond that point and
become personally empowered, to do what we need to
do as individuals and a group to make different changes
in our lives. I told a friend 'I think this idea of self-help
and talking with each other is only for people like you
and myself.' . . . My friend looked me in the eye and she
said: 'Who's hopelessness is it?' And it clicked: it was my
hopelessness.*

Cheryl Boykins, United States
North American Public Hearing

References

1. See Srilatha Batiwada, 'The Meaning of Women's Empowerment: New
   Concepts for Action', in Gita Sen, Adrienne Germain, and Lincoln C.
   Shen (eds.), *Population Policies Reconsidered—Health, Empowerment
   and Rights* (Cambridge, Mass., Harvard University Press, 1994).
2. Ibid.

Part IV

New Global Perspectives

14 Mobilizing Social Forces

Towards a New Social Contract

> *The role of the State is clearly important but, because of the magnitude of today's problems it is also important that NGOs be supported as a countervailing, co-ordinated force.*
>
> Cynthia Bautista, Philippines
> South-East Asia Public Hearing

> *The popular refectories of Lima are one response that the inhabitants of poor neighbourhoods found to solve problems collectively. Today 5,000 refectories prepare about a million daily rations of food. The refectories gave rise to other initiatives, such as the glass-of-milk committees and health-care for women.*
>
> Roelfien Haak, Peru
> Latin America Public Hearing

> *There is the rise of a global civic culture that is providing a transnational democratic foundation to challenge governments and to give them political space to act more decently and effectively. We have to remind those who think they have power that they have to really listen to the NGO world. That is where the guidance can come from. It can't come from the world, the G-7 world that they are listening to. There are a lot of people in government that feel the frustration and want to be helped from those outside.*
>
> Richard Falk, United States
> North American Public Hearing

❧ *Most pro-poor programmes and projects fail to recognize and develop the capacity of the urban poor towards self-reliance. The focus and emphasis shall be on self-reliance and mutual assistance. The Philippine Commission on Urban Poor aptly puts it: 'The poor can make it. The mystery of urban poverty lies in the fact that the poor are able to survive their present condition despite the almost inhuman situation they find themselves in. Any scheme for poverty alleviation should take cognizance of the primacy of the poor people not only in coping with their basic human needs but also in mitigating the inhuman elements in their environment so as to sustain their human dignity.'*

Cecile Joaquin-Yasay, Philippines
South-East Asia Public Hearing

❧ *The people of southern Africa have become weary of top-down policy implementations which impact directly on their lives. They want to be part of the process and not merely the passive recipient of well-intentioned, but often ill-conceived, population and quality-of-life programmes. The people of southern Africa want to be full and active participants in developing and implementing population and quality-of-life programmes which will make a real difference in their lives. The challenge is to the politicians who think vertically. We have the minister of industry, the minister of agriculture, of health. That is the problem, it is really the integration that is the challenge.*

Marvellous Mhloyi, Zimbabwe
Southern Africa Public Hearing

❧ *We live in a macro-culture that is racist, classist, and full of prejudices rooted deeply in ourselves. We have to break with this logic of domination if we are ever to be in a position to construct culture and society.*

Margarida Pisano, Chile
Latin America Public Hearing

The Need for New Societal Balance

We have created a thesis that deals with evolution amongst various societal groups. Before proceeding to a series of proposals as to how to implement much of what we recommend, let us take stock of where international society stands in terms of force mobilization.

Issues of 'population and quality of life', as we interwove them in Part II—'A Fresh Vision', and the policies that they imply require new perspectives on two essential factors constituting a revised *social contract*.

First, because any social contract concerns the paradigms operative between individuals and organized society, balance between different groups of the population is fundamental. Most traditions include in their founding myths an equilibrium between men and women, children and old people, those who are self-sufficient and those who depend on care by others, and between the concrete world and some of the transcendental elements of life. Some traditions remain part of our heritage, the task in our time being to find new but still adequate expression for them.

The transcendent element, characteristic of some great religions, has found a new focus in the integration of human beings within Nature and the universe beyond. Ecology (although a branch of science) is often how Nature is interpreted by society, while certain eclectic manifestations of individual beliefs are a phenomenon frequently exhibited.

In earlier chapters we saw how the men–women equilibrium is evolving, together with its shortcomings and its full potential. Figure 13.1 showed how the sexes are distributed in the political-power spectrum. On the basis of care, for instance, humankind has gathered elements of the Welfare State, one capable of guaranteeing to all at least a response to the need to survive. We have not yet dealt, however, with the equilibrium children–old people nor—for that matter—with an equilibrium between the living generation and what will be the differently structured age-groups of future generations.

There is a second basic factor in any contract between people and government: the relationship to property. The issues of its protection and security have been changed, over the past few centuries, by the advent of the concept of *market*; market has emerged as an autonomous element. With the end of the Cold War, a free market has become the world's dominant organizing principle in economic and social life. Competition, a critical constituent of the market system, has the extraordinary powers of:

- accelerating technological innovation;
- increasing efficiency;
- reducing the amounts of energy and materials used in production; and
- creating employment in developing countries that have healthy and educated work-forces.

❧

But we must learn to recognize the confines of markets and the ethical limits to competition. Some of the greatest challenges to modern government arise from problems that markets either cannot deal with or, in some cases, problems created by markets themselves: environmental damage, unemployment, social breakdown, crime. These undermine the caring capacities of entire societies. Considered traditionally as externalities, they cannot remain long with that status. Unless we internalize the social and environmental dimensions in the economic management of society, no real change can happen. Likewise, they cannot be resolved by unregulated markets. Only political means will assure market regulation. We should be aware, none the less, of new oversimplifications or new errors.

We urgently need a new synthesis, a new balance among the various forces that we call market, society, environment, efficiency and equity, wealth and welfare; a new balance between, on the one hand, economic growth and, on the other, social harmony and sustainable improvement in the quality of life.

We need new concepts, new instruments to enable governments to regulate markets, and sound finance so that markets will not jeopardize humankind's survival.

We need a new equilibrium capable of creating harmony among different age-groups throughout the ongoing democratic transition, between humans and Nature, between the created world and the differing forms of spiritual energy that surround and sustain our world.

Changes in Governance, At All Levels

We are witnessing in the 1990s a loss of control by national governments, together with a gradual but insidious erosion of the powers of conventional political institutions. This erosion has favoured less-publicly accountable, perhaps less-democratic, entities: banks, transnational corporations, media conglomerates. Despite the near-universal acceptance of democracy, representative government is at the same time showing signs of its incapacity in its management of some of the pressing problems of society: besides those already mentioned, such problems as increasing social disorder and the growth in drug-abuse.

The globalization process, furthermore, has so closely linked political, economic, and social activities across national frontiers that handling them demands a new system of global values and mechanisms of execution. But we run the risk of adopting mechanisms of political power devoid of the devices necessary to ensure protection and stability of the citizenry—and incapable, at the same time, of making the decisions necessary to the well-being of all countries.

Global change demands that the political class think further ahead than ever before, but we know that there is a loss of long-term vision. We have seen how electoral pressures force short-term survival tactics on people in power, enabling them to ride out periodic economic storms of various sorts. A political transition with new institutions and instruments of work is needed, combined with bold and imaginative leadership.

The three decades ahead may prove to be the most critical in history. Their primary moral challenge is to expand and realize fully our *caring capacity*:

- abolishing poverty;
- fulfilling for everyone all economic, social, and political rights; and
- improving generally the quality of life for all.

We need to find a new willingness to make sacrifices for the common good, a new surge in our caring capacity for both people and the Earth, but still remaining within the *carrying* capacity of the environment. Given that it is the responsibility of leaders to lead, what is sought is both a political climate and the kinds of institutions that will *empower people*—with participation as the central, integral feature of social interaction at all levels.

Problems build up when people are least free to publicize them, to protest. Hence democracy—freedom of association and assembly, free speech and a free press, free elections with universal suffrage, equal access to lifelong education and legal aid—is essential to humankind's ongoing adaptation to changing conditions.

The Nucleus of a New Social Contract

The social contract of the political philosophers (John Locke, Jean-Jacques Rousseau, and others) was a notional agreement that rationalized the creation of society and State. Citizens consented to be ruled by the State. In return, the State guaranteed security, justice, and the well-being of all. This (imaginary) contract thus translated into other terms the reality that States had emerged through conquest and imposed themselves without popular consent. Yet the idea of a social contract was a powerful factor in the historical shift from absolutism to democracy.

The world has greatly changed in the two centuries since Rousseau. Global interdependence now impinges on the powers of national governments, underlined further by the absence of worldwide mechanisms to deal with emerging phenomena such as planetary warming or global financial markets. Globalization has offered new opportunities, on the other hand, to tackle transnational problems that elude national solutions.

The objections frequently raised, within and among nations, concerning real power at different political levels today find adequate grounding in the original texts of, for example, Rousseau. While Rousseau listed, on one side of the ledger, what he termed *natural liberty* (what today we call total deregulation of all sectors, at all levels) and *man's limitless right to everything that is necessary to him* (today: over-consumption and the economic hegemony of several countries), he placed on the other side what we now call freedom of movement and international economic norms. So a new social contract should foresee adequate forms of individual citizenship, national sovereignty, and world order.

Given the multiple transitional processes active in a globalized world, it may now be the time to launch the concept of a *new social contract*, one forming a new basis for society's understanding of the new realities of the world. At its heart must be a new commitment to strive together for a better quality of life, and a sustainable one.

The Commission believes that a new social contract of this kind should extend to government, the population (all its men and women), Nature itself, and all the nations of the world.

Enhancing Citizenship

The basis of citizenship lies in a sense of identity, the feeling of belonging. We speak not only of belonging to the same nation or using the same language, but also of the historical events binding people together, along with the concerns they share about the future. When people belong, they care. When they care, they act— contributing to the well-being of society, acts that precede even participatory rights. Even people deprived of their civic rights sense that they are joined to all others by a kinship, that same sense of belonging. During the first free vote held in the Republic of South Africa, although it was the selection of political parties that was at stake, there was beneath this an overwhelming sensation of belonging. Making this feeling public for the first time was most important.

So the starting-point for a new social contract must be the pragmatic, and then legal, acknowledgement that sovereignty lies with the people. Political citizenship is made and remade from the bottom up, woven together from partial and sometimes contradictory efforts. This means, of course, that people are inevitably the authors of the improvement of their *own* quality of life. Empowering people to do so is not a wish; it is dialogue, action in the form of concrete projects, all within a legal framework.

Participation is still widely used as a development slogan, one not always practised meaningfully. Weak participation at the community level means that beneficiaries of a given scheme contribute their labour, cash, or land to build (or maintain) community facilities of common benefit—but with no say in their planning and management. This is an approach often used to reduce the costs of wells, health centres, primary schools, or rural roads.

Thus we see that participation may be promoted deliberately in development projects. The *level* of participation is variable, too, ranging from surveys of popular needs, through formal consultations, to rural appraisals that involve communities in direct identification of their needs, priorities, and resources.

Citizenship is, of course, part of the substance of democracy. In many countries where democracy is a recent phenomenon, citizenship is a factor that has been dignified during the process of preparing empowerment of the population. In other countries the feeling of belonging has mutated into *participation*—without implying necessarily a higher degree of full citizenship. In the latter case, democracy is not strengthened nor are the people *empowered*.

The Essentials of Participation

So that citizens' participation can become a universal right and practice, we need to build participation into government at every level, in both developing and developed countries.

Just as lack of participation induces a feeling of impotence, insecurity, and alienation, so participation brings a sense of *being able to control* what was previously thought to be beyond our influence. If participation is encouraged in one sphere of life, the attitudes that it creates carry over to other domains: from health and family-size to housing and environment. Participation means that people take an active part in the decisions closely affecting life at home, at work, and in the community. Strong local participation means that the people conceive, design, execute, manage, and evaluate local programmes. In the case of ongoing public services, the population helps set goals and their priorities, and assesses the quality of the services delivered.

So full participation at the community level by all sections of the population—including women, the poor, the landless—ensures that development responds to popular needs because planning is based on local knowledge and expertise as well as on the local cultural and economic realities. Participation can transform, thereby, communities from passive recipients of governmental activity into partners.

Real participation is found, one must add, throughout the developing countries. In burgeoning cities such as Lima and Manila people have spontaneously created organizations that fight for land rights or develop community services.[1] Encouraging participation is not, however, a question only of creating the proper institutional framework. It means, also, creating the conditions in which every individual and group can assume active roles.

Politically speaking, then, citizen participation signifies that people have the right to influence or decide policy—not only indirectly, through democratic representatives—but directly, too, via town meetings, public referenda, and the like. This is most important in an era when representative democracy is sometimes seen as *weak participation*: in most countries the proportion of people truly active in the democratic processes is, indeed, small.

Meaningful participation in the political process often includes writing letters of incitation, organizing petitions, creating organizations, producing pamphlets, *using* the existing legal and political frameworks. Needed for all such activities are information and education: exposure to civic rights and duties should be part of the curricula followed in primary and secondary schools. Developing all these different forms of participation only deepens and enriches representative democracy, integrally part of the new social contract.

Devolution of power is critical, even a pre-condition, to participation. Not simply handing over discretionary powers—but transferring real decision-making and tax-levying to locally elected, locally accountable bodies. In the industrializing countries devolution must also mean a fairer distribution of governmental spending between urban and rural areas—bringing services closer to their users, in direct response to need. In the European Union this principle (subsidiarity) has gained prominence as the means to ensure that decisions are taken, and implemented, at the lowest possible level.

Mobilizing the Social Forces Within Civil Society

The overwhelming interest and participation of all kinds of organizations in the UN global conferences organized in the 1990s is not accidental. This is the 'tip of the iceberg' in a wide social process affecting all the continents: the emergence of organized civil society.

The renewed interest in the effectiveness of civil society may have its origins in the partnership that developed, beginning in the 1950s, between some organizations in the North and the liberation movements of the South. After decolonization, the struggle for democracy and in defence of human rights provided a new impetus everywhere for organized forms of dissent or intervention. Since the 1960s development projects also have been in many cases opportunities to experience social transformation originating at the grass roots. Civil-society organizations in the industrialized countries, with their established history of the nation-state, of course, had an earlier start—sometimes centuries ago.

Whether in old States or new, however, the *raison d'être* for the organization and mobilization of civil society has been to defend causes and to supply goods or services that neither the State nor other established institutions could (or would) deliver. Motivations leading to the organization of civil-society entities are many in their orientation, scope, and dimensions. Some emerge from the desire to defend one's immediate condition, others by an inner conviction that 'things can change', while others express anger or revolt

Significance of the Phenomena of Civil Society

Any new social contract should be expected to transcend the relationships between a government and its people, an arrangement not to be equated with the so-called *social question* reflecting the capital–labour dichotomy of the past. Civil society conjures up, in other words, a picture of the *multiplicity of* interests and causes constituting societal structure, treating them as a continuous process of self-reproduction.

against what should be done but is not being done. Some of the motivations are political in origin; others have a moral or even religious impulse.

Civil society, we see, is not merely a juxtaposition of new institutions paralleling the State and the market institutions. Its landscape is varied, changeable. During periods of strong social movements an organized civil society seemed possible. Today the situation is different: civil-society groups vary in the causes they stand for, in their goals. Some are structured, capable of action with a sense of continuity; others are of a more 'prophetic' nature, likely to act intensively in a more episodic way. Still others endure changes from outside or within, intervening with forms of action that are permanent or else change during the entity's lifetime. Once empowered, citizens are quite capable of turning to those forms of organized action allowing them to apply pressure where they themselves are affected. The multiplicity of these forms of action, their cross-fertilization and their potential for confrontation create an enormous vitality within the social fabric. Only when all this comes to pass can we speak coherently of a *civil society*.

So it will be a new form of social contract that determines how civil society can be active throughout public life, expanding the rationale and developing the organization and functioning of its applications. It will be important, too, to find arrangements for the representation of civil society in an environment that is in constant flux. This is precisely what many such organizations, here and there in different countries and across national frontiers, are doing today more than ever before.

The work remaining to be done to put to work our fresh vision regarding population problems may well emerge from a vital civil society. Needed also to bring the social contract to life are firm commitments to the ideal of a right to the quality of life for all, and individual, group, and institutional caring capacity. Although we may not reach total social harmony in the process, we should move towards major changes that will strengthen social cohesion and promise a liveable future for the generations to come.

This report thus challenges the new, market-force governments to take on their part of the real responsibilities—and not regard private capital as an alternative to government itself.

❧ *In the process of re-democratization and increasing affirmation of citizen's rights in Latin America, it is important to analyse the other facet of citizenship—that of responsibility and the construction of spheres of public participation. These spaces and spheres are outside the family, they go beyond the domestic sphere, but they are not as distant as the State sphere. Reinventing the public sphere and spaces for public participation where the State can be present—by invitation—would represent a novelty that needs to be explored. I believe that the challenge for the 21st century is to think creatively about these different spheres of participation.*

Elisabeth Jelim, Argentina
Latin America Public Hearing

❧ *The devolution of responsibilities—delivery of basic services—and resources (a greater share from the national income, broader taxing powers) are radical changes considering our history of centralized government. But what is truly revolutionary about the Local Government Code is its philosophy of power and governance. Local Government Units 'shall promote the establishment and operation of people's organizations and non-government organizations to become active partners in the pursuit of local autonomy.' Democratization and empowerment, however, are not limited to the political aspect of governance. Public order, especially in the urban areas, is another area where the involvement of the community is essential. Hence, what the Code calls for is democratization—nothing less than a real 'power shift' from the national to local, from government to the people, from bureaucracy to citizen's organizations.*

Rafael M. Alunan III, Philippines
South-East Asia Public Hearing

❧ *I believe in the citizenry. I believe that, if the world wants to change, it has to begin with the citizen, but for that it is necessary that each person, each citizen, believes first and foremost in him or herself. That is what differentiates us from two extremes—on the one hand, from those who do not know that other people exist and, on the other, from those who only believe in institutions. For me today, the great avenue towards change is to manage to build a new culture, that is democratic culture, the culture of citizenship. . . .*

We are creating the cultural conditions for an extremely important change, for generating a new culture that has ethics as its base, that subordinates everything to ethics and that places the citizen at the centre of changing the world. For me, that is quite transparently clear, but every day I come up against thousands of people whose beliefs are those of the past, who still live by a culture of the past . . . This appeal to citizenry is completely new in Brazil. Here we were organised— like any modern society—into institutions.

In the family, there are persons, but outside the family what exists is the party, the trade union. . . . They forgot that there exists a thing called 'I', the individual, the person, the fundamental agent of all that happens in the world.

Herbert de Souza (Betinho), Brazil
Latin America Public Hearing

➤ *The basic social result of Russian transformations is the atomization and disintegration of society. We go to civil society from rigid society with unitarian and totalitarian features, paternalism and bureaucracy. Public relationships are being destroyed, an individual becomes unprotected from power structures (or their lack of power), from lawlessness and corruption, from bad economic development and poverty, from ecological and technological catastrophes. Only one structure turned out to be stable under such conditions. This is the family.*

Natalia Rimachevskaya, Moscow
Eastern Europe Public Hearing

➤ *Bearing in mind the need to broaden the concept (of civil society) and break out of the polarized straitjacket of public and private, where public is the State and private is profit—businesses operating on the market—we formulated and developed this concept of private initiatives in the public interest, which characterizes a third sector of society, coexisting with the public sector in the strict sense—the State—and with the private, for-profit sector—the market. This concept of a third sector seems to me to be far richer than the previous notion of organized civil society and, most importantly, it opens up the prospect of new, far more flexible interactions with the first and second sectors. The campaign against hunger and poverty in Brazil, the movement against violence in Rio de Janeiro, the experience of the popular canteens in Peru and the experience of job placement in Chile are several instances of this new formula.*

Miguel Darcy de Oliveira, Brazil
Latin America Public Hearing

References

1. Paul Harrison, *The Third World Tomorrow* (Harmondsworth, Penguin Books, 1980).

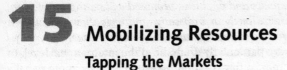

15 Mobilizing Resources

Tapping the Markets

> ❧ *It is not so much the North versus the South, I would*
> *say that it is the North of the North and the North of the*
> *South that are coalescing to oppress the South of the*
> *North and the South of the South.*
>
> D. Bandyopadhyay, India
South Asia Public Hearing

The Need for New Directions, New Departures

Over a substantial period of time enormous resources will be
needed to translate into reality the ambitious action-plans adopted
by the global conferences held between 1990 and 1995: on environment, population, human rights, social development, and women.
Rarely before has the financial impact of such multilateral policy
directives and recommendations been realistically costed.
(Heretofore, the foreseeable costs to society were expressed in
descriptive, non-operational terms. Potential overlaps and redun-
dancies were not taken into account.)

Throughout the present report, the Commission has identified
objectives and strategies intended to achieve a sustainable
improvement in the quality of life, including prescriptions
addressed to a variety of sectors of human activity. Many changes
in policy, priority, and approaches will be needed to enhance the
overall quality of life—and to extend it to the additional 4 billion
people who will be added to the world's population during the
coming five decades.

The Commission is aware that, in order to have the desired

impact, *the policies and measures proposed will require substantial resources, either directly or indirectly, and well above the current levels. These resources must be raised nationally or internationally.*

The needs are particularly dramatic at the international level. In recent years official development assistance (ODA, more usually known as aid) first stagnated then declined effectively in real monetary terms—despite a mushrooming of needs and demands for assistance. Better management and a higher level of efficiency of the present regime of aid will not, in itself, be sufficient to deliver the additional resources needed.

Rather, innovative mechanisms must be developed and put into operation, supplementing—and eventually replacing—the prevailing approach of relying on (sometimes mandatory, assessed) contributions by governments and the solicitation of private donations through NGOs.

The end of the Cold War signified not only that democracy had prevailed. It meant also that the markets, by now enveloping the whole world in an invisible web, had won the predominant organizing and allocating means to support the world's resources and economies. Hence it is only logical to stipulate that markets ought also to play a key role in generating the funds required to finance, on a sustainable and long-term basis, the staggering tasks already outlined.

The Self-Help Imperative: Mobilizing National Resources

All too often discussions on abolishing poverty or fulfilling rights claim that the job can be done only with a 'massive' transfer of resources from North to South. The first level of resource mobilization, however, is on the national plane.

Given the political will, countries whose annual income is on the order of $2,000–$3,000 per capita (expressed, again, in 'international' dollars at purchasing-power parity) should be in a position, theoretically, to fulfil most economic and social rights. This would be accomplished largely by designing effective policies, targeting available national resources in terms of funds and personnel, and then managing them with effect. A Norwegian study in 1995 revealed that for each tax dollar collected in Latin America, five tax dollars were collected in Europe.

But the poorer developing countries that have real per-capita incomes below $2,000–$3,000 are bound to experience difficult problems in improving the quality of life. At this level the potential for raising taxes is lower and the skills needed to staff public services are scarcer. Hence the poorer countries need to rely, to a considerable extent, on external resources.

Targeting National Resources

Prior to the World Summit for Social Development (1995), UNDP and UNICEF had proposed a '20 : 20 compact' under the terms of which donors would agree to give at least 20 per cent of their foreign aid for priority goals—basic education, primary health care, clean-water supply, family-planning services), while the developing countries themselves would earmark 20 per cent of their budgets for the same areas of activity. The corresponding shares operative during the early 1990s were 7 per cent of (foreign) development assistance and 13 per cent of the developing countries' budgets.[1]

At the Social Development Summit in Copenhagen this proposal was not accepted by all countries as a firm plan of action. It was seen, instead, as a recommendation that 'interested developed and developing country partners' might take up if they wished. The Commission now urges that all countries and international intergovernmental bodies accept and implement the 20 : 20 compact as a valuable policy target and that they integrate it within their policies.[2]

The Commission believes, however, that the 20-per cent target should be nothing less than a first step. A growing portion of national resources and external assistance should be devoted to sustainable improvement in the quality of life, especially for primary education, adult literacy, primary health care, family planning, basic housing, adequate nutrition, women's equality, fundamental legal services, and the building and support of NGOs and information services in order to support democracy.

Debt Relief: Freeing the Public Resources

High levels of debt are a serious obstacle to providing sufficient levels of national resources for improving the quality of life in poor countries. Indebtedness has risen ceaselessly, soaring to a record US$1,945 billion by April 1994, and entailing annual debt-servicing obligations of $199 billion. The total 'debt stock' of the thirty-two most severely indebted, low-income countries (twenty-five of them in Africa) quadrupled between 1980 and 1984.[3]

Therefore substantial debt relief, for both official and commercial debt, must remain a top priority—especially for the least developed nations, as this would free substantial resources for allocation to quality-of-life related sectors.

Several avenues are available to respond to this priority: rescheduling, outright cancellation, or forgiveness. Governmental and commercial debtors should implement the various terms devised for debt-repayment in a more comprehensive and meaningful fashion than prevails today. And, at long last, official and commercial debt-relief must be complemented through means intended to lower the burden of multilateral debt, hitherto treated as a taboo.

Depending on a country's specific situation, other, more innovative debt-reduction devices could be arranged. An attractive possibility is to swap commercial and official debt in exchange for a governmental undertaking to pursue certain programmes related to the environment or to social development. Such swaps meet a dual objective: they help to reduce debt, while financing commendable environmental or social endeavours, creating in turn substantial leverage in order to obtain donor funds.

International Trade: A Prerequisite for Generating Resources and Jobs

The most direct and effective way to generate the needed national resources and create more jobs is to enable developing countries to earn more through international trade. The anticipated benefits of a reduction by the North of tariffs and quotas on exports would dwarf the volume of official development-assistance flows.

A study by the World Bank of fourteen aid-receiving countries has shown that removing OECD trade barriers could lead to increases in annual exports equivalent to aid increases of between 46 and 623 per cent. In twelve of these countries trade liberalization would be equivalent to reducing the debt-service burden by more than half; indeed, in seven cases the liberalization would be worth more than complete cancellation of debt payments. The same study seemed to have had little impact, however, on the contents of the final package adopted because there remain many trade barriers against imports arriving from developing countries.[4]

So the conclusion of the GATT Uruguay round is nothing but the beginning of continuous trade-battles for the developing countries. Other measures must be urgently agreed to in order to improve developing-country access to industrialized markets for the commodities and other products of the Third World.

Further reduction of tariffs on agricultural, manufactured, and semi-manufactured goods need to be combined with a phasing out of subsidies for—and the dumping of—agricultural produce from the North. To this end, the World Trade Organization should initiate, without delay, new rounds of global-trade negotiations aimed at creating a 'level playing-field' for all countries and thus preparing the ground for the creation of new jobs.

The Role of Official Development Assistance (ODA)

In 1970 the UN General Assembly set out for the first time, through Resolution 2626 (XXV) on the International Development Strategy for the Second United Nations Development Decade, agreed targets for financial-resource transfers and ODA flows:

Each economically advanced country should endeavour to provide by 1972 annually to developing countries financial-resource transfers of a minimum net amount of 1 per cent of its gross national product at market prices in terms of actual disbursements . . . Those developed countries which are unable to achieve this target by 1972 will endeavour to attain it not later than 1975.[5]

In recognition of the special importance which can be fulfilled only by official development assistance, a major part of financial-resource transfers to the developing countries should be provided in the form of official development assistance. Each economically advanced country will progressively increase its official development assistance to the developing countries and will exert its best efforts to reach a minimum net amount of 0.7 per cent of its gross national product at market prices by the middle of the Decade.[6]

Since 1970 the target of 0.7 per cent of the GNP of industrialized countries to be devoted to ODA (comprising both bilateral and multilateral funding) has been reaffirmed, in many fora, with varying degrees of commitment. The latter is manifest in differently worded formulas that each time had to be (re-)negotiated painstakingly, be it at the 'Earth Summit' in Rio de Janeiro in 1992, the Conference on Population and Development (Cairo, 1994), or the World Summit on Social Development (Copenhagen, 1995).

A quarter-century after the adoption of this landmark resolution, its goals and targets remain elusive, unfulfilled by many countries. Only four industrialized nations (Denmark, Netherlands, Norway, and Sweden) have individually met—and even exceeded—the target of 0.7 per cent.

On average, the aggregate performance of the members of the Development Assistance Committee (DAC) of the OECD (the industrialized countries, to remind) fell far short of the target of 0.7 per cent. In 1975 the ODA portion stood at 0.36 per cent; it dropped in 1992 to 0.32 per cent, and hit bottom in 1993 at 0.30 per cent—less than 50 per cent of the solemn commitment made earlier. By applying the target figure of 0.7 per cent to the GNP of 1993 for all the OECD countries, the flow of ODA to the developing countries would have been $130.2 billion in that year, compared with the real $55.96 billion transferred.

The changed political climate in many of the donor countries presages an even further decline in commitment to development aid and probably increasing hostility to international institutions and multilateral causes. There is no doubt that escalating global needs are unlikely to be addressed with this shrinking fraction of the ODA target. Beyond the 'aid fatigue' felt in the donor countries, however, this trend also reflects a more fundamental turnabout in development funding, whereby private *investment* is replacing *aid* as the primary engine of economic development.

The Commission is concerned that the present trend in official-aid flows contravenes the spirit of all international agreements and solemn undertakings. Every effort must be made to arrest the downward trend and to work towards an early realization of the hitherto all-but elusive goal of 0.7 per cent of GNP donated by the industrialized countries. Even if new mechanisms were to be adopted, they will take time to become effective. Thus, ODA will need to continue playing a critical role in supplementing national resources.

Targeting ODA on the Quality of Life

In 1992 only 29 per cent of ODA went to human resources and agriculture. Within this percentage, a total of 8.4 per cent went to education and 3.7 per cent to health and population. UNDP calculated that during 1989–91 only 16 per cent of ODA was tabbed for social purposes: education, health and family planning, welfare, water, sanitation, housing and amenities, and social security. Much of this 16 per cent went to large hospitals and universities. A mere 7 per cent was allocated to assuring the most basic of the economic and social rights: basic education, primary health care, and clean water.[7]

In future, international grant-aid and concessional loans should be more consciously targeted towards sustainable improvement in the quality of life—especially by those not currently enjoying it, the poorest strata of the population in low-income countries.

Redirection of aid will require better statistics than those currently available on the uses to which foreign aid is put. Data are currently collected by the OECD's DAC. In DAC's annual *Development Co-operation* report there is no breakdown within each category. Education and health, for example, do not indicate the shares attributed to primary, secondary, or tertiary levels of teaching or to primary health care or hospitals.[8] The Commission recommends, therefore, that DAC initiate discussions intended to refine the statistics covering grants by donor nations, permitting a breakdown by purpose.

The Commission also believes that, at present, much aid is distributed in inverse proportion to needs. If we group countries by real income, the poor countries with incomes averaging under

$2,000 received only $8.23 per person in 1991. Those with per-capita incomes of $3,000–$4,000 received seven times as much, and those with per-capita revenue of $4,000–$5,000 obtained twelve times as much.[9] A more equitable distribution of existing assistance flows would make an enormous difference, in itself, to the poorest people in the poorest countries.

It is absurd, furthermore, that assistance and grants to areas such as Singapore, Hong Kong, and Israel be counted as 'development assistance' when these entities are richer than some donors of aid. To correct such imbalances, the Commission recommends that assistance flows to countries with real incomes of more than $3,000 per person (in 1992 international dollars at purchasing-power parity) should no longer be officially classified as ODA.

～

The geographical distribution of aid is of interest, because at present it does not always relate to needs. (See Figure 15.1) Botswana, one of the richest countries of sub-Saharan Africa (with real income per capita of $4,690 in 1992), received more than 3.5 times per person as Ethiopia—where income averaged only $340. Thailand received the same aid per person as Bangladesh, although Thai incomes were five times higher. Singaporeans received more aid per person than Nigerians, who had one-twelfth the income of the former.[10]

A redirection of aid of this sort could have an impressive impact. In 1991 almost $16 billion was given to countries with incomes averaging more than $3,000. Had this assistance been redistributed to countries where incomes averaged below $2,000 (leaving countries in the $2,000–$3,000 band unaffected), then aid per person in the poorest countries would have been 75 per cent higher. Further still, if half the aid to poor countries were redirected to the poor and vulnerable *within* these countries, then the impact of aid on raising the quality of life could be augmented by at least a factor of five.

Another innovative approach would be to earmark a percentage of ODA for monitoring its applications at the grass roots, helping to avoid misallocations and misuse of development funds.

It is in this spirit, therefore, that the Commission urges all donor countries to re-examine radically their bilateral aid programmes.

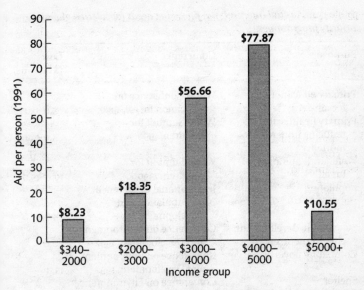

Fig. 15.1. Aid and real need, disparities between aid transferred and income level of recipients (1991). Does aid go where it is most needed?

The aim should be to shift priorities, phased over a period of three to five years, to improve the quality of life for the benefit of countries with real incomes (at purchasing-power parity, of course) below the $3,000 level, giving the obvious advantage to the most disadvantaged regions and groups within these countries.

Consolidating International Commitments

Estimates made in connection with recent international conferences on the cost of reaching their own sets of targets provide a glimpse of the volume of funds required. Table 15.1 lists, in an indicative manner only, some of the major commitments of the 1990s. The sums cannot be added to provide an arithmetical total because of overlaps or double counting. In too many cases no costing has been prepared, as in the instance of the conference on women held at Beijing (given the importance attached to the

Table 15.1. *Annual international financing needs for selected global-priority programmes.*[11]

Purpose	Conference	Cost ($ billions)
Primary education for all	World Conference on Education for All, 1990	5.0–6.0
Primary health care: reducing under-5 mortality	World Summit for Children, 1990	5.0–7.0
Water and sanitation for all	World Summit for Children, 1990	10.0–15.0
Population	International Conference on Population and Development, 1994	5.7
Sustainable development: environment, etc.	Conference on Environment and Development, 1992	80.0
Combating poverty	Conference on Environment and Development, 1992	15.0
Shelter	Conference on Environment and Development, 1992	25.0

empowering of women), or else price-tags were attached to only some elements of a programme.[12]

The Commission finds this situation untenable, undermining the relevance of and credibility of international conferences as corrective instruments. The Commission therefore calls on the Secretary-General of the United Nations to draw up—as a matter of urgency—a comprehensive and detailed inventory of all internationally agreed priority programmes, together with their cost estimates or financing commitments. The inventory should be established in conjunction with the component institutions of the UN system and other multilateral organizations. This exercise could then be followed up, ideally, by a system-wide consolidation of targets.

Where costings are presented, moreover, funds are lacking. It is increasingly apparent that internationally agreed programmes and their priorities, in the sphere of economic and social development as well as elsewhere, remain a dead letter because of a dearth of internationally provided resources. Action plans fail, for example, to specify concrete mechanisms as to how the requisite funding is to be obtained. There is routine reference to an ODA goal of 0.7 per cent, an affirmation that sounds more and more hollow since some countries have adopted an almost reflexive stance of resisting calls for any binding commitment whatsoever.

It is clear that the sums needed to meet globally agreed priorities in areas pertinent to quality of life greatly exceed what is currently available and what may (optimistically) be anticipated in the future on the basis of present approaches and funding mechanisms. Development assistance in 1993 totalled $56 billion. Even by making allowances for double counting and overlapping, the commitments shown in Table 15.1 approach $150 billion per year. This indicates the order of magnitude of the international funding resources that might be needed to reach a selected list of goals agreed upon globally. And this is not all.

A myriad other international commitments must be met, too: the budget (for organizational infrastructure) of the United Nations and its programmes, the specialized agencies, the regional development banks and other institutions, the costs of UN peacekeeping, These important activities are plagued by other problems as well, given that assessed and thus legally binding contributions are either not paid at all or are paid only partially—or not paid on time by a surprisingly large number of governments.

The sad fact is that very little additional resources have been mobilized in recent years to respond to the many needs identified at the UN Conferences in Rio, Cairo, Copenhagen, and Beijing. The only new mechanism so far is the Global Environment Facility (GEF). However, the funds available within GEF are limited, an estimated US$2 billion for the time period 1996–8 to assist developing countries to 'increment costs' associated with measures to protect the climate, biodiversity, and oceans. As an illustration, in the field of energy production alone, total annual investments in the world amount to US$60–70 billion, the vast majority of this still devoted to conventional fossil fuel energy. The resources of the GEF are marginal in this context and have little chance of making the required impact in the face of the enormity of the tasks and needs. Hence, if we are serious about the climate convention and other international commitments, there is an urgent need to explore ways to mobilize additional resources.

Alternative Mechanisms for Financing Global Priorities

The Commission is convinced that the world urgently needs new mechanisms for funding the global priorities (primary health care, water, basic education, family planning, and so forth). Relying on the faltering generosity and sagging payment morale of individual nations is no longer adequate. The globalization of economic, environmental, and other problems requires both global institutions commensurate with the task and financing mechanisms scaled to global dimensions. These mechanisms should be capable of delivering the kinds of sums involved; they should be free, also, of the budgetary constraints of individual countries—where foreign aid is inevitably an easy option in the reduction of funds.

This should be the hour of the markets, that is to say, those bodies that have been the principal beneficiaries of the globalization of virtually all activities, and that are dependent on a global network of interdependence—woven together, maintained, and continuously upgraded by multilateral co-operation.

Many suggestions have been put forward in recent years for novel mechanisms meant for global fund-raising. The Commission ordered a detailed, expert study on new funding mechanisms (see note 12). Some of the means proposed will involve formidable (and, sometimes, perhaps insurmountable) conceptual, technical, and political difficulties. For example: taxes on the international arms trade, or redirecting the 'peace dividend' into a Global Demilitarization Fund or else a Global Human Security Fund.[13] (See Fig. 15.2 for some comparisons.)

Other, more limited mechanisms might also be attractive: tradeable permits to emit carbon dioxide, issued to all countries on an internationally agreed basis, could be sold by poor developing countries to rich nations, yielding revenue to be earmarked for quality-of-life purposes. This measure would also improve inter-

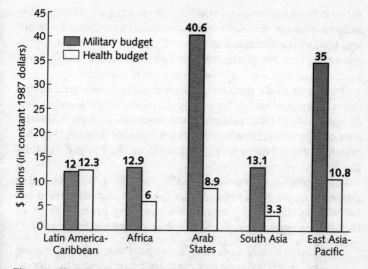

Fig. 15.2. Human security priorities (1990), contrasting military budgets with public-health expenditures.
Source: *World Military and Social Priorities* (1993).

national equity, while contributing to the reduction of greenhouse-gas emissions. The UN Conference on Trade and Development (UNCTAD) is currently developing a pilot scheme for such emission permits. The Commission encourages UNCTAD to proceed speedily with this project, although it should be borne in mind that tradeable permits of this sort would be bought and sold directly among the permit-holders. They would not yield funds to finance global-priority programmes.

Another novel instrument, debt-swaps, could help in the pursuit of the dual objectives of debt reduction and fostering sustainable improvement in the quality of life for individual nations. Their design and effects depend largely, however, on the circumstances surrounding each case and country. Funds released through such swaps are bound to benefit only the individual countries involved, and the funds are unlikely to accrue for the benefit of global programmes. Thus the potential of this instrument for raising funds meant to support international programmes is limited.

Other potentially promising schemes include levies on airline tickets or on aviation fuel; on international postage; and on the allocation ('sale') of telecommunication frequencies. There is also the idea of an international lottery, with the profits devoted to global priorities. Few of these proposals have been studied in detail thus far.

The Commission recommends that the UN General Assembly adopt an omnibus resolution requesting detailed study of the feasibility, potential yield, and eventual operating procedures of all these financing mechanisms with multilateral aims, specifically:

- the International Civil Aviation Organization (ICAO) should study various levies on passenger traffic and freight in international civil aviation, in consultation with the International Air Transport Association and the Airports Council International;

- ICAO, the UN Environment Programme (UNEP), and UNCTAD should examine a potential levy on aviation fuel;

- the International Maritime Organization of the UN should study a charge on international ocean freight and international ocean cruises;

- the International Telecommunications Union of the UN (ITU) should examine a potential levy on the allocation of international telecommunication frequencies and of subsequent annual user charges;

- ITU and the UN's Committee on the Peaceful Uses of Outer Space should study potential charges on communication satellites;

- the Universal Postal Union of the UN (UPU) should study a potential surcharge on international postal items; and

- the World Trade Organization of the UN and UNCTAD should study possible taxes on international commerce in goods and services.

All such studies should be submitted to the General Assembly not later than 1997.

The UN Secretary-General should also appoint a group of experts, with experience in national-lottery management, to develop concrete proposals for establishing an international lottery.

As to peacekeeping and peacemaking, the Commission recommends that—in order to instil an element of automaticity and allow for speedy deployment in peacekeeping operations—the United Nations be allowed recourse to Special Drawing Rights (SDR). To this end, the Articles of Agreement of the International Monetary Fund (IMF) would need to be revised so as to permit the allocation of SDRs in another way than currently envisaged, one restricted to peace-related activity. The allocation of such SDRs could be tied to a fixed life-span instead of being permanent—as is the case with SDRs at present. The possibility of extension, too, should be envisaged.

Tapping the Globalized Financial Markets

The Commission concludes that the most promising source of finance for global priorities, in terms of yield, would be an international charge on all transactions in the world's financial markets: currencies, bonds and other securities, derivatives, and stock shares.

This idea stems from a proposal made by the Nobel laureate James Tobin, who first suggested in 1972 that a tax on 'spot' dealings in the international currency market would discourage short-term speculation. In recent years Tobin has also suggested that such a tax might be a promising source of finance for the global priorities that pre-occupy us in the present report.[14]

Tobin's principal motive has remained, however, to dampen speculative activities that are considered destabilizing. Speculation of this kind has reached epidemic proportions in the recently deregulated markets, wreaking havoc with national economic policies.

The total turnover in currency markets alone is inflated far beyond the underlying economic realities: on a single day in April

1992 turnover totalled $880 billion—more than three times the GNP of the whole of sub-Saharan Africa.

Computed on an annual basis (240 working days) this sum translates as some $211 *trillion*, more precisely $211,200,000,000,000, or nearly ten times the entire world's GNP in 1992.[15] During a subsequent survey conducted in April 1995, the daily turnover on the same market soared to a mind-boggling $1.3 trillion, and present trends point to even stronger growth.

The revenue potential of a charge on currency transactions is evident. Even assuming possible evasion in the wake of imposition of the charge, independent brokers or dealers specializing in trading and technical adjustments may handle more than $100 trillion annually. A charge of a mere 0.01 per cent could conceivably yield $100 billion a year, or about twice the current level of ODA. At such a level the new charge would be unlikely to interfere with market activity, although it might have a moderating influence on the extent of speculation.

Depending on trading elasticities, there is a risk that speculators and other market actors might shift into other, non-taxed areas of the globalized financial markets. Given the interlinkages existing among the various sub-markets—those of currency exchange, securities and bonds, stock-shares, and derivatives—it is advisable not to deal with each of these market segments in isolation.

For this reason the Commission recommends that a flat transaction charge should be levied uniformly, equally, and universally on all present and future types of financial transaction occurring in the globalized market-place. If the levy were fixed at a rate of 0.01 per cent of each transaction, the potential yield is estimated to exceed, conservatively speaking, $150 billion annually. This sum, in itself, could go a long way towards financing all of the globally agreed priorities advanced in this report.

Many preliminary steps would be needed to prepare the ground for installation of the charge recommended. First required would be the collection of accurate and reliable data on financial transactions world-wide in all of the sub-markets involved. Data collection on financial transactions would need improvement over what exists. The Bank for International Settlements (BIS) and its members, together with the members of the G7 and G10 groupings as well as the members of the Interim Committee of the IMF, will have to play a leading role in this enterprise, together with the appropriate professional associations of the financial-services industry.

Software programming would also be needed to monitor dealings under way among a very large number of participants, operating in a decentralized and largely unregulated manner. The financial-services industry should develop and harmonize electronic dealing and trading programmes (or other electronic means) by which to capture all transactions with precision and rigour.

The fee charged would have to be collected by national central banks, and collection would be required of every member of the IMF or the World Bank as a condition for receiving loans from them. The proceeds of the collection could be deposited in a Global Priority Fund, for example, under the auspices of the BIS. Other institutional solutions are possible.

Finally, a new international authority would have to be created to administer the substantial funds collected, to review the mechanism's operation, and to distribute the proceeds in accordance with internationally agreed priorities. The membership, voting mechanics, and powers of such an authority would remain to be decided, but this would provide the opportunity to establish a novel structure involving all major stakeholders, including:

- representatives of civil society, including
- specific non-governmental organizations;
- the private sector;
- parliaments; and
- national governments.

Existing organizations, which would need to compete for the funds to be made available, would participate in an advisory capacity. The governing body would be charged with the setting of priorities, determining the specifics of operations, management, oversight, review and evaluation, and enforcement.

❧

Creating the basis for the global tax and its fund will doubtless be a lengthy process taking many years, possibly a decade. But a beginning must be made. And what better time is there than the very first years of the second half-century of the United Nations? The first five decades resulted in the emergence of powerful concepts of human rights and rights to quality of life. Many frustrations have been encountered, of course, and (most disturbing of all) poverty is mushrooming, as we have shown in our report. Now is the time to 'put teeth' in all the proclamations and action plans. Preparatory work for a global convention on transaction charges should begin, therefore, without delay.

To this end, the Commission recommends that a small group of high-level international financial experts be appointed under the auspices of the United Nations or the Bretton Woods institutions to study and report on the details of the introduction of a global transaction charge on the financial activities already described.

If international priority programmes could be financed by the money markets through the first truly international levy—globally agreed, globally paid, with genuine global ownership—the novelty would herald a revolutionary shift in international relations. Governments would no longer have the exclusive right, for instance, to decide about global priority programmes; nor would they have any longer the exclusive responsibility to fund such programmes—or not to finance them, as is so often the case.

These grand schemes and manifold proposals notwithstanding, ODA is bound to remain the backbone, for many years to come, of the international development effort. In order to preserve the viability of the present multilateral arrangements—no matter how unsatisfactory these may be—the Commission urges once again that a determined, international effort be the minimum action taken to arrest the present downward trend in ODA, inducing the industrialized countries to fulfil their commitment of 0.7 per cent of their GNP as quickly as possible.

With global wealth increasing by some $700 billion each year, the funds are there to end absolute poverty early in the twenty-first century and to conserve our planet's threatened biodiversity. The knowledge exists, together with the wherewithal. What must be added now are the will and the act. If we care enough, if we are committed enough, everything is possible.

References

1. UN Development Programme, *Human Development Report 1994* (Oxford, Oxford University Press, 1994).
2. *Programme of Action of the World Summit for Social Development* (Copenhagen, 1995).
3. World Bank, *World Debt Tables 1994–95* (Washington, 1995).
4. World Bank, *Global Economic Prospects and the Developing Countries 1993* and *Global Economic Prospects and the Developing Countries 1995* (Washington, 1993, 1995).
5. General Assembly Resolution 2626 (XXV) of 24 October 1970.
6. Ibid.
7. Development Assistance Committee, *Development Co-operation 1994* (Paris, OECD, 1994); UN Development Programme, *Human Development Report 1994*.
8. DAC, *Development Co-operation 1994*.
9. Calculations made by the Commission from World Bank, *World Development Indicators 1994* (data diskettes).
10. UN Development Programme, *Human Development Report 1994*.
11. UN Development Programme, *Human Development Report 1994*; *Report of the International Conference on Population and Development* (doc. A/CONF./171/13) (New York, UN, 1995); *Agenda 21*, Rio de Janeiro (UN, 1992).
12. Dragoljub Najman and Hans d'Orville, *Towards a New Multi-lateralism: Funding Global Priorities* (Paris and New York, Independent Commission on Population and Quality of Life, 1995).
13. See UN Development Programme, *Human Development Report 1994*.
14. James Tobin, *A Currency Transactions Tax* (paper prepared for the Conference on Globalization of Markets; rev.) (Rome, CIDEI University, 1995).
15. Bank for International Settlements, *Central Bank Survey of Foreign-Exchange Market Activity in April 1992* (Basel, 1992).

16 Conclusions and Recommendations

We have seen throughout this report how the relationship between population and quality of life leads us to be concerned with new and holistic perspectives. In 25 years more than 4 billion people will be most probably added to the 6 billion foreseen for the year 2000. These people must be free from want. How then do we reach such a goal when we have already today in our midst one poor among every four persons?

The task ahead is at the same time a qualitative one—to provide for every human being a life worth living—and a quantitative one—to move towards the stabilization of the global population.

Our attempt in this book is to show how the two goals are inter-twined and can be reached if some all-embracing, fundamental concepts and practices can be followed. Many factors are to be tackled if we want to seize this opportunity.

The many factors include: making life more liveable through improved individual and collective health and security; dealing with the scourges of poverty and exclusion; raising the levels of literacy, education, and access to needed information; rationalizing production and consumption in terms of what the planet's resources can continue to provide—and bringing fairness and equity to all through better-balanced exploitation and use of these resources (such as keeping more profits from raw materials 'at home'; utilizing them in a sustainable manner); more effective policies of aid and assistance; and finding new funding mechanisms between North and South. And last, but hardly least, caring for ourselves, our neighbours, and the environment by observing the rights pertaining to all of humankind.

Care is the antithesis of competition (a natural bent of the human species, essential to survival), and its reinforcement now will necessitate a dramatic change in mind-set. The transactional concepts of the past, excessive competition and the philosophy of ever more may destroy us. We need, therefore, to explore if and how the reservoirs of caring capacity can sustain us, and lift at the same time at least 1 billion people mired in poverty—and growing—from the level of eking out their survival and on to the path of sustainable improvement of the quality of life. This will require nothing short than *another kind of development* than hitherto pursued. Humankind faces challenges of a civilizational change. Its survival and existence in dignity requires a transition to a fundamentally new type of development—ecodevelopment—which should govern all forms of human activities and all interactions of people with nature.

In this quest, a few guiding principles set the ground rules. Equity, caring, sharing, sustainability, human security. *Equity* has a crucial, even overriding role in all efforts aimed at a sustainable improvement in the quality of life. We believe that without equity there can be neither *sustainability* nor *security*. Equity denotes a principle of fair and equitable treatment to all, to be respected equally by individuals, institutions, and States.

In addition to our fundamentally human consideration for care and caring, we have been guided in our analysis and conclusions by other elements not less important. These are *population as people* (and not only as numbers); *overcoming the North–South divide*; and *listening to the women's voice* because women are at the very centre of population policy and at the forefront of societal activities, particularly those influenced by the notion of caring.

Based on the findings of the Commission as they appear in the foregoing chapters, we advocate a series of policies, strategies, action programmes, or other measures which must be taken *now* at various levels to improve the quality of life in a world whose population—at nearly 6 billion human beings today—will continue to grow until it reaches some 9.8 billion in 2050, stabilizing perhaps one century later at about 11 billion.

Improved Security for a More Liveable World

We saw in Chapter 5 (Focusing the Goal: Sustainable Quality of Life) that sustainability is both a precondition and an integral component of quality of life, on which policy-making in all countries should focus. Sustainability and security are two main features and determinants of quality of life. As security transcends the traditional concept focusing on national sovereignty and military dimensions only, the Commission embraces a comprehensive definition of human security: it must also include the safety of people from the risks of injury or accident, disaster, disease, or violence, as well as from loss of livelihood or damaging environmental change.

The redefinition of security must include personal, economic, social, environmental, and military security and must affect security priorities at the national level. This will necessitate shifts away from military spending to areas with great impact: health, family planning, environment, crime prevention. As a minimal first step, all governments should aim to spend at least as much on health and education as on military programmes.

We join the international call that all governments not already doing so should lower military budgets, especially those of the developing countries and in regions where conflict and potential warfare are endemic.

Developed nations must contribute, actively and credibly, to the demilitarization of life—for no State that profits from war can convincingly argue for peace. It is not enough to admonish developing countries that their military expenditures must be reduced—as they indeed should be—or to introduce forms of conditionality to aid-and-assistance programmes. Military assistance, often under the 'cover' of development assistance, must decline further and be phased out.

We further propose that the concept of collective security be revisited accordingly. The Security Council of the United Nations, the body entrusted with the maintenance of international security and peace, should thus be enabled to address also threats to the socio-economic security of humankind.

In pursuing a sustainable improvement of quality of life, highest priority must be given to meeting the population's minimum survival needs. In order to make these needs operational, they should be related to *rights*—striking a balance between civil-political rights and economic-social rights.

The Commission urges that a major effort be mounted to universalize by the year 2000 the four great existing treaties embodying a range of rights relevant to the quality of life—the Convention on the Elimination of Discrimination against Women (CEDAW), the Convention on the Rights of the Child (CRC), the International Covenant on Economic, Social and Cultural Rights (ICESCR), and the International Covenant on Civil and Political Rights (ICCPR).

To this end, the number of signatory States must be increased and countries maintaining reservations must be persuaded to withdraw them. Countries should signify any reasons for non-signature, outlining what conditions would help them overcome existing obstacles.

The Commission urges speedy completion of an optional protocol of ICESCR, allowing complaints by affected individuals or groups. Similar protocols should be prepared for the three other international instruments and extended to include the right of States (already existing in the case of ICCPR) to bring complaints against other States.

Without enforcement, however, rights may remain unimplemented or dead letter. In the absence of effective machinery, direct and indirect approaches will need to be devised.

To increase pressure on countries to live up to their commitments, the committees established under the various treaties and conventions should be enabled to prepare regular, analytical summaries on the fulfilment of rights and on obstacles encountered.

The Commission calls on development agencies and NGOs concerned with social and economic needs (food, housing, health and family planning, education) to orient their activities more towards the internationally recognized rights. The force of rights should be added to those based on justice and equity. In that respect the organizations concerned should also submit reports and evidence to the committees established by the treaties.

We favour integrating the relevant rights within a single, all-encompassing concept representing a holistic approach that combines the economic, social, and political dimensions of quality of life. All these dimensions should be measurable and implementable.

This will allow the formulation of a strategy based on setting minimal quality-of-life standards applying to all nations, ones that can be measured and verified. A timetable should be agreed upon for bringing all parties to these minima. Progressively higher standards can then be set, while helping others lagging behind to attain the minima.

Targets and performance indicators concretize the various aspects of quality of life. *Indicators* offer mechanisms for governments to commit themselves to change and for civil society to hold governments accountable.

For each quality-of-life element, an international effort should be mounted to establish indicators and minimal standards. Civil society, including academic institutions, must be involved in the formulation and elaboration of indicators, spearheaded by governments and local authorities. Standards should be defined clearly, measurably; and schedules should be drawn up for meeting these standards that allow governments to set targets within a reasonable period. The targets themselves should be expressed as indicative parameters. Targets should not be averages for the entire country, but floor levels above which everyone is to be raised. This implies the need for disaggregated indicators, broken down by gender, ethnic or income groups, and region: making sure that every group surpasses the minima and that poverty is eradicated.

Individual nations must be at the front line of this effort, with the State as enabler and sustainer of people's capacities. This should facilitate the emergence of a favourable framework for policies, services and societal processes that would enable the people themselves to strive for and attain a higher quality of life. Once the quality-of-life rights have been assured for all, sustainable improvement of this quality should remain a primary goal of policy: a permanent process.

At the international level, inconsistencies and incompatibilities in targets must be ended. We recommend that targets and timetables concerning social and economic rights, already adopted by various UN conferences, be reconciled and consolidated.

National-level commitments of poor countries should be backed by an international compact, allowing foreign aid to be prioritized in order to supplement the national resources required to reach internationally defined minimal standards. For nations already above the minimum, governments should be held accountable by their own societies for developing programmes intended to raise the level of those social groups falling below the quality-of-life minima.

We recommend that reporting on the progress of these activities be done by bodies independent of the government of the moment, perhaps a Quality-of Life Ombudsman producing a periodic assessment, a 'Quality-of-Life Audit'.

GNP is not an accurate road-map for quality of life: it does not sum up national welfare, or whether welfare is sustainable. International comparisons of GNP do not reflect the current relative state of the quality of life amongst different countries. A step in the right direction would be the adoption, urgently, of the reformed System of National Accounts.

But more must be done. Parallel accounts should reflect environmental costs and depreciation of natural capital. Unless this is done, key policy decisions will continue to be made on the basis of false information. We should use the best economic and scientific expertise available to estimate the future costs of damage to the environment today.

We recommend also that steps be taken to measure unpaid caring services in the home and voluntary work in the community, and to value them in parallel accounts to be established nationally.

Equity is a central element for the sustainable improvement in the quality of life. Equity connotes real equality of opportunity, accepted by society when there is reasonable equality in the distribution of incomes, distribution of services, even wealth. Equity has to be applied each time that persistent discrimination becomes visible; it requires affirmative action—in itself a certain degree of inequality favouring those disadvantaged, excluded, or victims of past injustices. Equity is not a principle to be delayed until later stages of development; it corrects the inequalities present in all societies. Nor does it cease to matter once a country becomes 'rich'. Nations dealing effectively with equity, and whose other policies are sound, are rewarded with fast economic growth and high human security. And by applying measures of equity, nations redress inequalities and strengthen their social cohesion.

The Planet has its Constraints: Carrying Capacity

In terms of Respecting the Limits: The Carrying Capacity of the Earth (Chapter 6), we have recognized the limits that humankind can impose on the environment, which may be called carrying capacity. In scientific terms, however, it is impossible to calculate population ceilings for the world or for individual countries because ceilings are currently based on existing knowledge and technologies as well as on current patterns of production and consumption.

Agricultural feeding capacity

Since we face a probable population increase of some 4 billion people, keeping food production in step with the growth in population and consumption is crucial, especially to the growing ranks of the poor. This will mean a constant effort on all fronts, beginning with sound economic policies at the national level and ensuring market prices for farmers. Of the utmost importance will be raising the incomes of the poorest through employment, or by improved access to the most arable land through agrarian reform—while reducing the amount of land used to raise animal protein—and providing them with capital and technology.

International efforts must help to ensure food security for all. This may involve the redistribution of available supplies and crops in combination with fishery research as well as increased imports of food aid if necessary. Boosting national agricultural-research centres, and operating extension services to disseminate research results to farmers, should also command high priority.

Agricultural research has been central to increasing food production. It will be even more important in the future, as crops and farming methods have to be adapted to impending climate change. Focused not only on high-potential regions and on methods that only richer farmers can afford, research must produce plant varieties and technologies (biofertilizers, biopesticides) suitable for poor farmers, women farmers, and for use on marginal lands, ensuring that the genetic pool remains within the reach of people. A full implementation of the biodiversity Convention, adopted at the 1992 Earth Summit in Rio de Janeiro, will help ensure unimpeded access by indigenous people to these genetic resources. Research needs the full participation of farmers themselves, since they know best their traditions, current conditions, and future possibilities.

Given the enormity of the food challenge, secure and stable funding for the centres of the Consultative Group on International Agricultural Research (CGIAR) must be ensured at much higher levels than at present.

Because sustainability is critical in the realm of food, we must move towards more sustainable use of inputs to agriculture, more sustainable management practices—all to be devised with the full participation of all stakeholders. Soil and water conservation are indispensable to sustainable agriculture.

Water and other global commons

Future consumption levels of water will depend on the efficiency of its supply and use. Subsidies encouraging over-use of water, fertilizer, and fossil fuels should be discontinued.

Wasteful over-use of water in households abounds. Conservation measures must be complemented by the redesign of domestic appliances to achieve substantial savings.

Many industrial processes consume significant amounts of water, or use it as a cooling agent or to dispose of pollutants. Technical solutions to water shortage or pollution must be pursued, intensified, and linked to new research priorities that place emphasis on novel harvesting techniques (for example, capturing and exploiting rainwater, desalinization, introducing biofertilizers to agriculture).

An impending water crisis is not resolvable without major policy changes. Water can be treated and reused. Recycling must be made national policy, for example using waste water after treatment for irrigation, and reducing the problem of sewage discharged into the oceans.

The Commission, believing that the global commons must be managed sustainably, deems that such management requires appropriate institutions and rules. The Commission is further convinced that equity is essential in global agreements governing the use of the global commons.

A major challenge is to reduce the aggregate fishing around the world. Solutions to ocean problems should be based on multiple measures, including the development of effective market mechanisms to discourage over-fishing.

The time is ripe to consolidate the different exploitative activities, unifying scientific study of the seas and their problems, designing policies and institutions to deal with all of these questions. Part of the solution for many countries may be a switch to appropriate and environmentally balanced aquaculture—thereby reconciling nutritional, social, agricultural, and economic considerations, and avoiding potentially negative effects of overproduction.

It is incumbent on the industrial countries—principally responsible for the use and abuse of these commons—to reduce greenhouse-gas emissions per person to sustainable, equitable levels. Rather than relying on 'preaching' or simple, linear reductions, these decreases will require the advent of environmentally sustainable technologies and modified patterns of settlement. In the national and international area, 'tradeable quotas' could also be a measure to facilitate reductions in emissions levels.

Stabilizing the presence of carbon dioxide and other greenhouse gases at safe atmospheric levels will require a drastic reduction in emissions—which may not be possible without a correspondingly massive lowering of the use of fossil fuels, with the ultimate aim of phasing them out. This will require a rapid change in the production technologies together with a simultaneous reorientation of life-styles and consumption patterns.

A wide range of measures must be pursued towards lowering the use of hydrocarbons and introducing renewable energies at a large scale. A central priority must be to bring about a reduction in the costs of renewable-energy technologies. Prices of fossil fuels should internalize their ecological cost and should not benefit from subsidies, while offering incentives to energy-efficient technology (including the use of renewable energy sources). An 'ecological tax' reform, whereby taxes on labour are gradually reduced as the taxes on fossil-fuel energies are raised, may hasten the necessary transition.

Funding for the research and large-scale applications of renewable energies must be increased dramatically, requiring perhaps an international effort of the scale of the Manhattan Project of more than five decades ago. Such funding is a pre-condition for progress in research on solar, photovoltaic, thermal, and biomass energy technologies, and possibly nuclear fusion. But a boost in funds will also be required to reach higher levels of energy efficiency and conservation for present technologies based on fossil fuel use.

As part of a global undertaking, a network of research centres for renewable energy should be formed, drawing also on the expertise residing in developing countries in order to harmonize research objectives and concentrate on fields of priority. Centres would focus on specific technologies, be internationally funded, and their product made available at little or no cost to developing countries, thereby promoting transfer of the latest technologies.

The world's forests play a crucial role both in the climate equation and the sustainable improvement in the quality of life. Especially needed are national forestry strategies, policies and means of application to increase productivity, halt forest degradation, improve the benefits from forests, increase the incentives and efficiencies related to conservation, management, and sustainable development of forest resources. Forest management itself needs to be better balanced in terms of ecosystem protection—its objectives more broadly based than on wood production alone. All stakeholders, including the voices of care, must be fully involved in these processes.

The best way to preserve biological species is to protect their habitats through policies that slow their destruction: reducing the expansion of farmland in virgin areas of mainly forest cover, and managing sustainably already exploited tracts.

Throughout this chapter, we recommend that grassroot groups participate directly in the preparation of strategies to protect water, fish,

and forest resources, and that scientific research take into account endogenous traditions and belief systems affecting ecosystems reliant on water and woodland.

We advocate global agreements on the use of the commons, be they water and oceans, the atmosphere or forests. Equity will be an essential prerequisite for all such agreements.

Humanity has no Limits to its 'Caring Capacity'

Responding to Needs: the Caring Capacity of Humankind (Chapter 7) evoked a different series of conclusions because our Commission believes that we must transcend a narrow focus on the material basis of survival. We need now to establish our psychological, spiritual, and political capacities to care for each other as a determinant of progress and survival. The ethic of care—defining us as human beings—surmounts economic rationale: it can counteract individualism and greed. Caring for ourselves, for each other, for the environment is the basis upon which to erect sustainable improvement of the quality of life all round us. The care ethic now requires a drastic shift in paradigm.

Caring may be expressed otherwise: attitudes and actions acknowledging that humans, their communities and nations are not isolated, but are interdependent, aware of *otherness*, and ready to commit themselves to others. *Caring enough* enables society's members to care for each other: thus creating an enabling, empowering society.

We seek a new humanism to promote human rights not only in terms of legal guarantees but, more importantly, in the context of dignity. *Care* can provide the foundation for such a humanism. The notion of care for ourselves, for each other, and for the environment we occupy is the very basis on which the sustainable improvement of the quality of life must be developed.

Yet we are paralysed by a profound paradox: at one and the same time, we seem capable of solving our problems but, in fact, are unable to do so. We have the knowledge and the means—technology, financial resources, policy options—to make a difference, but we lack collective political volition, the will to act.

What we need is a new frame of mind, rejecting unalloyed selfishness. We seek a widely acceptable ethic of caring for our fellow beings, caring for our home on Earth. It is within such a value system of caring that sustainable improvement in the quality of life can become the central focus of policy.

Based as it is on constant interaction, *care* has the capacity to promote egalitarian attitudes and practices. We believe that care must be made visible. Even when money values cannot be attached, society must become aware of the cost incurred if caring services had to be procured at market prices.

We are thus convinced that care—by its attentiveness to the concrete needs of individuals and groups, by the responses implicit in order to meet these needs, by the steadfastness of this commitment—provides the foundation for future societal activity. Care supremely overrides the macro-economic goal of an improved quality of life at a 'sometime' in the distant future.

We maintain that social policy lies at the heart of the State's responsibilities. Social policy may be translated as pro-active strategies implemented by the State or by private means—with the State setting a regulatory framework that ensures equity. A central government cannot withdraw from assuring the means and financial obligations of the socially conscious State (education, public health, public housing, urban renewal), although these should be assured at lower levels of government in keeping with the subsidiarity principle and the better capacity to deliver. Such services are inevitably better assured with the full participation of the people involved.

Our Commission understands that the socially caring State model is not the same as that known by the name of welfare State. We suggest, as more countries embark on the way to economic development and industrialization, that they apply intelligent reform of this model as the point of departure in developing ever more humane social policies.

With the 1995 Copenhagen Summit as background, we urge intensified efforts to shift spending priorities and pursue new approaches to combat social exclusion in whatever form this takes.

We consider it imperative to implement, without delay, the Copenhagen agreement to remove all barriers currently preventing people from escaping from poverty, and eradicating *absolute poverty and exclusion* by target dates set by individual countries.

Finally, we endorse the idea that each country should produce a national development plan covering all the major elements involved in quality of life (poverty, work, food; children, women; reproductive rights), specifying targets, timetables, and indicators for monitoring the plan's progress.

Towards a New Understanding of Population

As the sequel to the analysis of population policies in Chapter 8, we noted a remarkable, recent shift in attitudes concerning population change. The effective delivery of contraceptives and related informational and motivational services, which lowered fertility, was not accompanied by supportive measures drawing upon social and economic change. The status of women in the 1970s emerged as a major determinant of fertility, but the choice of indicators defining status led to much debate. After the initial parameters relating to literacy, education, and marriage age were developed, others, such as economic participation, education and health, were added gradually.

A modification in views occurred in the brief time between 1974 and 1984. On the one hand, massive structural changes in the world economy and the onset of globalization brought development to an impasse. On the other hand, the women's movement emerged, becoming an influential and decisive force. Almost suddenly, women's reproductive rights became the basis for decisions on population and development—of, in fact, population policy. The affirmation of a woman's inviolable right to reproductive choice thus put population policies in a new context—nothing short of a paradigm shift.

We recommend that implicit and explicit policies concerning population and its relationship with quality of life be regarded as a responsibility of governments and situated at a high level of governmental structure (with concomitant parliamentary debate and decision, especially when it involves the setting of budgetary priorities). Such a role should not be relegated to advisory bodies only.

We further recommend setting up a Joint Committee consisting of WHO and UNICEF with the participation of representatives from the United Nations Commission on Human Rights and the Commission on the Status of Women to draw up international ethical standards covering currently available new reproductive technologies (NRTs). These standards should include the human-rights perspective, be gender-sensitive, and furnish guide-lines for future development in terms of scientific research and the anticipated evolution of NRTs.

We recommend that research-sponsoring agencies, both national and international, initiate studies on the use (and abuse) of NRTs and make their findings public.

We recommend constituting, at the national level, an independent, interdisciplinary council (as has been done in some countries) to scrutinize the social and ethical implications of biotechnologies on both those new technologies which concern the reduction of fertility and those new technologies designed to overcome infertility.

We interpret the use of coercion, whether direct or indirect, in the application of population policy and programming as a violation of human rights; we recommend its abandonment in favour of measures advocated by us, those favouring public debate and supportive social policy that promotes voluntary limitation on the size of families.

We further recommend, to correct imbalances in the information currently available, research on inter-regional and global migration among developing countries. We also recommend special studies of female migration from developing countries, at both departure and terminus, in order to identify needed policy support.

Work, Paid and Unpaid, also Assumes new Definitions

Readers will note that the Commission made a particular effort in Redefining Work (Chapter 9), whence come the following recommendations.

We propose to redefine work in a broad sense, encompassing a wide spectrum of activities, of which conventional employment and unpaid activities benefiting society at large, families, and individuals are the most visible part, and ensuring an equitable distribution of the wealth thus generated. The value of this unpaid work—performed mainly by women all over the world—must be incorporated into national accounting systems, as we suggested earlier.

In view of the changed nature of work from how it was perceived early in the Industrial Revolution, we surmise that work can no longer be defined in traditional terms. We suggest, rather, that work be perceived as a continuum and that economic value be attached to its segments: from jobs for mere survival to meaningful employment and other roles (for example as unpaid housewife or, much less frequently, volunteer) that satisfy human needs or empower people. The task of work in developing countries is to create livelihoods that will end poverty, absorb unemployment and underemployment, and keep pace with the future growth of the labour force.

The same attention must be given to creating jobs in urban areas by a new focus on small enterprises and the informal sector. Much of the informal sector is part of the hidden economy. We believe, too, that another solution to this problem is to account economically for the informal sector, along with recognizing other small-scale enterprises that follow the rules.

We welcome growing international support for the creation of credit schemes for micro-firms. These schemes benefit the poor, especially poor women. The Commission calls for expansion of such programmes (thus far concentrated in Asia), and urges bilateral and multilateral donors to provide the necessary funding. Governments of developing countries, for their part, need to ensure the necessary legal and political environment that enables micro-credit structures to flourish.

Unemployment in most industrialized countries is not a matter of work shortage or the wealth of some. Correcting the maldistribution of work and income is the greatest social challenge facing today's developed countries.

We propose, therefore, that the potential of work-sharing be explored and adopted by a large number of enterprises, and even governments, as a means to relieve unemployment in both North and South. Work-sharing will have to be complemented by plans to provide for profit-sharing. Rising unemployment rates sometimes contrast sharply with the realization of high profits too, a paradox creating unbearable tensions inside the labour/capital environment.

To complement such novel approaches, we recommend major changes in the regulation of work, important increases in the availability of education and training throughout life, and significant shifts in tax and benefits systems.

Industrialized countries also need a different kind of labour flexibility, whereby workers' skills are constantly upgraded on or off the job. This means large increases in employees' training schemes and in the vocational curricula offered by colleges and universities.

We hold that the redistribution of existing jobs solves only part of the problem; there is an urgent need to create entirely new jobs. The Commission believes that this offers much scope for innovative public–private or community partnerships.

⁃

We are convinced that sustainable improvement in the quality of life, and thus of people everywhere, will reduce all types of migration and its attendant pressures.

Urban growth poses tremendous challenges with severe social and environmental impact on municipalities, which must be given the means and assistance to resolve these problems—now bordering on the apocalyptic. The State, in dialogue with civil society, must strive for a more balanced distribution of population.

We propose that rural areas and the urban poor obtain—especially under conditions of structural adjustment—their fair share of governmental expenditures. These cannot be 'safety nets' of a temporary nature only. Priority should be accorded to decentralizing responsibilities and resources to municipalities and poor districts.

Migration (including immigration, refugees, and labour mobility), and its relationship to livelihoods, must receive priority attention at the international level with special attention to migrant labour by women. The Commission calls on the United Nations, regional organizations, and informal groupings (for example the Group of Seven) to address these problems in an effort to devise workable and humane solutions appropriate to this age of globalization.

We believe that the transfer of jobs should not occur at the cost of working conditions or safety. A few transnational corporations have shown that profitability and responsible employment practices can go hand in hand. Other firms should adopt similar standards—possibly guided by a voluntary code of conduct. This should lessen growing pressure in industrialized countries to raise non-tariff barriers on goods produced in developing countries under what is perceived as exploitative conditions; this could complement existing ILO conventions suffering from lack of implementation and enforcement.

Increased benefits from freer global trade must accrue to the benefit of developing nations. We call on all international organizations, including those of the private sector, to examine the implications of such trends and to take energetic action to prevent the development of new cleavages between rich and poor.

We propose that, under the auspices of the World Trade Organization, negotiations be resumed without delay to facilitate further access to industrialized markets of products coming from developing countries.

Alternative Educational Approaches: The Promise of New Technologies

Our group has given considerable thought to the possibility of new directions Towards an Alternative Educational Policy (Chapter 10), and our conclusions are the following.

The primary challenge during the decades between 1996 and 2015 is to realize the *right to education* for all those not having access to schooling, including those who have failed the first time round. The wastage represented by drop-outs and repeaters calls for action. We deem that education is to be perceived as a continuum and treated as a right belonging not to a specific age-group (childhood and youth), but a life-long right that can take many forms until old age. Basic education for adults, therefore, must be closely geared to the real needs of their communities.

We are convinced that a massive resort to educational technologies including new information technologies can help introduce higher degrees of flexibility and responsiveness to societal needs. We urge the international development agencies to resume pilot projects using new educational technologies—including teacher training meant to familiarize and engage the instructors themselves. The inertia of educational systems is often attributed to its labour intensity. We are aware of a number of projects undertaken during the 1970s that failed largely because of teacher resistance. If new educational technologies are appropriately integrated, the role of the teacher is bound to change: this means that teachers must be trained differently.

One of our concerns is that the right to education is largely unrealized, causing educational deprivation. Enrolment rates at primary level in developing countries are projected to remain stable until 2015, so that the situation is not likely to improve in the immediate future. We are deeply concerned about this, with about 1.5 billion children and adults in the category of illiteracy or on their way there.

Shortages of teachers and buildings may be mitigated by raising class size (not beyond forty students), introducing morning and afternoon sessions. The strategy should not be pushed to the overloading of teachers. Older children and educated volunteers can be used as monitors to teach younger children, siblings still at home and children out of school. Day-care centres may enable parent girls to remain longer in school and provide their own, limited, preschool education to reduce the handicap suffered by children of non-literate backgrounds. All this would raise productivity, lower the cost of education, and improve both 'internal' and 'external' efficiencies in terms of the educational processes.

We are convinced that achieving universal primary education should have top priority everywhere; we strongly endorse the proposals made in international fora concerning policies and targets in this respect, intended to eradicate relentlessly all analphabetic conditions. Education itself needs an approach committed to advancing standards, overcoming the resistance of teachers (and sometimes parents); an approach based on clear targets and timetables at both national and international levels.

We recommend, therefore, that UNESCO and other qualified organizations adopt jointly, as soon as possible, an effective strategy of Education for All by the Year 2010. Its adoption would be conditioned, of course, by the introduction of an alternative educational policy (say 80 per cent of primary-school enrolment for boys and girls), or one complementing or supplementing the formal-education system. Preparations should begin immediately by declaring the ten years of 2001–10 the Decade of Universal Basic Education.

We contend that, if the international community is serious about influencing demographic growth-rates, it has a moral obligation (and material self-interest) to help developing nations eradicate illiteracy and achieve universal primary education. The Commission believes further that, as a minimum to strive for, the recent downward trend in overseas-development assistance be reversed quickly. Aid should be targeted in a co-ordinated way on those countries unlikely to reach their targets without outside help.

We are convinced, too, that the education of women has a powerful effect on the health and education of their children, who are likely in turn to be healthier and more educated than others. Women's education may be the most effective way of empowering women and constitutes, in itself, a *right*. Women's education, furthermore, is probably the most important measure possible to enhance the quality of life of women, children, and future generations as a whole—as well as a factor contributing to the stabilization of the world's population. We strongly urge, too, that special efforts be made in the education of boys and male adolescents throughout pre-school, school, and professional training concerning gender issues, women's rights and social responsibility.

Given the decisive role of education in regard to population and quality of life, we are convinced that the political will must be rallied to launch alternative approaches and policies in regard to education: funded globally; implemented nationally, regionally, and locally; and especially made accessible to the poor. Governments, qualified international organizations, research and media institutions should undertake studies immediately as to how the immense potential of the newest media can be utilized for the equalization of education, life-long training, and social integration, and how the large-scale infrastructures necessary can be implanted.

We deem it desirable, at the same time, to undertake systematic study of the consequences of violence, sexuality, and consumerism in the media.

We emphasize, as well, the critical function of educational systems in promoting the universal values essential to sustainable improvement of the quality of life. The Commission believes that an *ethic of care* needs to be taught throughout primary and secondary education and beyond, to the level of adult education.

If education should promote the development of a caring society, then education is no longer a commodity for self-advancement and mainly of economic value. We must now concentrate on education's unquestioned potential to teach all how to teach themselves.

We call, therefore, on the community of educators, scholars, and students at all levels to extend their concerns beyond the curriculum, using their institutional, individual, and other participative resources to promote the values that ensure a sustainable improvement in the quality of life.

New Obstacles to Health Care

We turned next to areas relating to the physical condition of humankind, From Medical to Health Care (Chapter 11). Our conclusions are as follows.

We reiterate the need to adopt the primary health-care model, including the best of traditional and alternative therapies, while developing in a balanced way medical and hospital care accessible to all—physically and financially speaking. We call, further, for a concerted redistribution of public expenditures towards and within the broader social sector of education, housing, employment, and environmental activities.

We believe it is vital that basic preventive and curative services be made available to all in order to avoid any form of two-tiered delivery of health.

We advocate a shift of financial resources from the overdeveloped curative, hospital-based model to primary-care community clinics, home-care programmes and preventive initiatives.

To counter the negative impact of structural adjustment in developing countries, we see a great and urgent challenge in protecting and, if required, restoring, the share of resources devoted to health and education, and to health and education for women, in particular.

- We are convinced that prevention demands strong health education campaigns and making health education a compulsory subject in school.

- We note that lifestyle transitions induce 'health transitions', a shift of attention from mainly communicable diseases to chronic and chiefly non-communicable illnesses, as well as those associated with longer life-spans.

- We conclude that the various determinants of good health mean that health policy must be co-ordinated across a broad field; health policy must be as holistic as population policy. Health policy focused on curative intervention is bound to fail, whereas one that includes preventive public health is more likely to succeed; one capable of dealing with a variety of social factors affecting health is the most likely to be a success.

We recommend that a comprehensive health policy and the community services corresponding to women's needs include nutrition, family planning, and safe motherhood, as well as food-price policy, the prevention of smoking amongst young women and girls, the promotion of sport and exercise, and proper transport and environmental facilities. While such policy should include the de-medicalization of the normal processes associated with women's health, from adolescence and pregnancy through menopause to ageing, it should also give medical attention to health problems more prevalent in, or unique to, women.

We hold, then, that health is more than a matter to be handled by health ministries. It is a societal challenge, cutting across many sectors, and a goal in the programmes of varied governmental services: agriculture, environment, food, transport, industry, and education.

It is our belief that measures need to be taken towards the realization of the most important objectives of the revolution in primary health-care:

- ensuring equity, in favour of those most in need of health services;
- stressing prevention and self-help;
- increasing participation, and devolving both powers and budgets downwards; and
- changing the culture of medical care by concentrating on the patient.

We suggest, moreover, that objectives and targets be combined with timetables at national and international levels, co-ordinated with outside aid. The Commission calls on all countries to take concrete steps, at long last, to translate the objectives of the Declaration of Alma Ata (1978) and in the Ottawa Charter (1986) into reality.

We urge international financial institutions and donor countries to desist from seeking reductions—within the context of structural adjustment programmes—in existing levels of health spending. This substantiates our view of the need for a policy of partnership among people's organizations, legitimate authority-structures at the community level, professional institutions that can provide knowledge, and other resources and funding agencies within or outside governments. Such organic links are essential to make the primary health-care model universally adaptable to differences in local situations and affordable, and to bring about the revolution in the culture and power structure of health services that has become essential. This applies also to the power structure in medical education, now totally globalized and thus in need of substantial change.

We suggest, to conclude this section, that all countries of the international community develop research and specific programmes that concentrate on controlling new and re-emerging diseases.

Human Reproduction: The New Element of Human Rights

Closely linked with the reforms seen as necessary in the general field of good health for all, the Commission examined carefully the question of Reproductive Choices (Chapter 12). In this area, we believe that sexual education is absolutely necessary in all societies; such education can impart to all an appreciation of the true dimensions of personal freedom *and personal responsibilities*.

We point out that 'free choice' carries socially constructed expectations; it suggests that, through a reaffirmation of individual rights, *reproductive rights* acquire a new quality among human rights. Inherent among the reproductive rights is the affirmation that women, in all societies, must be treated as full citizens on a par with men and not only on the basis of their capacity for procreation.

We suggest that the notion of the non-negotiability of reproductive rights as human rights is supported by several fundamental, ethical principles: the dignity of the individual, equity and non-discrimination, participation and solidarity.

We further suggest that the idea of the non-commercialization of reproductive rights as human rights is sustained by the same basic principles.

Our Commission calls for urgent remedial measures to correct a number of practices impinging on women's reproductive rights. We concur fully in the Action Programme adopted at the Beijing World Conference on Women and Development (1995) to the effect that reproductive health care is a critical part of health care. We believe further that a call for *choice* must be balanced by the notion of *availability*, bearing in mind that many countries face critical constraints in resources meant to ensure reproductive services. Absolute priority to an ever-growing range of choice in services supporting reproductive health could result, otherwise, in the neglect of other important zones of health care.

We consider it desirable that a group of like-minded countries initiate the adoption of a statement on reproductive health rights, laying out the rights to free choice and primary health care for reproductive needs, aiming also at safeguarding the quality of service and assuring user participation. The statement should cover counselling and the provision of services from adolescence to old age ensuring informed consent prior to any intervention, and outlaw all coercive practices.

We recommend that UNFPA, in collaboration with WHO, UNICEF,

and UNIFEM define a model of reproductive health care constituting a minimum to be accessible to everyone. We believe, besides, that priority must be given to extending reproductive health services (within accessible distance) to groups not currently provided for (men, unmarried people, adolescents); to reducing costs to affordable levels; and to broadening the range of services as much as possible.

We strongly reject abortion as an instrument of population control. Abortion should not be a means of contraception or to exercise choice of the sex of unborn children. These practices defeat the very purpose of seeking safety in abortion as a 'health right' of women. Nor does the Commission support an 'abortion culture' driven by the unavailability of contraceptives which, in turn, stems from societal and governmental neglect of women's—and especially girls'—needs.

The Commission recommends that abortion be decriminalized and made available, to ensure its safety, within the context of health services. Penal measures against sex-specific abortions may, however, be necessary to prevent abuse.

We advise that all aspects of the abortion problem, especially those involving health hazards, must be considered while deciding on its form of legislation. Social, religious, and other cultural leaders have a special responsibility in this respect, to weigh the range of arguments possible in making recommendations to policy-makers.

We believe that civil society, especially its religious and cultural authorities, cannot remain blind to social realities and needs—those that governments should seek to address by providing safe reproductive-health services.

We are convinced that the all-embracing concept of reproductive health-care is critical to the quality of life of women, men, and children. Its components are among others family planning, safe motherhood, fertility–infertility, and prevention or treatment of sexually transmitted disease.

We endorse fully the proposal that reproductive health should not be a separate domain, one fenced off from the rest of health care and requiring its own delivery system. This will require, therefore, an understanding of the model of primary, reproductive health care to be offered. The model should not aim at providing all aspects of such care; it should be limited to promoting prevention and the most basic treatment for common complaints. Higher levels of the health service should be consulted on complex diagnosis or treatment in cases of problem pregnancies, contraceptive clients in search of more durable methods, or antibiotic treatment of infertility resulting from sexually transmitted disease.

We believe that prevention of infertility and basic treatment of curable, sexually transmitted disease (thanks to universal access to ensuring safe-motherhood) must be integral to reproductive health services. We suggest that an appropriate balance be established between fund allocation to primary services and to expensive, high-technology treatment—including research on sterility. We wish to help infertile women, but we insist that priority be given to primary health care.

We deem that voluntary family-planning programmes are far more effective than those involving coercion to promote sustained use of contraceptives and the value of having small families. We note also that incentive payments and promises of promotion, or threats of sanction to health workers, invite abuse and reduce the amount of funds needed elsewhere.

We are convinced that community involvement is important to effective self-service delivery and in defining and resolving socio-cultural resistance, rooted mostly in fears reflecting ignorance of the psychological processes. This is why we learned with interest of successful family-planning approaches through collective incentives by local self-government to improve the quality of life, especially that of children.

We maintain, furthermore, that improving the quality and credibility of information, education, and counselling in reproductive health care for individuals enables them to make ethically and socially responsible choices concerning pregnancy and childbirth. There exist innovative social-development models to these ends. Sustained involvement of research and teaching institutions to improve the quality of information, education, and counselling within the community is sure to have a positive effect on their basic functions.

The Empowerment of Women—A New Social Force

Because human reproduction and the well-being of new generations depends on women's status, we next turned to enabling women to participate fully in community and political life and in work—sharing equally with men in the worlds of education, industry and trade, the service sector, and decision-making in all public affairs (Empowering Women, Chapter 13). The Commission has, as a consequence, a number of concrete recommendations to advance in order to allow women fully to benefit from improved quality of life.

The central role of women's rights must be fostered in all societal processes, linking personal rights and liberties with entitlements. There is a need to continue to build a sense of solidarity among women, a phenomenon historically new—while raising awareness among men and boys to avoid resistance to the empowerment of women.

Equal-pay legislation should be adopted and expanded everywhere, incorporating the principle of equal pay for equal work. Affirmative action should be the policy until the elimination of inequalities in pay and status—with specific goals, timetables, and monitoring of progress. Such action might include providing day-care for children and flexible working hours for mothers; women's quotas in recruitment, promotion, training, and retraining; and outlawing sexual harassment at work.

Labour laws should be broadened to provide improved conditions, benefits, and job security for domestic and agricultural workers, part-time, temporary and at-home workers, and employees in export-processing zones.

New development initiatives and economic and social policies, including structural adjustment programmes, should be subject to gender audit—with women's participation—to assess their effects on women's quality of life.

The formulation of a comprehensive global-action plan for children and adolescents, with a special focus on girls, will be a critical component in redressing the injustices faced by women. Elements already exist in various international documents, but they must be integrated within a single framework, and like-minded governments and NGOs should take initiatives in this direction.

NGOs and women's associations should promote activities to increase women's awareness to enter the political arena and learn the necessary skills therefor. Women must be encouraged to engage directly in political activities (including standing for elections), earning them a new status in public life and decision-making. Attention must also be paid to men and boys so as to create a supportive environment and to reduce resistance to change.

Governments, the banking sector, and international agencies must help give meaning to women's empowerment through a radical shift in economic, especially financial, policies; changing priorities in national budgets, extending credit to women's collective initiatives, and changing the conditions pertinent to international lending. By moving from a one-sided, technocratic balancing of budgets, these important economic actors will bring about new policies for improving the opportunities for all women to exercise their proper rights.

Mobilizing All of Humankind for a New Social Contract

We come next to the Mobilizing of Social Forces—Towards a New Social Contract (Chapter 14).

Given the multiple transition processes emerging in a globalized world, now may be the time to launch the idea of a new social contract: one forming a new basis of society's self-understanding that corresponds to all the new realities.

The starting-point of a new social contract will be the legal and pragmatic acknowledgement that sovereignty rests with the people: it is people who must become the subjects of the enhancement of the quality of life. Empowering people is not an abstract wish; it consists of countless dialogues and actions, concrete projects, all within legal frameworks.

We urgently need a new social contract—a new synthesis, a new balance between markets, between society and environment, between efficiency and equity, between wealth and welfare; a new equilibrium between economic growth on the one hand, and social harmony and sustainable improvement in the quality of life on the other. We need new concepts too, new instruments enabling governments to regulate markets, as well as sound finance so that markets neither jeopardize our survival nor take precedence over a sustainable quality of life.

This contract shall also articulate a new equilibrium able to create harmony between different age-groups throughout any demographic transition: between human beings and nature, between men and women, between adults and children, between the created world and the various forms of its ambient, spiritual energy.

It is our conviction that concrete meaning must be given to the notion of a new social contract. It should be applicable to governments and people, people and nature, as well as to entire nations and the world community.

At the heart of the social contract would be a new commitment by all to strive together towards improvement, sustainably, in the quality of life everywhere.

While it is the responsibility of our leaders to *lead*, leadership requires a political climate and institutions empowering people. Popular participation must become a central, integral feature of people's activities at all levels of society. Problems tend to build up where people are least free to publicize them or to protest about them. Hence the features of democracy (freedom of association and assembly, free speech and a free press, free elections with universal adult suffrage, equal access to legal systems, and life-long education) are all essential to successful adaptation by all concerned.

Encouraging participation is not simply a question of creating the right institutional framework. It means also creating the conditions in which every individual and group is enabled to participate. There is a need therefore, to evolve forms of citizens' participation that enrich and deepen the effectiveness of democracy.

A precondition for such participation is the devolution of power supported by the necessary resources: each decision should be taken as closely to the people affected by it as possible.

Citizens' participation, as a consequence, must become both a right and a practice universally. We need to strengthen citizens' participation in the structure of governance at every level, in both developing and developed countries.

Once empowered, citizens turn to forms of organized action by which they will exercise power on the issues affecting them most. The multiplicity of such forms, their cross-fertilization (or sometimes even confrontation), should create an enormous vitality within the social fabric. Only in these circumstances can we speak of a truly *civil* society.

At the global level, ways and mechanisms must be found to overcome the exclusive nature of activities, negotiations, and dialogue—especially within the UN system. The United Nations should build and draw on the resources residing with NGOs and solidify the constructive and uplifting experiences made with contributions by NGOs at the World Conferences held in Rio, Vienna, Cairo, Copenhagen, and Beijing. The patronizing attitudes by Governments and the leadership of many international organizations must be transformed into **real** and **lasting** partnership for the common good. This must eventually also permeate the permanent structures and machinery of these organizations.

For these purposes and to establish legitimacy and political weight, the criteria for representation of NGOs at the international level has to be carefully defined, with an adequate process of consultation among all concerned.

Finding the Resources

We come finally to the material substance of our thesis, **finding the means to help the world achieve most—if not all—of the things that we have proposed, suggested, recommended, or declared to be imperative and urgent in the previous chapters. We have called the penultimate section of our report Mobilizing Resources—Tapping the Markets (Chapter 15).**

The Commission is aware that in order to have the desired impact, the policies and measures proposed will require substantial resources, either directly or indirectly, well above the present levels of assistance flows. The resources must be raised either nationally or internationally—and unless these resources can be found, the world and our quality of life will be worse off.

New and innovative mechanisms will need to be developed and put into operation, supplementing—and eventually replacing—the prevailing traditional approach of relying on voluntary (or sometimes mandatory, assessed) contributions by governments, and the solicitation of private donations through NGOs.

Markets ought to play a key role in generating the funds required to finance on a sustainable and long-term basis the internationally agreed priorities. Markets have been the principal beneficiaries of globalization of virtually all activities, which are dependent on the global network of interdependence woven, maintained, and continuously upgraded by multilateral co-operation. Therefore, the private sector must be engaged and induced to take an interest in the financing of the national and international activities outlined in this report.

Official Development Assistance (ODA)

With respect to traditional financing modalities, we are concerned that the present trends in official development assistance flows are in contravention of the spirit of all international agreements and solemn undertakings. Every effort must be made to arrest the recent downward trend and to work towards an early realization of the hitherto all but elusive 0.7 per cent of GNP goal for ODA by industrialized countries.

International grant aid and concessional loans should be more consciously targeted towards a sustainable improvement in the quality of life, especially by those who do not yet enjoy them—by the poorest people in low-income countries.

A redirection of aid will require better statistics and improved quality of information on the uses to which aid is being put. We therefore recommend that OECD-DAC initiate discussions towards refining statistics by donor countries to allow a breakdown by purpose.

We believe that at present much aid is distributed in inverse proportion to needs. A more equitable distribution of existing assistance flows by itself would make an enormous difference to the poorest people in the poorest countries. To correct imbalances, the Commission recommends that assistance flows to countries with real incomes of more than US$3,000 per person (in 1992 international dollars at purchasing power parity) should no longer be officially classified as ODA.

Another innovative approach would be to earmark a percentage of ODA to empower and strengthen the capacity of civil society to control and monitor developments. This would help avoid the misuse and misallocation of development funds by governments and would raise awareness among people.

In this spirit, the Commission urges all donor countries to make a radical re-examination of bilateral aid programmes. The aim should be a shift, phased over a three to five year period, towards priority for improving quality of life, priority for countries with real incomes (at purchasing power parity) below US$3,000, and priority for disadvantaged groups and regions within those countries.

The Commission further suggests that:

- countries with annual income in the order of US$2,000–3,000 per capita (at purchasing power parity) should be in a position to pursue on their own equitable and redistributive policies aimed at a sustainable improvement in the quality of life and at fulfilment of the various economic and social rights;

- an effective national system for the collection of income and other taxes is the key to providing the wherewithal for the policies and programmes necessary to improve the quality of life. When such a system is not in place, it must be put in place speedily, and countries with an existing system should revive their structures with a view to reinforcing them and to maximizing domestic revenue collection;

- all countries and international organizations should accept and implement the 20:20 compact as a valuable policy target for the allocation of resources to basic social policies;

- the 20 per cent target should, however, be only a first step: a growing proportion of available national resources and external assistance should be devoted to the sustainable improvement in the quality of life, which comprises not only social policies but also other areas, such as environmental protection. These resources may be devoted to the broad range of needs identified: primary education, adolescent and adult literacy, primary health care, family planning, basic housing, adequate nutrition, women's equality, basic legal services, water and sanitation, environmental protection, social information and communication to strengthen democracy and the building of NGOs.

Substantial debt relief—for official and commercial debt—must be provided by Governments, banks, and international financial institutions to the least developed countries, especially in Africa. There must be an end to the drawn-out piecemeal process which results in a never-ending proliferation of rescheduling and relief terms, only marginally different from each other; this tinkering must come to an end once and for all and be replaced with a stable solution.

The burden of multilateral debt, especially for African countries, which hitherto had been a taboo in the debt-relief debate, must also be tackled and lowered effectively; initial ideas emanating in 1995 from the World Bank must be brought to fruition, as a matter of priority.

Depending on the specific situation of a country, other more innovative debt-reduction modalities can be devised. One attractive possibility is to swap commercial and official debt in exchange for a Government undertaking to pursue certain environmental or social-development-related programmes. Swaps meet dual objectives: they help to reduce debt while financing worthwhile environmental or social activities, with substantial leverage for donor funds.

Other measures must urgently be agreed to improve access to industrialized markets for the commodities and products from developing countries. Further reductions in tariffs on agricultural, manufactured, and semi-manufactured goods need to be combined with a phasing out of subsidies for—and the dumping of—Northern agricultural produce. To that end, the World Trade Organization should without delay initiate new rounds of global trade negotiations, aimed at creating a level playing field for all countries and preparing the ground for job creation and an integration of environmental protection concerns. The potential impact of such measures can already be highlighted by the anticipated monetary benefits of a reduction in Northern tariffs and quotas on exports from developed countries under the terms of the Uruguay round, widely perceived as unsatisfactory for developing countries; these approach the volume of ODA flows.

Also, existing commodity agreements aimed at a stabilization of export revenue by developing countries should be fully implemented.

The Need for New Funding Mechanisms

Increasingly, internationally agreed programmes and priorities—in the areas of economic and social development and in other areas—remain dead letter for the lack of internationally provided resources. We call on the United Nations Secretary-General to draw up, as a matter of urgency, a detailed and comprehensive inventory of all present, internationally agreed priority programmes and their cost estimates or financing commitments.

At the international level, we are convinced that the world urgently needs new mechanisms for funding global priorities, complementing the present approaches. Relying on the faltering generosity and the sagging payment morale of individual nations is no longer adequate. The globalization of economic, environmental, and other problems requires both commensurate global institutions and global financing mechanisms and the involvement of all players and stakeholders. The new mechanisms should be capable of delivering the kind of sums required and should be free of the immediate budgetary constraints of individual countries, where foreign aid is always an easy option to cut.

In terms of potential yield, the Commission concluded that the most promising source of finance for global priorities would be an international charge on all transactions in the global financial markets, i.e. including currencies, bonds and securities, derivatives, and stocks. We believe a flat transaction charge levelled uniformly, equally, and universally on all present and future types of financial transactions in the globalized marketplace, would be the most appropriate approach.

We are conscious of the fact that the application of such a charge will require a comprehensive, legally binding, and truly universal agreement or convention. Universal validity would pre-empt the diversion of funds to countries or offshore centres that are not party to the agreement.

Likewise, a new international authority might have to be created to administer the substantial funds collected, to review the operations of the mechanism, and to distribute the proceeds in accordance with internationally agreed priorities. The membership, voting structure, and powers of such an authority would remain to be decided, but it would provide the opportunity to set up a novel structure involving all major stakeholders, including representatives of civil society, non-governmental organizations, the private sector, parliaments as well as governments.

We recommend that a small group of high-level international financial experts be appointed under the auspices of the United Nations or the Bretton Woods institutions to study and report on all details of a global transaction charge on financial activities.

If international priority programmes could be financed by the markets through the first truly international charge—globally agreed, globally financed, with true global ownership—it would herald a revolutionary shift in international relations.

The Commission further recommends that the UN General Assembly should adopt an omnibus resolution requesting detailed studies of the objectives, feasibility, potential yield, and eventual modalities of various innovative financing mechanisms from the following agencies and bodies of the UN system, but not restricted to these agencies: the International Civil Aviation Organization (ICAO), the United Nations Environment Programme (UNEP), the International Maritime Organization, the International Telecommunication Union (ITU), the Committee on the Peaceful Uses of Outer Space, the World Trade Organization, and the United Nations Conference on Trade and Development (UNCTAD).

We also encourage UNCTAD to proceed speedily with its pilot project on tradeable emission permits—another modality to generate funds of benefit to developing countries.

We also call for intensified studies on the possible access and use of special drawing rights (SDR), under the auspices of the International Monetary Fund (IMF), for activities related to the broad area of collective peace and security, as redefined in this report.

❧

All these schemes and proposals notwithstanding, official development assistance (ODA) is bound to remain for many years to come the backbone of the international development effort. To preserve the viability of the present multilateral arrangements—no matter how unsatisfactory they might be—the Commission urges once again that a determined international effort be made as a minimum to arrest the present downward spiral in ODA; and to induce industrialized countries to realize their 0.7 per cent commitment as quickly as possible.

The Commission considers that these aspects of mobilization and allocation of resources are a *sine qua non* for the sustained improvement of quality of life and, at the same time, for the acceleration of the changes needed to reach the stabilization of the world's population.

APPENDIX

ORIGINS OF THE COMMISSION

The *Independent Commission on Population and Quality of Life* was launched at the initiative of several organizations that had been involved for many years in the population field and that felt the need for answering the compelling questions in the population/family-planning fields and programmes. Two preparatory meetings were held which finally led to the creation of the Commission.

The first preparatory meeting was held in **London, 3 December 1991**, under the auspices of the Rockefeller Foundation. Experts and representatives of main organizations involved in population activities took part. *For international organizations*: Nafis Sadik and Jyoti Shankar Singh, United Nations Population Fund; Ann O. Hamilton, the World Bank. *From the bilateral development agencies*: Amb. Nicolaas H. Biegmann, The Netherlands; Duff Gillespie, United States of America; Jacques Martin, Switzerland; David Nabarro, United Kingdom; Carl Tham, Sweden. *From ministries of foreign affairs*: Amb. L. O. Edström, Sweden; Akura Kitamura, Japan. *From NGOs (including private foundations)*: Peter Goldmark, President, Kenneth S. Prewitt, Vice-President, Robert S. Lawrence, and Steven W. Sinding, the Rockefeller Foundation; Carolyn Makinson, the Andrew W. Mellon Foundation; Carmen Barroso, the MacArthur Foundation; Jose Barzelatto, the Ford Foundation; Hafdan Mahler, Secretary-General, the International Planned Parenthood Federation; George Zeidenstein, President, the Population Council. *Invited international experts*: Robert McNamara, Manuel Urbina Fuente, Sandra Mostafa Kabir, Jacqueline Pitanguy, Shigemi Kono, Richard Sandbrook, Elizabeth Preble.

The purpose of the London meeting was to assess the population and family-planning situations world-wide, define new opportunities for both, and identify constructive ways to take advantage of the opportunities. The principles governing the organization of the Commission and its composition were also agreed upon.

The second preparatory meeting took place at the **Bellagio Study and Conference Center, 4–5 March 1992**. Its purposes were to define the main parameters which should guide the Commission to be created. The terms of reference thus drawn were to constitute the Mission Statement for the new initiative—the Independent Commission of Population and Quality of Life. The meeting further constituted a list of names of potential candidates for the chair, defined the functions and the composition of the secretarial staff, and considered the need to raise funds besides those already committed by governments and institutions whose representatives were present at the preparatory meetings.

The participants of the Bellagio meeting were: *For International Organizations*: Nafis Sadik and Jyoti Shankar Singh, United Nations Population Fund; Ann O. Hamilton, the World Bank. *From the bilateral development agencies*: Christoph Allison, the United Kingdom; Amb. Nicolaas H. Biegmann, The Netherlands; Michael Bonnet, Germany; Duff Gillespie, United States of America. *From ministries of foreign affairs*: Amb. L. O. Edström, Sweden. *From NGOs (including private foundations)*: Peter Goldmark, President, and Stephen W. Sinding, The Rockefeller Foundation; Carmen Barroso, the MacArthur Foundation; Jose Barzelatto, the Ford Foundation; Faith Mitchell, The Hewlett Foundation. *Institutions dealing with Population Issues*: Shigemi Kono, Institute of Population Problems, Japan; Mark Laskin, the International Planned Parenthood Federation; Maher Mahran, Egypt National Population Council; Haryono Suyono, National Family Planning Coordinating Board of Indonesia; Manuel Urbina-Fuentes, Consejo Nacional (Mexico) de Población; George Zeidenstein, President, the Population Council. *Invited international experts*: Jacqueline Pitanguy, Elizabeth Preble.

COMPOSITION OF THE COMMISSION

President

Maria de Lourdes Pintasilgo

Born 1930. Chemical engineer and Ambassador. Chair, Portuguese National Commission on Status of Women, 1970–4. Minister of Social Affairs, 1974–5. Ambassador to UNESCO, 1976–80. Prime Minister, 1979–80. Adviser to the President, Republic of Portugal, 1981–5. Member, United Nations University Council, 1983–9. Member, the InterAction Council of Former Heads of State and Government since 1983. Member, European Parliament, 1987–9. Chairman of the Board, World Institute for Development and Economic Research, UNU/WIDER, 1990– ; Member, high-level group of experts on Women and Structural Change in the 1990s, OECD, 1990–1; Member, National Council of Bio-ethics, 1991–6; Chairperson of the working group on Equality and Democracy, Council of Europe, Strasbourg, 1993–4; President of the 'Comité des Sages', European Union, 1995–6.

Members

Monique Bégin

Born 1936. University studies in Canada, France. Consulting sociologist, 1963–7. Executive director, Royal Commission on the Status of Women in Canada, 1967–70. Executive Director, Royal Commission on the Status of Women in Canada, 1967–70. Assistant Director of Research, Canadian Radio and Television Commission, 1970–2. Member of Parliament, House of Commons, Ottawa, 1972–84. Parliamentary Secretary to External Affairs, 1975–6. Minister of National Revenue, 1976–7, of National Health and Welfare, 1977–84. University professor (Notre Dame, McGill, Carleton, and Ottawa), 1984–90. Dean, Faculty of Health Sciences, University of Ottawa, 1990– . Co-chair, Ontario Royal Commission on Learning, 1993–4.

Ruth Corrêa Leite Cardoso

Born 1930. Anthropologist. Senior researcher in anthropology, CEBRAP (Brazilian Centre for Analysis and Planning), 1985– ; assistant and associate professor, 1972–86. Member Advisory Council of foundation monitoring Public TV-2, 1984–9. Member, National Council for the Rights of Women, 1985–9. Editorial board member, several scholarly journals. Associate of social programmes promoted by the Brazilian government, 1994– .

Karina Constantino-David

Born 1946. Sociologist and community organizer; composer and guitarist; author and editor. President, Caucus of Development NGO Networks; Vice-Chair, Women's Action Network for Development (WAND). Deputy Minister, Social Welfare and Development, 1986–7. General consultant, Philippine Development Plan for Women, 1988–9. Member of Inang Laya, female-protest song duo. Executive director, Harnessing Self-Reliant Initiatives and Knowledge (HASIK). Currently professor of Community Development, University of the Philippines. Consultant, long-term Plan for Gender Development, 1995.

Eleanor Holmes Norton

Congresswoman, District of Columbia, 1991– ; civil-rights and women's leader. Chair, Equal Employment Opportunity Commission under President Jimmy Carter. Chair, Post Office and Civil Service Subcommittee on Compensation and Employee Benefits; Chair, Subcommittee on Judiciary and Education, District of Columbia Committee. Award, Lawyers Committee on Civil Rights under Law, for helping secure passage of the Civil Rights Act, 1991; named by the *Ladies Home Journal* as one of the hundred most important women in the United States. Holds nearly sixty honorary degrees. Professor of Law, Georgetown University.

Maria Anna Knothe

Born 1951. Training in history, women in leadership, management of NGOs. Researcher in Polish history, old graphics, peasantry, immigration, 1973–91. Specialist in women's NGOs, Government Plenipotentiary for Women and Family Affairs, 1991–2. Founder-president, Centre for the Advancement of Women, Warsaw, 1992– . Participant in numerous national, international conferences on women's and historical issues. Author of research articles and studies.

Bernard Kouchner

Born 1939. Doctor of medicine. Founder-Chairman, Médecins sans Frontières, 1971–9; Founder-Chairman, Médecins du Monde, 1980–8. Humanitarian missions to Biafra, Jordan, Lebanon, Syria, Kurdistan, Chad, Eritrea, Vietnam, Cambodia, Thailand, Uruguay, Peru, Guatemala, San Salvador, Honduras, elsewhere, 1968–96. Secretary of State for Social Insertion, 1988, for Humanitarian Action, 1992–3. Executive Committee, UN High Commissioner for Refugees, General Assembly of the UN, 1988– . Author of several books.

Vina Mazumdar

Born 1927. Taught political science, Indian universities, 1951–72. Secretariat, University Grants Commission, 1965–73, Committee on the Status of Women, 1973–5, director of women's studies, Indian Council of Social Research, 1975–80; founder-director, Centre for Women's Development Studies, New Delhi, 1980–1; National Fellow, Indian Council for Social Science Research, 1992–4; member, Board of Trustees, Population Council, New York, 1976–85; National Consultant (Hon.), ILO, 1981–91; member, various working groups, Indian Planning Commission and Ministries of Human Resource Development, of Rural Development, of Labour and Employment, 1977–93; founder-secretary, Indian Association for Women's Studies, 1982–5. Recipient, awards for outstanding leadership, UNIFEM and Association for Women in Development (AWID).

Hanan Mikhail-Ashrawi

Born 1946. Dean, Faculty of Arts, Birzeit University. Palestinian negotiator in meetings leading to Madrid Conferences; official spokesperson of the Palestinian side during bilateral and multilateral peace-process negotiations. Member, Birzeit University Human Rights Action Project; active in community services. President, Palestinian Association for Human and

Citizen's Rights. Writer on literature, culture and criticism, intifada, the peace process, fiction, and poetry. Honoured by the Palestinian community, named Woman of the Year in Arab-world media. Recipient of Marisa Bellisario Award (Italy) for role as woman in international politics. Member of Parliament.

Taro Nakayama

Born 1924. Doctor of medicine. Osaka Prefectural Assembly, 1955–68; House of Counsellors, National Diet, 1968–86. Vice-Minister of Labour, 1971; Chairman, Committee on Cabinet Affairs, 1976; Chairman, Steering Committee, 1979; Director-General, Prime-Minister's Office; Director-General, Okinawa Development Agency, 1980; Chairman, Diet Affairs, 1985); member, House of Representatives, 1986– . Chairman, Research Committee on Ethics, Brain Death and Organ Transplants, Liberal-Democratic Party, 1988– , and LDP Finance Committee, 1988. Foreign Minister, 1989–91. Chairman, LDP Research Commission on Foreign Affairs, 1994– . Books: *Brain Death and Organ Transplants*, *Starting from Zero*, and *Changing the World through Science and Technology*.

Olusegun Obasanjo

Born 1937. Retired military officer. Served with UN peace-keeping force, Congo, 1960–1; general officer commanding Nigerian 3rd Marine Commando Division during Civil War, accepting surrender of Biafran forces, January 1970; general officer commanding Army Engineers, 1970–5; chief of staff at Supreme Headquarters, 1975–6; head, Military Government, and Armed Forces Commander-in-Chief, 1976–9; presided over transition to civil rule. Farmer since retirement. Member, Palme Committee on Disarmament and Security Issues, 1983–9; member, InterAction Council of Former Heads of State, 1983– ; Director, Better World Society, 1987–91; Founder-Chairman, African Leadership Forum, 1987– . Since 1995 this member has not been permitted to rejoin the Commission, having been arrested, jailed, and later secretly tried for alleged involvement in a plot against his country. The Commission has reason to believe in the falsity of the charges.

Jan Pronk

Born 1940. Economics graduate of Erasmus University, 1964. Research assistant to Nobelist Jan Tinbergen, attached to the Development Programming Centre and the Netherlands Economic Institute; lecturer, Erasmus University. Labour Party member, Parliament, 1971–3, 1978–80, and 1986–9. Professor, international economic policy, Institute of Social Studies (The Hague), 1980–6. Assistant Secretary-General, UN, and Deputy Secretary-General, UNCTAD, 1980–6. Professor, theory and practice of policy-making, University of Amsterdam, 1988–9. Minister for Development Co-operation, 1989– .

Pu Shan

Born 1923. Ph.D., Harvard University. LL D, Carleton College. President, Chinese Society of the World Economy, 1985– ; President, Graduate School, Chinese Academy of Social Sciences, 1991– . Member, National Committee, Chinese People's Consultative Conference, 1988– , and member, Standing Committee of the same Conference, 1993– .

Augusto Ramirez Ocampo

Doctor of economics and legal studies, Javeriana University. On various occasions Delegate-Minister for Presidential Affairs (Colombia); Minister of Foreign Affairs; Mayor of Santafé de Bogotá; delegate, Constitutional National Assembly; Director, Inter-American Development Bank; personal representative, Secretary-General of the UN for the Special Plan for Economic Development in Central America; personal representative of the Secretary-General of the Organization of American States. Chief of Mission for the Restoration of Democracy in Haiti. Director, UN Development Programme, Latin-American and Caribbean region. Ambassador to various international agencies. Chief of the UNSAL Peace Mission in El Salvador. Member of Parliament; member, National Reconciliation Commission.

Juan Somavia

Founder, Executive Director, and President, Latin American Institute of Transnational Studies, 1976–86. President of the international commission of the democratic opposition in Chile, 1983–90. Founder, secretary-general, South American Peace Commission, 1986– . Permanent representative of Chile to the UN, 1990– . President, UN Economic and Social Council, 1993–4; Chairman, UN World Summit for Social Development (Copenhagen), 1995. Awarded the Leonidas Praño Prize of the Latin American Human Rights Association. Member, International Foundation for Development Alternatives, the MacBride Commission (UNESCO), the Committee for a Just World Peace, and several NGOs.

Aminata D. Traoré

Born 1947. Doctorate, social psychology; diploma in psychopathology. Specialized in the fields of women, youth participative development, culture, and environment. Research assistant, University of Abidjan, 1974–88; director of studies and programmes, Ministry of Women's Affairs, Côte d'Ivoire, 1975–86; consultant to UN Development Programme, UNFPA, UNIFEM, UNICEF, African Development Bank,

Netherlands and Swiss development-assistance agencies, and Oxfam. Interior designer and owner of two gallery-restaurants in Bamako.

Beate Weber

Born 1943. University of Heidelberg and Pädagogische Hochschule (Heidelberg), 1968–79. Teacher, 1968–79. City Councillor, Heidelberg, 1975–85. Deputy chair, Federal Council, SPD political party since 1975. Member, European Parliament (vice-chair, then chair, of its Committee of Environment, Public Health and Consumer Protection), 1979–90. Member, German National Committee of Habitat II. Mayor of Heidelberg, 1990– .

Anders Wijkman

Born 1944. Bachelor of Arts, University of Stockholm. Member, Swedish Parliament (Moderate Party) 1970–8, Secretary-General of Swedish Red Cross, 1979–88. President, Disaster Relief Commission, International Committee of the Red Cross, 1981–9. Secretary-General, Swedish Society for Nature Conservation, 1989–92. Member, Royal Swedish Academy of Sciences, 1988– . Director-General, Swedish Agency for Research Co-operation with Developing Countries, 1992–5. Member, Club of Rome, 1992– . Assistant Secretary-General of UN and Director, Bureau for Policy and Programme Support, UN Development Programme, 1995– . Published author on environment, sustainable development, disaster prevention, AIDS.

Alexander Nikolayevitch Yakovlev

Born 1923. Doctorate in history. After the Second World War, served as party functionary, journalist, teacher. Worked alternatively at the Academy of Social Sciences and the Central Committee of the Communist Party of the Soviet Union, 1953–73. Ambassador to Canada, 1973–83. Director, Institute for the World Economy and International Relations, 1983. Elected Secretary, Central Committee and member, Politburo, 1985, then appointed to Presidential Council. Expelled from Party for attempting to create another party, 1991. Currently Chairman, Presidential Committee on Rehabilitation of Political Prisoners. President, International Foundation for Charity and Health. Author of works on international relations, democratic processes in Russia, global social and economic problems.

Advisers

Dragoljub Najman

Born 1931. Law, Diplomacy, French and Italian languages and literature, University of Belgrade (1950–6); Fellow, Centre for International Affairs,

Harvard University. Chief of mission (Zaïre); director, higher education; Assistant Director-General, then on special leave, UNESCO, 1957–86. Staff member, Independent Group on Financial Flows to Developing Countries, 1988–9. Member, steering group, A World in Need of Leadership: Tomorrow's United Nations, 1990–1. Member, Board of Directors, Peace and Crisis Management Foundation. Vice-President, The African Leadership Forum; member, Academic Council, European Centre for Peace and Development; consultant, InterAmerican Development Bank and UN Development Programme; lecturer on macroeconomics, international debt, and foreign direct investment, University of Belgrade.

George Zeidenstein

Doctor of laws, Harvard University (*cum laude*). Private law practice, 1954–65. Volunteer lawyer in Mississippi and Arkansas, supporting voter registration, 1964. Country director (Nepal), then Regional Director-Designate, East Asia and the Pacific, Peace Corps, 1965–8. President, Brooklyn Linear City Development Corporation, 1968–9. Resident representative (Bangladesh), later Deputy Head, Asia and the Pacific, Ford Foundation, 1969–76. President, Population Council, 1976–93. Distinguished Fellow, Centre for Population and Development Studies, Harvard University, 1993– .

Secretariat

Executive secretary:	Pierre de Senarclens (1992–4)
Senior staff adviser:	Stafford Mousky (1992–3)
Population specialists:	Christopher Allison, on secondment from the Overseas Development Agency, United Kingdom (1992–5). Alain Mouchiroud, on secondment from UNFPA (1993–4)
Gender specialist:	Martha O. Garcia
Human-resources specialist:	Laura Faxas
Development specialist:	Anne Baer
Communication:	Nadia Khouri-Dagher, assisted by Sophie Lavoute
Consultants:	Leonard Appel, Hans d'Orville, Pierre Henquet, A. M. A. Muhith
Administration:	Samy Bernardout
Assistant to the Chair:	Françoise Brunel
Support staff:	Margaret Hoareau, Kristi Hampton, Roza Agrane, Diana Heath, Sonali Munasinghe

The Report was prepared by a task force of the Commission, on the basis of a larger report by Paul Harrison, and finalized by Dragoljub Najman and Hans d'Orville, with Jacques Richardson as editor.

MANDATE

The Commission defined the main foci of its working as they resulted from the mandate given to it. The main features of the mandate were for the Commission twofold:

— to search for a 'fresh vision' of population matters that would include all the factors interacting with population and to elaborate the phenomena in their interfaces;

— to listen to the broadest possible audiences and to try both to gather data from their experience as well as to disseminate the Commission's own vision on the issues raised.

In a shorter and simplified form, the mandate of the Commission was, thus, the following:

Purpose. The purpose of this Independent Commission is to develop and disseminate a fresh vision of international population matters that engages, inspires, and commits, deeply and firmly, a large and broad constituency world-wide.

Context. The interactions among population numbers, economic development, environment, and human welfare are now extremely complex. It remains beyond debate, nevertheless, that sustainable improvement in the quality of life and survival of our world stand above all other goals.

The world's survival now requires unprecedented, collaborative solutions that unite all nations in a shared commitment to adapt production and consumption patterns, as well as addressing population issues, in ways that foster equitable development and respect rights.

High fertility is associated with two factors: lack of family-planning services and underlying socio-economic disparities. It is therefore essential to provide family-planning services of good quality and to improve living conditions with particular regard for health, nutrition, and education. At the same time, however, concern is voiced that financial and other support for developmental work in the social sectors is inadequate and not always well deployed. Ways and means are sought to pursue an economic growth that promotes equity and allows for the provision of humane, good-quality social services—especially health and family-planning services.

It is in this context that the Commission is established to develop and disseminate—in fact, to promote—both a vision and immediate, concerted action that recognize and build upon synergistic relationships among all pertinent elements involved.

Policy considerations. The Commission will keep in mind the following:

- The commitment of governments must be strengthened to formulate policies, and of both governments and NGOs to improve their institutional and technical capacities to implement programmes deriving from these policies.
- Common ground must be developed among multiple constituencies to promote harmonious action and generate the necessary support, including increasing the financial resources available.
- There is a need to focus on the individual, on the family, and on the capacity of individuals and couples to realize their own reproductive objectives in all population policies and programmes to achieve, on the one hand, individual freedom and better conditions for the family, and, on the other, a sustainable growth-rate of population.
- The importance of reproductive choice and sustainable population growth and size as essential elements in a broad strategy of development must be emphasized.
- Women are often the poorest of the poor, too often denied equal rights with men. The Commission must make progress in righting such undeniable wrongs.

Outputs. Social, economic, educational, and cultural factors need to be identified and discussed as to how they interact with fertility behaviour. Sexuality, gender–power relationships, discrimination and violence against women, equity, the dynamics of population change, and individual–collective ethics should be important components of the Commission's deliberations.

Approach. The Commission will seek, with vigour, to learn and reflect the experience and views of concerned groups and individuals in governments, multinational, and non-governmental organizations. The Commission will strive especially to hear and integrate the views of women in every aspect of its work. Towards this end, the Commission will hold intensive hearings at selected sites in representative countries round the world; it will interview multiple constituencies, inside and outside government, to learn their perceptions of issues related to population, development, and reproductive health; it will commission studies and other written materials.

The audience for the Commission's effort will be policy-makers and decision-makers, agenda-setters, and leaders of public opinion throughout the world. Public communications will be an especially important feature of the Commission's work from the outset: the Commission will seek to communicate through appropriate channels with the widest possible public everywhere.

SESSIONS OF THE COMMISSION

The Commission met every six months to elaborate a shared vision and to formulate its message to be disseminated mainly via its Report.

The Commission held its first session in **Paris, 21–23 April 1993**, to define the perception of, and a common methodology for, the work to be done. The members exchanged experience and views regarding population matters and quality of life, and their relationships with human rights, socio-economic development, and environment.

The second session was also held in **Paris, 13–15 October 1993**. The Commissioners confirmed their decision to take the concept of Quality of Life as the firm thread of their work. In that context, the concept of population was clearly refocused on people and their life conditions, beyond the mere play of numbers. As a consequence, the Commission decided to give priority to the grass-root work and set the guide-lines for Public Hearings to be organized in several regions of the world, with a desire to spread its auditions as widely as possible.

The third session took place in **New Delhi, 28–30 April 1994**, immediately following the Commission's South Asian Regional Consultation. The outcome of this session was an agreement on the outline and general content of the Report, on the basis of which the Commission's secretariat was to elaborate its first version.

This first version was presented at the fourth session, held in **Sintra, Portugal, 4–7 February 1995**, and the title of the Report, *Caring for the Future*, was adopted. During this session the Commission had the opportunity to discuss the Summit's state of affairs with Juan Somavia, member of our Commission and Secretary-General of the World Social Summit on Development scheduled in Copenhagen, March 1995.

At its fifth session, held in **Paris, 26 June–1 July 1995**, the Commissioners agreed on the ultimate formulation of their conclusions and planned the dissemination of the report. It was decided to appoint a Task Force of five members of the Commission to review the report in detail and propose a specific orientation of its final text.

The sixth and final session, also held in **Paris, 2–4 February 1996**, reviewed, adjusted, and adopted a new and final draft of the Report.

REGIONAL PUBLIC HEARINGS

As a consequence of the decision taken at the second session to give priority in its approach to the people and representatives of institutions directly involved, at the grass-root level, with population matters, a series of Public Hearings was organized in seven different regions of the world. In each instance a specific theme—a result of the analysis of the most pressing problems connected with 'population' questions in the region—was deepened and enriched by the contributions of representatives of NGOs, scientific communities, officials from public administration, religious and political leaders, organizations of women and of young people. The witness thus gathered has been embodied in the Report.

Moreover, videos were made by local teams at every Public Hearing. It is the intention of the Commission to prepare a series of book-magazines on each Public Hearing, the first one—on the basis of the Public Hearings held in Zimbabwe and in Mali—being already published with the title *Qui écoutera ma voix?/Who will listen to my Voice?*, in a bilingual edition.

Present at each hearing were the President, a few Commission members, and two advisers. Local groups were called upon to help organize the entire process under the guidance of the members of the Commission from the region. The Commission was thus able to evaluate perspectives that are, in fact, a host of reflections on the voice of the people.

Southern African Public Hearings, at Harare (Zimbabwe), 10–11 December 1993

Theme:	Population and quality of life: key regional issues.
Issues covered:	Environment. Women. Youth. Population and health.
Organized by:	Olusegun Obasanjo and Aminata Traoré (members of the Commission), with the National Association of Non-Governmental Organizations of Zimbabwe (NANGO), Africa 2000 Network, Environment, Zimbabwe Women's Resource Centre and Network, Department of Sociology of the University of Zimbabwe, Zimbabwe Public Health Association, and Zimbabwe Council of Churches.
Participation:	Tendai Bare, Deputy Minister for National Affairs and Employment; Victoria Chitauro, Deputy Minister of Public Service, Labour and Social Welfare; Stanislaus S. P. Matindike, co-ordinator of the Hearing, chairperson, National Association of Non-Government Organizations (NANGO), Zimbabwe. With: the Tsholotsho Group; the Iluba Elimnyama Group; Sibonelelo Group; Mutoko-Patikayi Group; Ngome

Group; Bhopoma Group; Nyota Group; Nyachityu Group; Mwenezi Group; Sweetwater Group; Zimbabwe Women's Bureau; Adult Literacy Organisation of Zimbabwe; Young Women's Christian Association; Black Sash of South Africa; UNIFEM; Presbyterian Church Choir, Mbare, Zimbabwe; ZACT, Zimbabwe; YMCA Highfield Youth Group, Zimbabwe; Chitungwiza Youth Group, Zimbabwe; Youth Forum; National Council of Women Societies, Nigeria; Women and Children Programme, Arusha, Tanzania; UNESCO sub-regional office, Harare, Zimbabwe. Individuals from Botswana, Ethiopia, Kenya, Mauritius, Namibia, Nigeria, Senegal, South Africa, Tanzania, Uganda, Zambia, Zimbabwe.

Meeting	T. Stamps, Minister of Health and Child Welfare.
Media coverage:	by television, radio, and articles in the local press.

Western Africa Public Hearings: Bamako (Mali), 22–25 February 1994

Theme:	Are we poor because we are too many? For a shared vision of population in sub-Saharan Africa.
Issues covered:	Reproduction and health. Socio-cultural aspects. Education as a factor of change. Family planning.
Organized by:	Olusegun Obasanjo and Aminata Traoré (members of the Commission), with the Centre Amadou Hampate Ba pour le Développement et la Qualité de Vie.
Participation:	Modibo Sidibé, Minister of Health, Solidarity and Elderly People. With A. Adepoju, Professor, Director IDEP, Senegal; Emma A. Agounke, Unité de recherches démographiques, Université du Bénin; Mamadou Y. Ba, OMS, Mali; Boubacar Bah, BECIS, Mali; Birama Bakayoko, BECIS, Mali; Rose Bastide, Centre Djoliba, Mali; Jean C. Berberat, Coopération suisse, Mali; Bernard A. Boa, CCD, Côte d'Ivoire; Amidou Berthe, GIE, Sema Saniya; Brunet-Jailly, ORSTOM/INRSP; J. Bugnicourt, ENDA-Tiers Monde, Senegal; Stephano Capotorti, Tierra Nueva, Mali; Samuel Carlson, The World Bank, Mali; N'golo Coulibaly, Ministère de l'éducation de base, Mali; Djibril Dembele, CIE 'Avenir', Torokorobougou, Mali; Seydou O. Diall, OMS, Mali; Doucoure A. Diallo, MSSPA, Mali; Fanta S. Diallo, Carrefour Reconversion, Mali; Gaoussou Diallo, Centre AHB,

Mali; Agnés Diaroumeye, Director, MULPOC, Cameroun; Sory I. Diarra, BAARA, Mali; Jean Dufriche, MSSPA, Mali; Duponchel, Fac/SPS, Ministère de la Santé, Mali; Habimana Gaudence, Office national de la population, Rwabda; Isaiah A. Ebo, FNUAP, Mali, A. W. El Abassi, UNICEF, Mali; Carol Hart, USAID, Mali; Keumaye Ignegongba, CERPOD, Mali; Aminata Konate, Centre Amadou Hampato Bâ, Mali; Abdoulaye Lansar, AHB, Mali; Oumar T. Ly, secretaire général, Présidence, Mali; Fatoumata S. Maiga, OMS, Mali; M. Maiga, ASACOBA, Mali; Lucy Mire, USAID, Mali; Rokia Niare, Centre Djolida, Mali; A. G. Rhaly, Koulouba, Mali; Jess Sah Bi, artiste, Mali; Bintou D. Sidibe, GP/JE, Mali; Malaye Sidibe, GIE, Torokorobougou, Mali; Tinga Sow, AHB, Mali; Joseph A. Tembely, GIE Badala Saniya, Côte d'Ivoire; Korotimi Tera, AHB, Mali; Marcio Thome, Population Council, CERPOD, Mali; Andre Tioro, MBDHP, Burkina Faso; Aminata N. Toure, Mali; Kadiatou P. Toure, Coopération suisse, Mali; Alfousseyni Traore, AHB, Mali; Boubacar M. Traore, FNUAP, Mali; Gaoussou Traore, AHB, Mali; Moukoro Virginie, Centre Djoliba, Mali. Individuals from Cameroon, Côte d'Ivoire, Mali, Rwanda, Senegal, and Togo.

Meeting: Audience with H. E. Alpha Oumar Konaré, President of the Republic of Mali.

Special session: 'Table-ronde' with national decision-takers and representatives of international agencies.

Media coverage: extensive TV and press coverage, including French-language Africa newspapers; radio interviews with the Commission's President.

North-America Public Hearings, Washington (DC), 28–30 March 1994

Theme: Unmet needs, innovative projects and public policy.

Issues covered: Reproductive health care for vulnerable population. Gender, sexuality, and family. Adolescents and sexuality. Population and quality of life; urgent issues.

Organized by: Monique Bégin and Eleanor Holmes Norton (members of the Commission), with The Development Group, Alexandria, Virginia.

Participation: Jocelyn Elders, Surgeon-General of the United States;

Faith Mitchell, Global Affairs, Department of State with: Marie-Marthe Saint-Cyr, Iris House, East Harlem, New York; Claudette Dumond-Smith and Elaine Johnston, Aboriginal Nurses Association of Canada, Ottawa, Canada; Cheryl Boykins, Center for Black Women's Wellness, Atlanta, Georgia; Virginia Ramirez, A Su Salud, San Antonio, Texas; Susan Jackiewicz and Jeanette McDonald, Office of Quality Enhancement, Department of Mental Retardation, Boston, Massachusetts; Mary Chung, National Asian Women's Health Organization and Asian Immigrant Women Advocates, Oakland, California; Heidi Hsia, Barbara Shine, and Sandra Bowman, Montgomery County Department of Addiction, Victim and Mental Health, Rockville, Maryland; Mary Jacksteit and Karen Sirker, Search for Common Ground, Washington DC; Shree Mulay, National Action Committee for the Status of Women, Montreal Canada; Claude Aguillaume, Population Council, New York; Eleanor Morrison and Melanie Morrison, Leaven, Lansing, Michigan; Juliette Martin Thomas, Shade Tree Family Resource Center, Milwaukee, Wisconsin; Perdita Huston, the Global Family Project, Washington DC; Charlie Lord, Jessica Beels, Jwahara Coleman, Mark Jennings, Sarah Nicholas, and Courney Snowden, Children's Express, Washington DC; William Johnson and Nkechi Ukeekwe, Teen Council, Washington DC; Blanca Diaz, Yossinia Menjiva, Linda Ohmans and Linda Preece, Latin America Youth Center, Washington DC; Franca Bertoncin and Nancy Hall, Health Promotion, North Shore Health Centre, Vancouver, Canada; Barry Hargrove and N-ya Finley, Shiloh Baptist Church, Washington DC; Clifford Johnson, Children's Defense Fund, Washington DC; Maria Antonietta Barriozabal, City Council of San Antonio, Texas; Aziza Al'Hibri, Daniel Maguire, Peter Paris, and David Sapperstein, Religious Consultation on Population, Washington DC; Cece Modupe Fadope, Women of Color Coalition for Reproductive Health and Rights, Washington DC; Luz Alvarez Martinez, National Latina Health Organization, Oakland, California; Phyllis Creighton and Natasha Feder, Ontario Conservation Council, Canada.

Individuals from community-based groups in the United States and Canada (Aboriginals, Haitian, Asian-American, African-American, Hispanic), as the most vulnerable populations in North America today.

Special Sessions: (a) Group of thinkers on fundamental issues of population at the global level;

(b) Round-table with a group of US-based international agencies and private foundations specializing in population matters.

Media coverage: by TV and radio, and in the local press.

South Asia Public Hearings, New Delhi, 25–27 April 1994

Theme: Population and quality of life: a South Asian perspective.

Issues covered: Perspectives on quality of life. People-centred strategies: quality, quantity, opportunities. Lessons from the past. Participation and roles of different actors. Perspectives on youth.

Organized by: Vina Mazumdar (member of the Commission), with the Centre for Women's Development Studies and the Council for Social Development. Organising Committee: *Centre for Women's Development Studies*: N. K. Banerjee, Nirmala Buch, Malavika Karlekar, Lotika Sarkar, Kumud Sharma (Director), C. P. Sujaya. *Council for Social Development*: Muchkund Dubey, Honorary Director. *Planning Commission*: Sarala Gopalan.

Participation Shri Pranab Mukherjee, Minister of Commerce and Deputy Chairman of the Planning Commission.

Bangladesh Zaffrullah Choudhury, Gonoshasthya Kendra; Nasreen Huq, Naripokkho; Hamida Hussain, Ain-o-Salish Kendra; Tehmina Hussain, Joint Secretary, Ministry of Health and Family Welfare.

Nepal Meena Acharya, Institute for Integrated Development Studies; Manisha Aryal, Himal; Dilli Raj Khanal, Executive Director, Applied Research and Development Study Centre; Kehm Raj Nepal, Joint Secretary, National Planning Commission; Devendra Raj Panday, Rural Self Reliance Development Centre; Shahana Pradham, Member of Parliament; Subodh Raj Pyakurel, Informal Sector Service Centre; Purushotam Risal, Chairperson, Women in Development.

India Poromesh Acharya, Abantika Abasan, Calcutta; Bina Agarwal, Institute of Economic Growth, Delhi; Indu Agnihotri, Fellow, Centre for Women's Studies, New Delhi; N. H. Antia, Foundation for Research in Community Health, Bombay; D. Bandyopadhyay, Calcutta; Nripen Bandopadhyay, Centre for Studies in Social Sciences; D. Banerjee, New Delhi; Narayan Banerjee, Centre for Women's Development Studies; Nirmala Banerjee, Centre for Studies in Social Sciences, Calcutta; Alaka Basu, Institute of Economic Growth, Delhi; Jyotsna Chatterji, Joint Women's Programme; Anjali Deshpande, India Press Agency, New Delhi; Vasudha Dhagamwar, Director, Multiple Action Research Group, New Delhi; Kamala Ganesh, Head, Department of Obstetrics and Gynaecology, New Delhi; Sanjoy Ghose, Urmul Trust, Rajasthan; Brinda Karat, All India Democratic Women's Association, New Delhi; Malini Karkal, Bombay; Primila Loomba, National Federation of Indian Women, New Delhi; Subhash Medhapurkar, Sutra, Himachal Pradesh; Kalpana Mehta, Saheli, New Delhi; Razia Patel, Pune; Imrana Quadeer, Centre for Studies in Community Health and Social Medicine, New Delhi; Asha Ramesh, Multiple Action Research Group, New Delhi; Vinod Raina, Eklavya, Madhya Pradesh; Joy Ranadive, Senior Fellow, Centre for Women's Development Studies, New Delhi; Amit Sengupta, Delhi Science Forum, New Delhi; Veena Shatrughna, National Institute of Nutrition, Hyderabad; Mira Shiva, Voluntary Health Association of India, New Delhi; Brinda Singh, Mobile Creche, New Delhi; Usha Sonker, Shakti Shalini, New Delhi; Husna Subhani, Mahila Dakshita Samity and All Indian Muslim Women's Association, New Delhi; T. Sundararaman, Pondicherry Science Forum, Pondicherry; M. S. Swaminathan, M. S. Swaminathan Research Foundation, Madras; Dr Vaasanthi, Editor, *India Today* (Tamil), Madras; V. S. Vyas, Director, Institute of Development Studies, Jaipur.

Pakistan Shagufta Alizai, Member, Shirkatgah; Hina Gilani, Director, Women's Legal Aid Cell, Human Rights Commission.

Sri Lanka Radhika Coomaraswami, Research Director, International Centre for Ethnic Studies;

Swarna Jayaweera, Coordinator, Centre for Women's Research; Wijetunga Mudalige Karunaratna, Asian South Pacific Bureau of Adult Education; Sepali Kottegoda, Joint Co-ordinator, The Women and Media Collective.

Observers from Donor Agencies in New Delhi R. K. V. Banerjee, Public Health Specialist, The World Bank; Tewabech Bishaw, Acting Chief (Health), UNICEF; John Dumm, USAID, American Embassy; Latika Padagaonkar, UNESCO; Ena Singh, UNFPA; John Watts, First Secretary, British High Commission, British Council Division.

Invitees from Youth Organizations Rajender Parihar, Secretary, Chatra Janata; Bratin Sengupta, Joint Secretary, Students Federation of India.

Meeting:	with Mrs Basawarajeshwari, State Minister for Women and Child Development, and Shri Arjun Singh, Minister for Human Resource Development.
Media coverage:	extensive coverage in the local press and on radio and TV, and by BBC-TV.

Latin America Public Hearings, 14–18 August 1994

Theme:	Strategies against poverty and social exclusion, a Latin-American approach to population and quality-of-life issues.
Issues covered:	Poverty and social exclusion. Ethnic and sexual discrimination. Violence against children and women. Health and reproductive rights. Safeguarding the habitat.
Organized by:	Ruth Corrêa Leite Cardoso (member of the Commission) and Rosiska Darcy de Oliveira, with the Instituto de Acção Cultural.
Participation:	Walter Barelli, former Minister of Labour, Brazil; Maria Bethânia Ávila, sociologist, Brazil; José Blanes, anthropologist, Bolívia; José Augusto Assumpção Brito, Director of SEBRAE, Brazil; Paulo Bussi, physician, Brazil; Nadia Cardoso, anthropologist, Grupo Axé Brasil, Brazil; Wanda Engel, Brazil; Rubem César Fernandes, anthropologist, Brazil; Brígida Garcia, sociologist, México; Roelfien Haak, social scientist, Director of 'Fomento La Vida', Peru; Rigoberta Menchú, Nobel Peace Prize, Guatemala; Ceclia Lopez Montaño, economist, Colombia; Ana Maria Pisarro,

physician, Nicarágua; Juan José Rivas, Chile; Edna Roland, sociologist, Comissão de Cidadania e Reprodução; Brazil; Herbert de Souza-Betinho, social scientist, Director of IBASE, Brazil; Célia Sterenfeld, psychologist, Brazil; Marta Suplicy, journalist and psychoanalyst, Brazil; Rodrigo Uprimny, laywer, Columbia; Ana Vasconcelos, sociologist, Casa de Passagem, Brazil; Alejo Vargas Velásquez, political scientist and social worker, professor Universidad Nacional de Colombia. Testimony heard from individuals and groups from the following countries: Argentina, Brazil, Chile, Columbia, Guatemala, Mexico, Nicaragua, Peru, Uruguay.

Meetings:	Audience with Itamar Franco, President of Brazil. Meetings with Henrique Santillo, Minister of Health, and Celso Amorin, Minister of Foreign Affairs.
Special session:	Round table with a group of thinkers.
Media coverage:	Extensively by the national press, the largest-circulation Latin-American magazine (*Veja*), and Portuguese media.

South-East Asia Public Hearings, Manila, 20–23 September 1994

Theme:	Organization and threats to human security and survival.
Issues covered:	Situation of the vulnerable populations. Threats to human survival. Government intervention. The urban poor. Women. Children and adolescents. Quality of life from the perspective of cultural workers.
Organized by:	Karina Constantino-David (member of the Commission), with Harnessing Self-Reliant Initiatives and Knowledge (HASIK)
Participation:	Juan Flavier, Secretary of State for Health; Rafael M. Alunan III, Secretary, Department of Interior and Local Government; Aniceto Sobripena, Deputy Director-General, National Economic Development Authority; Teodoro C. Bacani, Jr., Auxiliary Bishop of Manila, responsible for the Church's position on population issues. With: Alejandro Apit, Executive Director, Kamalayan Labor Center with Jose Caberos and Enrica Albes; Teodoro Bacabi, Auxilliary Bishop of Manila, Philippines; Maria-Teresa Banaynal-Fernandez, Executive Director, Lihok-Pilipina, Cebu City, Philippines; Agnes V. Camacho, Research

Officer, SALIN-LAHI Foundation, Philippines; Anita Celdran, National Campaigns Coordinator, Green Forum, Philippines; Eleonor Conda, Executive Director, Women's Legal Bureau, Philippines; Beverly dela Cruz-Perez, Legal Advocates of Talanay, Community-based Para-legals, Philippines; Marilen J. Dañguilan, MD, Office of the Senate President; Philippines; Lita J. Domingo, Associate Professor, Population Institute, University of the Philippines; Raquel Edralin-Tiglao, Executive Director, Women's Crisis Center, Philippines; Eduardo Estores, Mindanao Land Foundation, Davao City, Philippines; Anwar Fazal, Regional co-ordinator of Asia Pacific 2000, Manila, Philippines; Jaime Galvez-Tan, Under-Secretary, Department of State, Philippines; Wardah D. Hafidz, sociologist, Jakarta, Indonesia; Alex Hermoso, Programme Director, PREDA Foundation, Olongapo City, Philippines; Rina-Jimenez-David, chairperson, Pilipina-National Capital Region, Philippines; Cecile Joaquin-Yasay, Executive Director, Commission on Population, Philippines; Maximo T. Kalaw, 'Green Forum', Philippines; Alexander L. Mendoza, Executive Director, KAMPI, Federation of Disabled Persons in the Philippines; Leopoldo M. Moselina, Urban Basic Services and Street Children, UNICEF, Manila; National Coalition of NGOs for monitoring the Convention on the Rights of the Child, Philippines; Prapapat Niyom, Associate Professor, Faculty of Architecture, Chulalongkorn University, Thailand; Carmelita Nuqui, Executive Director, BATIS Centre, Philippines; Teresita Marie Pena-Bagasao, Executive Director, Kabalikat ng Pamilyang Pilipino, Makati, Philippines; Sri Eni Purnamawati, Medan, Indonesia; Mary Racelis, Assistant Representative, the Ford Foundation, Manila, Philippines; Yulfita Raharjo, Director, Center for Population and Manpower Studies, Indonesia; Evita Ramirez, Member, Ugnayan, Philippines; Corazon M. Raymundo, Executive Director, Population Institute, University of the Philippines; Rita Reddy, UNICEF, Bangkok, Thailand; Remedios Rikken, National Coordinator, Pilipina; Rosenna Sanchez, Development of People's Foundation, Philippines; Mary Alexis M. Salinas, Lankguman

Women's Collective for Action, Philippines; Patricia Mangrobang Sarenas, Executive Director, Kahayag Foundation, Davao City, Philippines; James Sherman, Center for Alternative Development Initiatives (CADI), Philippines; Maria Lourdes Sindico, Executive Director, Langkuman, Philippines; Aniceto Sobrepeña, Deputy Director General, National Economic Development Authority, Philippines; Florence M. Tadiar, Executive Director, Women's Health Care Development Foundation, Philippines; Joaquin Tan, President, CADI, Philippines; Nguyen Thi Canh, Deputy Head, Development Research Department, Institute for Economic Research, Ho Chi Minh City, Vietnam; Cecilia C. Villa, Executive Director, Foundation for Adolescent Development, Philippines; Junya Yimprasert, Friends of Thai Women Workers in Asia, Nonthaburi, Thailand. And with Joey Ayala, artist, singer; PETA – Philharmonic Educational Theatre Association; INANG LAYA, performing artists; GARY GRANADA, performing artists; EDRY ABRAHAM and the KONTRA-GAPI, College of Arts and Letters. The following countries were represented: Indonesia, Laos, Malaysia, Philippines, Singapore, Vietnam.

Media Coverage: Extensive in the regional media.

Eastern Europe Public Hearings, Moscow, 17–24 October 1994

Theme: Socio-economic transformation, population and quality of life.

Issues covered: The problems of childhood and youth. The situation of women. The elderly. The family in Eastern Europe.

Organized by: Alexander N. Yakovlev (member of the Commission) and Natalia Rimashevskaya with the Institute of Socio-economic Studies on Population, Russian Academy of Sciences.

Participation: Valentin A. Koralov, Deputy Chairman of Parliament, Russian Federation; Marja Lauristen, Member of Parliament, Estonia; Metropolitan Pitirim, Orthodox Church, Russian Federation; Kasimira Prunskene, President of the 'Lithuania-Europe' Institute, Lithuania. With: Valentin A. Koralov, Deputy Chairman of Parliament, Russian Federation; Marja Lauristen, Member of Parliament, Estonia; Metropolitan Pitirim, Orthodox Church, Russian

Federation; Kasimira Prunskene, President of the 'Lithuania-Europe' Institute, Lithuania, former Prime Minister. Natacha Aleksakhina (witness), Institute for population studies, Russia; T. Ananieva (witness) a mother; Rimma Antchipalovskaya (witness), gynaecologist, Russia; Vladislav Berzrukov, Director of Gerontology Institute, Kiev, Ukraine; Irina Bulantseva (witness), Institute for socio-economic population studies, Russia; J. Diskin (132); Natalia Gaidarenko, The Centre 'Sisters', Moscow, Russia; Goncharov (128); Irina Goryacheva (witness), Institute for socio-economic population studies, Russia; Inga Grebesheva, President, The Russian Association 'Family Planning', Moscow, Russia; Malgojata Halaba, Federation for women and family, Warsaw, Poland; O. Kadamsteva, engineering programme designer, Russia; Natasha Kaulina (witness), economist, Russia; Adisher Sergeyevich Kandelaki, Georgian building and placement of health resorts; Georgia; Zoia Khotkina, senior researcher, Centre for gender studies, Moscow, Russia; L. Khrapylina, Council for Social Policy, Moscow, Russia; A. Khvostova (witness), physician and teacher, Russia; N. Kolcheva (witness), employee in large factory making leather goods; Igor Kon, Professor, Institute of Ethnography and Anthropology, Moscow, Russia; Maria N. Krilova (witness); Boris Levin, Head of Laboratory, Institute of Sociology, Moscow, Russia; Natasha Logvinenko (witness), accountancy programme designer, Russia; Yuri Mitev, President, Municipal committee on social security, Taganrog, Russia; Marina Mozhina, Head of Laboratory, Institute for socio-economic population studies, Moscow, Russia; Maia Pankratova, senior researcher, Institute of Sociology, Russian Academy of Sciences, Moscow, Russia; Dr Nazarov, Historian, Kirgizia; Oleg Pchelintsev, Head of department, Institute for Economic Forecasting, Moscow, Russia; Marina Pisklakova, Crisis Centre for Women, Moscow, Russia; Andrei Popov, senior researcher, Institute for Economic Forecasting, Moscow, Russia; Natalia Rimashevskaya, Director of the Institute for socio-economic population studies; Russian Academy of Sciences, Moscow, Russia; Tania Shalakova, senior researcher, National Centre for Health Information, Sophia, Bulgaria; Donat Konstantinovich Sidorov, President, Moscow Fund of Aid to the war-disabled persons; Nina Simonova, senior researcher, Institute for socio-economic population studies, Moscow, Russia; Jadviga Slavinska, professor, Warsaw University, Poland; Vlada Stankunene, chief of department, Institute of Philosophy, Sociology, and Law, Tallin, Lithuania; Maria Vavrejnova, Institute of Economics, Prague, Czech Republic; Galina Vitkovskaya, senior researcher, Institute for Economic Forecasting, Russian Academy of Sciences, Moscow, Russia. Individuals represented the following countries: Bulgaria, Czech Republic, Estonia, Georgia, Kirgizia; Lithuania, Poland, Russian Federation, Ukraine.

Special session:	Round table with thinkers.
Media coverage:	Press conference and articles in the leading newspapers, including *Pravda, Izvestiya,* and *Literaturnaya Gazeta, Moskovsky Komsomolets, Nezavisimaya Gazeta.*

CONSULTATION OF EXPERTS

The Commission consulted experts on population issues, specialists from a broad spectrum of disciplines. Thematic panels were organized, in addition to direct consultation with individuals.

A panel on *Population Policies and Governance* was organized in **Bellagio (Italy), 27–30 September 1993**, to consider the evolution of population policies and measures adopted by different countries in the second half of the twentieth century, and to analyse their interconnections with governance and ethics. In addition to members of the Commission and the advisers, the experts present were D. Bandyopadhay (India), George Benneh (Ghana), Ana Maria Brasileiro (USA), John Hobcraft (UK), Musharaf Hossain (Bangladesh), Raj Karim (Malaysia), Kelley Lee (UK), Thérèse Locoh (France), Walter Mertens (USA), Nico van Nimwegen (Netherlands), Manuel Urbina Fuentes (Mexico), and Helen Ware (Australia). The Rockefeller Foundation played host at its Seminar Centre.

A second panel took place in **Stockholm, 18–20 May 1994**, addressing *production and consumption patterns in relation to the Earth's carrying capacity and their impact on the quality of life.* The aim was to present and analyse possible strategies to modify current production and consumption patterns, taking into account ethical and environmental concerns.

The experts participating were Anil Agarwal (India), G. Corea (Sri Lanka), S. Karezi (Kenya), Khor Kok Peng (Malaysia), A. Khosla (India), Maneka Gandhi (India), Manfred Max-Neef (Chile), Kirith S. Parikh (India), S. Hansen (Norway), Carl Folke (Sweden), Li Jinchang (China), Liu Wen (China), Paul Harrison (UK), Samuel Nana-Sinkham (FAO), Maciej Nowicki (Poland), R. Sandbrook (UK), J. H. Spangenberg (Germany), and Wouter van Dieren (Netherlands).

Most important were the meetings convened during some of our Public Hearings with 'thinkers' of the region.

- Within the **West Africa Public Hearings**, there was a round table on 'Health and Education' with Aderanti Adepoju, IDEP, Senegal; Emma Akoua Agounke, Unité de recherche démographique, Université du Bénin, Togo; Boubacar Bah, BECIS, Mali; Rose Bastide, Centre Djoliba, Mali; Bernard Ano Boa, CCD, Côte d'Ivoire; J. Brunet-Jailly, ORSTOM/INRSP, Mali; Samuel Carlson, the World Bank; Jacques Bugnecourt, ENDA/Tiers-Monde, Sénégal; N'Golo Coulibaly, Ministry for Basic Education; Doucouré A. Diallo, MSSPA, Mali; A. W. El Abassi, UNICEF, Mali; M. Maïga, ASACOBA, Mali; Gaudence Habimana Nyirasafari, ONAPO, Rwanda; Thérèse Locoh, INED/CEPED, Paris; Oumar T. Ly, Secrétaire général, Présidence, Mali; Agnès Rhaly, MSSPA, Mali; Marcio Thome, Population Council, Mali.

- In **Latin America**, the participants at the round table, chaired by Professor Rosiska Darcy de Oliveira, writer, Brazil, were: Elza Berquó, demographer, senior researcher CEBRAP, Miguel Darcy de Oliveira, political scientist, President of the Instituto de Ação Cultural (IDAC) and Co-Presidente do CIVICUS, Brazil; Joaquim de Arruda Falcão, lawyer, President of the Fundação Roberto Marinho, Brazil; Vilmar Faria, social scientist, senior researcher at CEBRAP, Brazil; Elizabeth Jelin, sociologist, senior researcher CONICET, Argentina; Ricardo Melendez Ortiz, economist, President of the Fundação Futuro da América Latina, Colombia; Paulo Sérgio Pinheiro, political scientist, Director of the Núcleo de Estudos da Violência, Brazil; Margarida Pisano, architect, Director of the Centro La Morada, Chile; German Rama, sociologist; David Tejada, former Minister of Health (Peru).

- In junction with the Commission's Northern American Public Hearings, there was a meeting with invited experts from diverse fields to assist the Commission with development of a new vision of population and the quality of life. They were: Patricia Baird, Royal Commission on New Reproductive Technologies, Canada; Lester Brown, Worldwatch Institute, Margaret Catley Carlson, Population Council; Carmen Delgado Votow, Girl Scouts of America; Richard Falk, Princeton University, Robert Gnaizda, Public Advocates, Inc., Hazel Henderson, economist and futurist; Luke Lee, US Department of State, Don Michael, University of Michigan, professor emeritus; Michael Murphy, St Peter's Hospice; Claire Randall, Church Women United; Jonas Salk, professor, the Salk Institute; Susan Stamberg, National Public Radio: Billy J. Tidwell, Urban League; and Dhyani Ywahoo, Sunrise Meditation Society. There was also a round table in the Population Reference Bureau to exchange views. Present were: Faith Mitchell, Global Affairs, Department of State; Robert Blancato, Director of the White House Conference on Aging; Michael Fix, lawyer and immigration policy researcher with the Urban Institute; Martha Farnsworth Ritchie, demographer (prepared the US National Report on Population for submission to the International Conference on Population and Development); Jeannie Rossof, Alan Guttmacher Institute; Frank Sharry, Director of the National Immigration Forum. A meeting was also held with United States based agencies representatives with the participation of Nils Daulaire (Policy and Program Coordination Bureau), Elisabeth Maguire (Office of Population), Amanda Classman, USAID; Joseph van Arendonk, UNFPA, Alene Gelbard, Population Reference Bureau; Ranjit Attapatu, UNICEF; Margaret Catley Carlson and John Bongaards, the Population Council; Steve Sinding and Sara Seims, the Rockefeller Foundation; Thomas Merrick, Minh Chan Nguyen, Robert Goodland, the World Bank.

- In **South-East Asia Public Hearings**, the participants at the 'thinkers' round-table with facilitator Maria Anna de Rosas-Ignacio, National Coordinator of the Partnership of Philippine Support Agencies, Philippines, were: Maria Cynthia Rose Banzon-Bautista, Sociologist and professor at the University of the Philippines, Philippines; Jacquelyn Chagnon, Consultant and Associate in Development of the Asia resource Centre, Laos; Solita Collas-Monsod, Economist, Professor and Expert in Economic Development Econometrics, Philippines; Marilen J. Dañguilan, medical doctor, Philippines; Anwar Fazal, Economist, Malaysia; Wardah D. Hafidz, independent researcher and consultant for women and gender issues, Indonesia; Aurora Javate-de-Dios, Commissioner of National Commission on the Role of Filipino Women, Philippines; Rina Jimenez David, feminist and journalist, Commissioner of the National Commission on the Role of Filipino Women, Philippines; Maximo T. Kalaw, Jr, president of four NGO's, Philippines; William S. W. Lim, founder member and president of the Singapore Heritage Society, Singapore; Sanmuga Raja S. Paramasivam, Expert in Population Studies, Malaysia; Yulfita Raharajo, Center for Population and Manpower Studies, Indonesia; Corazon M. Raymundo, president, Population Institute, Philippines; Nguyen Thi Canh, Institute for Economic Research, Ho Chi Minh City, Vietnam; Surichai Wun'gaeo, Chulalongkorn University, Bangkok,

Thailand; Yu Yongding, Institute of World Economics and Politics, China.

- The participants to the 'thinkers' round table within the **Eastern Europe Public Hearings** were, under the chairmanship of Professor Natalia Rimashevskaya, Director of the Institute for Socio-Economic Studies of Population, Russian Academy of Sciences; Marja Lauristen, Member of Parliament, Estonia; Kazimira Prunskene, President of the 'Lithuania–Europe' Institute, Lithuania, former Prime Minister; G. Diligensky, professor, Director of the Centre of Socio-Economic and Political Research, Chief Editor of the magazine *World Economics and International Relations*; Josif Diskin, Deputy Director of Institute for Socio-Economic Studies of Population, Russian Academy of Sciences; Father Georgy, Russian Orthodox Church; George Goncharov, Archpriest, Public Department of Moscow Patriarchate; Boris Mikhailovich Levin, professor, Head of Department, Institute of Sociology, Russian Academy of Science, Moscow; Yuri Mitev, President of the Municipal Committee on Social Security, Taganrog, Russia; Jadviga B. Slavinska, professor of the Warsaw University, Poland; Olga Vershinskaya, Institute for Socio-Economic Problems of Population, Russian Academy of Sciences; Anatoly Vishnevsky, Director of the Centre of Demography and Human Ecology, Institute for Economic Forecasting, Russian Academy of Sciences; Tatiana Volgina, Russian Orthodox Church.

DESK STUDIES PREPARED FOR THE COMMISSION

In order to gather the 'state of the art' concerning population science and neighbouring disciplines, a series of topical papers was ordered from a broad array of specialists from around the world. These commissioned studies cover diverse topics spanning a multitude of population and quality-of-life concerns, the Commission's desire having been to call upon as many local researchers as possible in a diversity of geographical areas. Some of the studies have been of a cross-regional nature.

List of Studies and their Authors

Author	*Title*
Adepoju Aderanti	Poverty, Structural Adjustment Programmes, Population and Quality of Life in Sub-Saharan Africa
Bandyopadhyay D.	Powerlessness and Fertility
Bandyopadhyay D.	Impact of Structural Adjustment Programmes: Survival Strategies
Bautista Rose Banzon, *Cynthia* Maria, and *Samson* Laura Lorenzo	Family, Population and Quality of Life in East and South-East Asia: Dynamics, Changes and Family Life Alternatives and Strategies
Behnam Djamchid	Réflexions sur l'évolution de la famille dans un monde en changement
Benneh George	Demographic Changes and the Role of Government
Berquó Elsa	Family and Household Structure in Brazil, 1970–89
Bose Ashasi	Gender Issues and Population Change: Tradition, Technology and Social Turbulence
Briones Prof. Leonor M. and *Chavez-Malaluan* Jenina J.	New Social and Political Challenges within the Framework of the Structural Adjustment Process in South-East Asia (with focus on the Philippines): Effects on New Population Trends and Quality of Life
Castelain Meunier Christ.	Un premier regard sur la paternité contemporaine à travers le monde
Colombo Daniela	Structural and Functional Changes within the Family in Western Europe.
Cooks Rebecca and *Dickens* Bernard	The State and Reproductive Self-determination
Cosio-Zavala M. E.	Les transitions démographiques dans les pays développés et le monde en développement
Costas-Centivany Cynthia	Education and Population
de Coulomne-Labarthe G.	Approche globale pour un 'mieux-être' des 'enfants de la rue' dans le monde. Analyse, tendances et prospective.
Demeny Paul	An Assessment of Population Policy Dialogue
Dyson Tim	Reproductive Choice

Author	*Title*
Dyson Tim	World Population Growth and Food Supplies
Fausto Ayrton	Niños y Niñas de y en la Calle en Brasil
Garreton Manuel	Economic, Political, and Socio-cultural Change in Latin-American Societies in the Last Decades
Garreton Manuel and *Malva* Espinoza	From Adjustment Policies to the new State–Society Relations
Gilbert Alan	Human Resources: Work, Housing, and Migration
Hamza Nabila	Structural and Functional Changes Within the Family in Arab Countries
Harrison Paul	Northern Consumption and Production Models in Relation to the Carrying Capacity of the Earth
Hopkins Michael	A Global Perspective on Population and Employment
Jaubert Ronald	Population et plan de lutte contre la désertification
Kaddar Miloud	Population et santé en Afrique
Ladjali Malika	Santé sexuelle et reproductive des jeunes—mythes et réalités
Lapeyronnie Didier and *Martucelli* Danilo	Le débat population et qualité de vie dans un monde en changement
Lengyel Peter	Quality of Life: The Emergence of a Concept
Livi-Bacci Massimo	Population Policies: A Comparative Perspective
Locoh Thérèse	Familles africaines, population et qualité de vie
Lush Louisiana	The Health Implications of Future Demographic Change—1992–2025
McNicoll Geoffrey	Population and Institutional Change
Mertens Walter	Pathways for the Exploration of Population Policies
Mohsin Nadeem	Street and Working Children in South Asia
Najman Dragoljub and *d'Orville* Hans	Toward a New Multilateralism: Funding Global Priorities. Innovative Financing Mechanisms for Internationally Agreed Programmes
van Nimwegen Nico	Population-related Policies and Quality of Life. The Case of the Netherlands

Author	*Title*
Noin Daniel	Geography of Population and Quality of Life
de Oliveira O., *Ariza* Marina and *Gonzalez de la Roche* M.	Family Population and Quality of Life in Mexico, Central America, and the Caribbean
Orivel François	Population et éducation en Afrique sub-saharienne
Palloni Alberto	A Study on Mortality Trends and the Effect of Selected Policies
Palomba Rossela and *Sabbaddini* Linda Laura	Family, Population, and Quality of Life in Western Europe: Dynamics, Changes, New Family Life Alternatives, and Strategies
Palriwala Rajni	Changing Family and Gender Relations in South Asia
Pool Ian	The World's Caring Capacity: Population Compositional Aspects
Pool Ian	Quality of Life, Caring Capacity, Public Policy and Population Reproductive Choice
Pugh Cedric	Housing, Population, and Quality of Life
Rama Germán W.	Human Resources, Education, and Employment in Latin America
Rath Ferdinand J. C. M.	Coherence, Cooperation, and Coordination in Internationally Assisted Population Activities
Sachs Ignacy	Population, Development, and Employment
Sachs-Jeantet Céline	Humaniser la ville: Les enjeux de la citoyenneté et de l'urbanité
Safilio-Rothschild C.	Family, Population and Quality of Life in the United States and Canada
Silvestre Emmanuel	The Child in Latin American and Caribbean Streets in the Current Context of Political and Economic Change
Sinding Steve W.	The Role of Government and Demographic Change
Sonko Sheriff	Fertility and Culture in Sub-Saharan Africa: A Review
Stolnitz George J.	International Population, Labor Force and Child Labor Patterns: Trends, Perspectives, Interrelation

Author	Title
Tabah Léon	Vers la nouvelle Conférence internationale sur la Population et le Dèveloppement au Caire en septembre prochain
Author	Title
Tabah Léon	Les interrelations population–environnement–développement: état de la question et perspectives
Valdes Teresa and **Weinstein** Marisa	Cambios en las familias en America Latina: Procesos sociales y culturales
Valenzuela Eduardo	Crise et pauvreté en Amérique latine
Vichnevsky A.	Evolution de la famille et changements des structures familiales en Russie
Youego Christine	Evolution du statut de la femme et la qualité de vie en Afrique sub-saharienne au regard des transformations structurelles de nature économique et politique actuelles
Zlotnik Hania	International Migration, Population, and Quality of Life in a Changing World

MAIN COMMUNICATION ACTIVITIES

A *Newsletter*, informing about the Commission's activities and tackling controversial issues related to population, was disseminated to 25,000 organizations and individuals, mainly NGOs in the South and to media groups. Four issues were published in English and French: *Labour, New Trends*; *Parenthood Today*; *Young People's Sexuality: A Taboo Subject?*; and *Production and Consumption Patterns: More of the Same Won't Do*.

The Commission has made a **video of each Public Hearing** and is still conducting consultations about their diffusion. Leonard Appel, consultant to the Commission, prepared a bilingual book-magazine—English and French: *Who will listen to my voice/Qui écoutera ma voix?*, the first one of six of an intended series, *La Voix des Sans-Voix/The Voice of the Voiceless*, edited by *Le Fennec Editeur, Thionville, France*.

To mark the ICPD event, a special issue on *Women, feminisms, feminities* was published in September 1994 by international newspapers in collaboration with World Media Network.

For the Cairo Conference, the Commission produced an **8-minute video film**, *Moments of Youth*. During the conference, one 'dazibao' per day was presented on the ICPQL stand in Cairo, with quotes extracted from the Public Hearings.

A photographic exhibition, **Living Together—Testimonies of A Population Revolution**, was organized together with the Gamma Liaison photographic agency. It was shown in Cairo (ICPD) and Paris (Arche de la Défense), and was made available to the Musée de l'Homme (Paris) for a large scientific exhibition, *6 Billion People*, held in Paris from September 1994 to December 1995. (The photographic collection remains available for further use.)

A **seminar for journalists** on the theme: *Informing on Population Issues: A Challenge for the Media?*, was organized on 28 June 1994 at the Arche de la Défense in Paris, moderated by Robert Stolé, editor-in-chief of *Le Monde*. The meeting brought together sixty people, mainly media representatives, population specialists, and scientists such as Jacques Magaud, Director of INED, the (French) National Institute for Demographic Studies. As a result of this event, the interviews given by the Chair to the BBC World Service and to Radio France Internationale have both centred around the world event that ICPD was to constitute.

A press conference was organized at the end of the first three sessions of the Commission with several interviews of the participants.

FINANCIAL CONTRIBUTIONS

Funding of the Commission's work came from the governments of **Canada, Germany, Japan, the Netherlands, Norway, Sweden,** and the **United Kingdom;** from international organizations: the **International Planned Parenthood Federation,** the **United Nations Population Fund,** the **World Bank;** and from private foundations: the **Ford** Foundation, the **William and Flora Hewlett** Foundation, the **MacArthur** Foundation, the **Andrew W. Mellon** Foundation, and the **Rockefeller** Foundation.

INDEX

ACKNOWLEDGEMENTS

Many people contributed to this book. First, and most importantly, are the hundreds of witnesses who voluntarily testified during the regional Public Hearings held by the Commission, recounting courageously their personal experiences and offering to evaluate the reasons underlying many unbearable situations. Experts, whom we consulted individually or in groups, gave generously of their knowledge and advice.

The advisers to the Chair contributed decisively to the work of the Commission. George Zeidenstein brought in his experience in population matters and was a permanent pillar at the Public Hearings. Dragoljub Najman always showed his superior talents in the interdisciplinary and managerial functioning of the Commission.

Paul Harrison, Drago Najman, Hans d'Orville, and Jacques Richardson contributed intensively and in record time their assigned tasks in the preparation of the report: this book.

Leonard Appel helped to shape most of the Public Hearings and recorded the findings with precision and sensitivity. Last, but not least, Françoise Brunel demonstrated at all times her utmost dedication to our mission. I welcomed her numerous suggestions and her real capacity to organize with despatch our administrative obligations.

The Commission wishes to express its gratitude to the large number of institutions and other organizations that provided support and advice when these were required. Without the intervention and help of hundreds of people, the holding of regional consultations, the meetings with specialized bodies—and even the preparation of this report—would not have been possible.

The Commission regrets not being able to name all these co-operative contributors. Special thanks and consideration, nevertheless, go to UNESCO and its Director-General, Federico Mayor, for having facilitated the activities of the Commission's secretariat through the Funds-in-Trust mechanism.

OXFORD

MORE OXFORD PAPERBACKS

This book is just one of nearly 1000 Oxford Paperbacks currently in print. If you would like details of other Oxford Paperbacks, including titles in the World's Classics, Oxford Reference, Oxford Books, OPUS, Past Masters, Oxford Authors, and Oxford Shakespeare series, please write to:

UK and Europe: Oxford Paperbacks Publicity Manager, Arts and Reference Publicity Department, Oxford University Press, Walton Street, Oxford OX2 6DP.

Customers in UK and Europe will find Oxford Paperbacks available in all good bookshops. But in case of difficulty please send orders to the Cash-with-Order Department, Oxford University Press Distribution Services, Saxon Way West, Corby, Northants NN18 9ES. Tel: 01536 741519; Fax: 01536 746337. Please send a cheque for the total cost of the books, plus £1.75 postage and packing for orders under £20; £2.75 for orders over £20. Customers outside the UK should add 10% of the cost of the books for postage and packing.

USA: Oxford Paperbacks Marketing Manager, Oxford University Press, Inc., 200 Madison Avenue, New York, N.Y. 10016.

Canada: Trade Department, Oxford University Press, 70 Wynford Drive, Don Mills, Ontario M3C 1J9.

Australia: Trade Marketing Manager, Oxford University Press, G.P.O. Box 2784Y, Melbourne 3001, Victoria.

South Africa: Oxford University Press, P.O. Box 1141, Cape Town 8000.

POPULAR SCIENCE FROM OXFORD PAPERBACKS

THE SELFISH GENE

Second Edition

Richard Dawkins

Our genes made us. We animals exist for their preservation and are nothing more than their throwaway survival machines. The world of the selfish gene is one of savage competition, ruthless exploitation, and deceit. But what of the acts of apparent altruism found in nature—the bees who commit suicide when they sting to protect the hive, or the birds who risk their lives to warn the flock of an approaching hawk? Do they contravene the fundamental law of gene selfishness? By no means: Dawkins shows that the selfish gene is also the subtle gene. And he holds out the hope that our species—alone on earth—has the power to rebel against the designs of the selfish gene. This book is a call to arms. It is both manual and manifesto, and it grips like a thriller.

The Selfish Gene, Richard Dawkins's brilliant first book and still his most famous, is an international bestseller in thirteen languages. For this greatly expanded edition, endnotes have been added, giving fascinating reflections on the original text, and there are two major new chapters.

'learned, witty, and very well written . . . exhilaratingly good.' Sir Peter Medawar, *Spectator*

'Who should read this book? Everyone interested in the universe and their place in it.' Jeffrey R. Baylis, *Animal Behaviour*

'the sort of popular science writing that makes the reader feel like a genius' *New York Times*

POPULAR SCIENCE FROM OXFORD PAPERBACKS

THE AGES OF GAIA

A Biography of Our Living Earth

James Lovelock

In his first book, *Gaia: A New Look at Life on Earth*, James Lovelock proposed a startling new theory of life. Previously it was accepted that plants and animals evolve on, but are distinct from, an inanimate planet. Gaia maintained that the Earth, its rocks, oceans, and atmosphere, and all living things are part of one great organism, evolving over the vast span of geological time. Much scientific work has since confirmed Lovelock's ideas.

In *The Ages of Gaia*, Lovelock elaborates the basis of a new and unified view of the earth and life sciences, discussing recent scientific developments in detail: the greenhouse effect, acid rain, the depletion of the ozone layer and the effects of ultraviolet radiation, the emission of CFCs, and nuclear power. He demonstrates the geophysical interaction of atmosphere, oceans, climate, and the Earth's crust, regulated comfortably for life by living organisms using the energy of the sun.

'Open the cover and bathe in great draughts of air that excitingly argue the case that "the earth is alive".' David Bellamy, *Observer*

'Lovelock deserves to be described as a genius.' *New Scientist*

OXFORD PAPERBACK REFERENCE

From *Art and Artists* to *Zoology*, the Oxford Paperback Reference series offers the very best subject reference books at the most affordable prices.

Authoritative, accessible, and up to date, the series features dictionaries in key student areas, as well as a range of fascinating books for a general readership. Included are such well-established titles as Fowler's *Modern English Usage*, Margaret Drabble's *Concise Companion to English Literature*, and the bestselling science and medical dictionaries.

The series has now been relaunched in handsome new covers. Highlights include new editions of some of the most popular titles, as well as brand new paperback reference books on *Politics*, *Philosophy*, and *Twentieth-Century Poetry*.

With new titles being constantly added, and existing titles regularly updated, Oxford Paperback Reference is unrivalled in its breadth of coverage and expansive publishing programme. New dictionaries of *Film*, *Economics*, *Linguistics*, *Architecture*, *Archaeology*, *Astronomy*, and *The Bible* are just a few of those coming in the future.

**Oxford
Paperback
Reference**

CONCISE SCIENCE DICTIONARY

New edition

Authoritative and up to date, this bestselling dictionary is ideal reference for both students and non-scientists. Fully revised for this third edition, with over 1,000 new entries, it provides coverage of biology (including human biology), chemistry, physics, the earth sciences, astronomy, maths and computing.

* **8,500 clear and concise entries**

* **Up-to-date coverage of areas such as molecular biology, genetics, particle physics, cosmology, and fullerene chemistry**

* **Appendices include the periodic table, tables of SI units, and classifications of the plant and animal kingdoms**

'handy and readable . . . for scientists aged nine to ninety'
Nature

'The book will appeal not just to scientists and science students but also to the interested layperson. And it passes the most difficult test of any dictionary—it is well worth browsing through.'
New Scientist

OXFORD

RETHINKING LIFE AND DEATH
THE COLLAPSE OF OUR TRADITIONAL ETHICS

Peter Singer

A victim of the Hillsborough Disaster in 1989, Anthony Bland lay in hospital in a coma being fed liquid food by a pump, via a tube passing through his nose and into his stomach. On 4 February 1993 Britain's highest court ruled that doctors attending him could lawfully act to end his life.

Our traditional ways of thinking about life and death are collapsing. In a world of respirators and embryos stored for years in liquid nitrogen, we can no longer take the sanctity of human life as the cornerstone of our ethical outlook.

In this controversial book Peter Singer argues that we cannot deal with the crucial issues of death, abortion, euthanasia and the rights of nonhuman animals unless we sweep away the old ethic and build something new in its place.

Singer outlines a new set of commandments, based on compassion and commonsense, for the decisions everyone must make about life and death.

OPUS

A HISTORICAL INTRODUCTION TO THE PHILOSOPHY OF SCIENCE

John Losee

This challenging introduction, designed for readers without an extensive knowledge of formal logic or of the history of science, looks at the long-argued questions raised by philosophers and scientists about the proper evaluation of scientific interpretations. It offers an historical exposition of differing views on issues such as the merits of competing theories; the interdependence of observation and theory; and the nature of scientific progress. The author looks at explanations given by Plato, Aristotle, and Pythagoras, and through to Bacon and Descartes, to Nagel, Kuhn, and Laudan.

This edition incorporates an extended discussion of contemporary developments and changes within the history of science, and examines recent controversies and the search for a non-prescriptive philosophy of science.

'a challenging interdisciplinary work'
New Scientist

MEDICINE IN OXFORD PAPERBACKS
MEDICAL DICTIONARY
Fourth Edition

Written without the use of unnecessary technical jargon, this illustrated medical dictionary will be welcomed as a home reference, as well as an indispensible aid for all those working in the medical profession.

Nearly 10,000 important terms and concepts are explained, including all the major medical and surgical specialities, such as gynaecology and obstetrics, paediatrics, dermatology, neurology, cardiology, and tropical medicine. This third edition contains much new material on pre-natal diagnosis, infertility treatment, nuclear medicine, community health, and immunology. Terms relating to advances in molecular biology and genetic engineering have been added, and recently developed drugs in clinical use are included. A feature of the dictionary is its unusually full coverage of the fields of community health, psychology, and psychiatry.

Each entry contains a straightforward definition, followed by a more detailed description, while an extensive crossreference system provides the reader with a comprehensive view of a particular subject.